WINNING
with
MUTUAL FUNDS

by the Editors of **Money** Magazine

**Edited by
Junius Ellis**

Oxmoor
House®

Library of Congress Catalog Number: 87-061719
ISBN: 0-8487-0722-2

Manufactured in the United States of America
Second Printing 1987

Published by arrangement with Oxmoor House, Inc.
Book Division of Southern Progress Corporation
P.O. Box 2463, Birmingham, Alabama 35201

Executive Editor: Ann H. Harvey
Production Manager: Jerry Higdon
Associate Production Manager: Rick Litton
Art Director: Bob Nance

Winning with Mutual Funds

Editor: Vicki L. Ingham
Editorial Assistant: D. Lynne Hopkins
Designer: Earl Freedle
Illustrator: Michael Alfano

Money Staff

Managing Editor: Landon Y. Jones
Executive Editor: Frank Lalli
Assistant Managing Editors: Richard A. Burgheim, Frank B. Merrick
Senior Editors: Joseph S. Coyle, Caroline Donnelly, Augustin Hedberg,
Niles A. Howard, Robert J. Klein, Tyler Mathisen
Senior Writers: Jerry Edgerton, Richard Eisenberg, Marlys Harris, Michael Sivy
Staff Writers: Greg Anrig, Jr. (Washington), William C. Banks, Diane Harris,
Robert McNatt, Robin Micheli, Andrea Rock, Eric Schurenberg, Suzanne Seixas,
John Stickney, Denise M. Topolnicki, Candace E. Trunzo, Walter L. Updegrave,
Leslie N. Vreeland
Chief of Reporters: Katharine B. Drake
Senior Reporters: Jordan E. Goodman, Lani Luciano
Reporters: Martha J. Mader (deputy chief), Jan Alexander, Caroline Baer,
Debra Wishik Englander, Carla A. Fried, J. Howard Green, Bruce Hager,
Daphne D. Mosher (letters), Jeanne L. Reid, Caren M. Weiner, Holly Wheelwright,
Sarah Button White

Editor's Note

Congratulations! With this book, you have taken an important first step toward investing in your future. *Winning with Mutual Funds* will tell you everything you need to know about the most popular investment of our time. Diversification and professional management of investments, once reserved only for the rich, are now available to almost everyone through mutual funds. And today there are more funds for you to choose from than there are companies listed on the New York Stock Exchange. With more choices have come more opportunities—and more risks.

How can you take advantage of the opportunities and minimize the risks? Which funds are right for you? The purpose of *Winning with Mutual Funds* is to help you answer those questions simply and successfully. Here you will find out how a mutual fund works, how the various kinds of funds differ from each other, how to size up the ones that best fit your investing objectives, how to manage your portfolio, and how to sell your funds at the right time. Our premise is simple: no matter what your objectives are or how inexperienced you may be as an investor, you *can* make money in mutual funds.

The Editors of *Money* are delighted to offer this book in collaboration with Oxmoor House. To prepare it we have drawn upon the insights of Wall Street experts as well as the experiences of people who invest the same way you do. As a result, you will find practical advice on every aspect of investing in mutual funds.

We are confident that you will find this book a valuable resource. Good investing and good fortune!

Landon Y. Jones
Managing Editor, *Money*

Contents

The New World of Mutual Funds

In much the same way that credit cards radically changed Americans' spending habits, mutual funds are fundamentally altering the way that they invest. Nowhere is this transformation more apparent than in the new iconography of investment. For years newspaper and television advertisements for financial services were dominated by symbols of venerable Wall Street brokerage houses—from Merrill Lynch's raging bull to Smith Barney's grizzly John Houseman. Today these emblems of stock market prowess are all but lost in the clutter of sales pitches bearing the Dreyfus lion, the Fidelity pyramid, and the Vanguard flagship—to name just a few of the biggest beneficiaries of mutual funds' dramatic emergence as Everyman's investment of choice.

Indeed, there were some 46 million shareholder accounts for mutual funds at the start of 1987, an increase of more than 400% over the number 10 years earlier. During that period, mutual funds' total assets under management soared from $51 billion to $716 billion, an incredible gain of fourteenfold. And the mutual fund growth curve, if anything, is getting steeper: investments in stock and bond funds in 1986 totaled $216 billion, nearly double the record-setting level in 1985 of $114 billion. (See figure 1.) To put this explosive growth into perspective, consider the fact that sales of funds in 1985 and 1986 combined exceeded those for all previous years combined since the founding of the first mutual funds in the 1920s!

Why the stampede into funds? The most compelling reason is the enticing investment returns made possible by the prolonged bull market in stocks and bonds that began in 1982. In 1986 the market, as measured by the Dow Jones industrial average, extended its winning streak to five years in a row, a feat unprecedented in the postwar era. It was a period in which historically high interest rates tumbled—from about 12% at the start of 1982 to around 6% in mid-1987—resulting in a correspondingly sharp rise in long-depressed prices of stocks, bonds, and the funds that invest in them. Moreover, the stocks that funds typically favor—those of large, well-established companies commonly known as blue chips—became the rage on Wall Street once again, in part because of corporate takeover fever. The buying spree accelerated with the once-strong dollar's decline in value abroad, which made U.S. securities comparatively cheap for foreign investors in search of bull market profits.

The resultant—and often robust—overall appreciation in the prices of securities was particularly tempting for millions of savers who previously had earned fairly high returns from essentially riskless bank certificates of deposit and money-market funds. Faced with the progressively lower interest rates paid on their savings, they increasingly forsook safety for the riskier but potentially more rewarding returns offered by stock and bond funds—small investors' most accessible proxies for owning securities

FIGURE 1. Net Sales of Mutual Funds

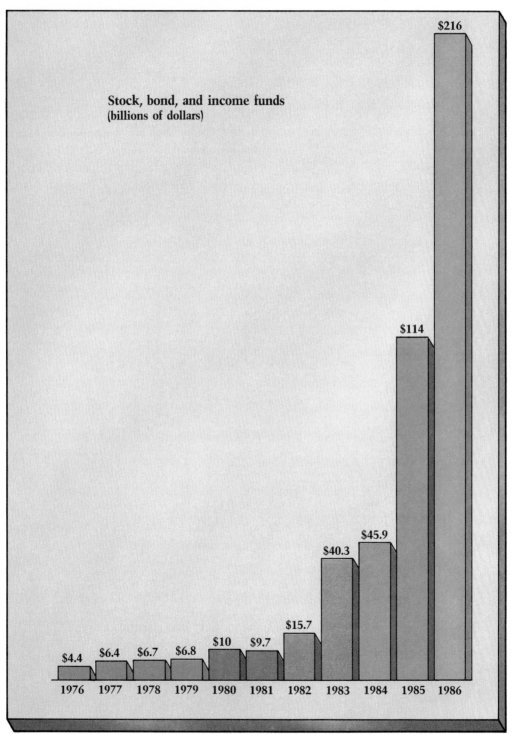

Stock, bond, and income funds
(billions of dollars)

outright. This mass conversion of savers to investors accounts for the fact that three out of every four dollars flowing into these funds in 1985 and 1986 went to fairly conservative, income-oriented funds that invest in bonds and dividend-paying stocks.

In fact, investing in a fund these days is almost as easy as putting your cash into a savings account; with many funds you can get your money back in a day or two by making a telephone call or writing a check. Shares in mutual funds traditionally have been bought and sold through stockbrokers or directly from the funds themselves via the telephone or the mail. But people who prefer to comparison shop in person for their investments can now ask questions, obtain literature, and purchase fund shares at centers operated by many of the major fund companies.

For example, at Fidelity's Investor Center in New York City—one of the busiest of the firm's 44 walk-in offices nationwide—about a thousand people drop by each day (including Sundays) to pick up brochures, talk to sales representatives, or call up the current values of a third of Fidelity's 100 or so funds on colorful video monitors. The throngs of buyers and browsers passing through this slickly designed investment emporium contribute to an air of expectancy remarkably similar to that found at the perfume and cosmetics counters at Bloomingdale's and other nearby department stores. To John O'Brien, a Fidelity managing director, that sense of anticipation reflects the reasons people are buying funds now: they represent neatly wrapped packages of hope and a piece of the future.

The greatest solace for a fund's shareholders, however, is that its portfolio of securities is professionally managed and sufficiently diversified for safety. For a modest initial investment—usually $1,000 or less—a fund's manager relieves you of the exacting, time-consuming chore of researching and assessing the outlook for companies whose stocks or bonds you might otherwise buy on your own. Because the portfolio typically consists of 50 or more securities, your investment is diversified, which means that a disaster in one stock will not deliver the knockout punch that it might if you owned only a few. You thus avoid the danger of buying into a company that has unforeseen problems or choosing the rare turkey in an industry that is flying high. You also benefit from the deep-discount brokerage commissions available to funds, pension plans, and other large institutional shareholders.

Professional management and diversification have always been the main selling points of mutual funds. But these attributes are particularly attractive to small investors at a time when the stock and bond markets are increasingly dominated by institutions that buy and sell millions of securities daily. Such voluminous trading, often triggered by computers programmed to detect the slightest market shifts, can send stock and bond prices shooting up or spiraling down too fast for even the most alert individual to react. Take for example the 87-point plunge of the Dow Jones industrial average on September 11, 1986. The value of shares on the New York Stock Exchange fell 4.6% that day, while funds invested in stocks for long-term growth dropped 3.7% on average.

Still, you must choose a mutual fund with care and periodically check up on its performance to make sure the manager is doing a good job. If you cannot be bothered with such a routine, or if you cannot bear the thought of your investment declining in value, as all stock and bond funds eventually—though temporarily—do, you probably should keep your cash in a riskless money-market fund, bank certificate of deposit, or savings account. There it will grow slowly but steadily, more or less in step with inflation, without subjecting you to restless nights spent worrying about the wisdom of your fund investments.

For investors who are prepared to ride out market fluctuations, the challenge is to make intelligent choices among those funds that not only match your financial goals and tolerance for risk but also have produced above-average returns over time. The task is more difficult than you might expect. Since 1982 most stock and bond funds have scored gains that, while impressive, have nonetheless fallen short of the market averages. In 1986, for instance, only one in six funds that invest primarily in stocks outperformed the 18.7% total return—or price appreciation plus reinvested dividends—of the bellwether Standard & Poor's 500-stock index of mostly blue-chip companies. The comparable figure for the average stock fund was 13.4%. Funds that invest mainly in bonds lagged even further. A popular bond index compiled by Salomon Brothers, a leading Wall Street investment bank, produced a total return of 16.4%, compared with 12.7% for bond funds as a group.

One explanation for this comparatively poor showing is that many funds cannot invest the flood of money from new shareholders fast enough to keep abreast of rising stock and bond prices. While this cash awaits investment, it usually is parked in a low-return money-market fund, a performance-depressing handicap that does not apply to an unmanaged market index. Furthermore, as the number of funds and the size of their portfolios have swelled, the probability that any one of them will outpace the market has declined because collectively they are such an integral part of it.

The Investment Company Institute, the industry's trade association, reports that between 1976 and 1986 the number of its member funds quadrupled to 1,843—more than the number of companies listed on the New York Stock Exchange. (See figure 2.) Many of these funds are relatively new types and invest in everything from government-backed mortgages to tax-exempt municipal bonds to such narrow slices of the stock market as shares of airlines or computer makers. While the proliferation of choices can be confusing, diligent investors are almost certain to find a fund—or collection of funds—that suits their particular goals and tolerance for risk.

Consider Anne Clark, 83, a Lubbock, Texas, resident who until 1984 kept her retirement savings in bank certificates of deposit and would have been hard pressed to explain what a mutual fund was. On the advice of a financial planner, she invested $100,000 in Colonial Government Securities Plus, a U.S. Treasury bond fund that returned 7.7% in the 12 months to April 1987. That income covers more than half of her monthly living expenses, with Social Security providing the rest. She had been earning 14% on her CDs, but each time they matured, rates dropped further. The mutual fund turned out to be a reasonably safe alternative that would still provide her with a good income.

Then there is Bill Blankemeier, 32, of Naperville, Illinois. He began investing in mutual funds in 1983, after deciding that the demands of his job as a regional sales manager for an equipment manufacturer left him with too little time to

FIGURE 2. **Number of Mutual Funds**

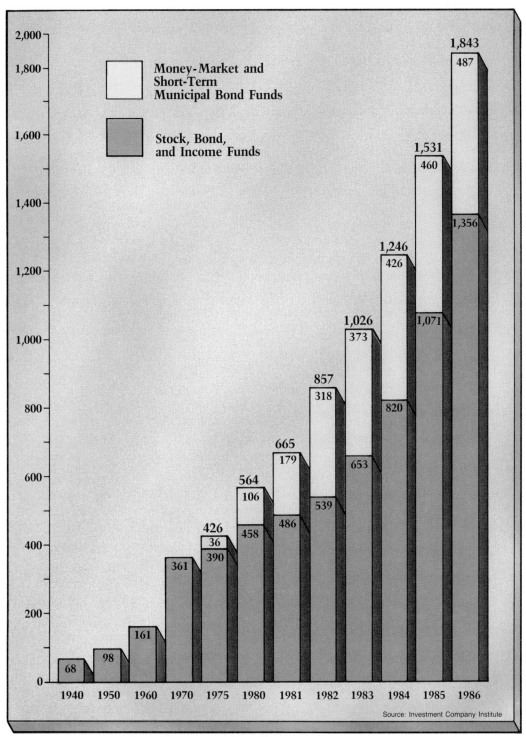

Source: Investment Company Institute

manage his stocks. Now he switches his money three to four times a year among six or more stock and bond funds, seeking the highest possible returns according to his assessment of which ones will perform best. Blankemeier says that using funds has reduced the time he spends on investments each week from two hours to one. More important, he has boosted his average annual return from 11% to 18%.

Winning with Mutual Funds can help make you a successful investor, whether you are just starting out or are fairly experienced. The explanations and insights it provides will assist you in developing a strategy that meets your financial objectives—capital growth, income, or a combination of the two. And it will teach you how to select funds that will help you realize those goals without subjecting you to added risk.

Subsequent chapters will describe how a mutual fund works, how to determine what kinds of funds are best for you, and how to size up a fund that seems promising. You will learn how to monitor your fund's performance, how you can switch your money among different types of funds to boost your returns, and when to sell your fund shares. Then, in chapter 10, mutual funds are ranked according to how well their three-year total returns to April 1987 compared with those of funds having the same objectives. An alphabetical listing of 738 funds follows the rankings.

This guide should not only answer just about any question you have concerning mutual funds, but also help you to be more demanding of the ones in which you put your money. No one knows better than fund managers how quickly knowledgeable investors pull their money out of a fund that does not keep up with its competition. John Bogle, chairman of the Vanguard group of 45 funds, admits that the message from customers comes through loud and clear: the management had better keep its act together if it wants to keep their business. This book will also prepare you for the major changes in store for funds. Among the most important that fund specialists say you can expect in coming years are the following.

• There will be even fewer no-load funds—those that do not impose sales charges. No-load stock and bond funds increased their share of mutual fund dollars between 1976

and 1983, when they had 31% of fund investments. But by
1986 that percentage had slipped to 24%, and most fund
specialists think the decline will continue. Many no-load
funds are adding sales commissions of 1% to 3%, plus such
charges as exit fees, which you pay when you sell your
shares. Fund managers say they need the money to pay for
stepped-up advertising and marketing campaigns to com-
pete with load funds, which are sold—often aggressively—
by brokers and financial planners. The trend will make it
more important than ever that you pay close attention to a
fund's fees, which reduce your return.

● A growing number of funds will be marketed by banks
and insurance companies. The 1932 Glass-Steagall Act has
prevented Federal Reserve member banks from directly
marketing and distributing mutual funds. But banks seem
likely to persuade Congress to change the law. Several
banks, including Chemical Bank in New York City and
Security Pacific National Bank of Los Angeles, have already
signed agreements with such fund companies as Fidelity
and Dreyfus to disseminate sales materials to depositors.
Insurance companies are getting into the act too. As Stanley
Egener, president of the Neuberger-Berman fund family,
explains, insurers already have excellent distribution net-
works that they can use to market funds. For example, in
1986 Liberty Mutual acquired the Stein Roe fund family,
enabling its agents to sell Stein Roe funds. This develop-
ment will be good news for investors who prefer to deal
with a local bank or insurance agent rather than by mail
with an impersonal fund company.

● Technological advances and improvements in services
will make fund transactions more convenient. Several large
fund families, including Fidelity, Neuberger-Berman,
T. Rowe Price, and Vanguard, already offer a touch-tone
telephone equivalent of banks' 24-hour automatic teller
machines. You call the fund at any time and punch in your
personal identification number to, say, find out current
share prices, buy additional shares, or switch your money
between funds. Some systems offer investors the ultimate
convenience—letting them sell shares by phone and have
the proceeds transferred directly to their bank accounts.

ONE

What a Fund Is
and
How It Works

A mutual fund is a company that consolidates its share-holders' money and buys and sells securities on their behalf. When you put money into a fund, you receive shares representing part ownership of the fund's securities and of any profits they produce. These profits can take the form of stock dividends, interest paid by bonds and money-market instruments, or capital gains realized from selling securities for a higher price than the fund originally paid for them.

In effect, the fund transforms you from a solitary small investor into a part owner of a multimillion-dollar portfolio whose value fluctuates with changing market conditions.

No stock or bond fund can guarantee that you will not lose money, as is the case with bank savings accounts and certificates of deposit. But it does give you many advantages that are normally available only to the wealthiest investors, including professional management, diversification, and reduced brokerage fees.

The concept of mutual funds originated in England in the late nineteenth century. Some of the earliest British and Scottish investment pools, called trusts, contributed to the financing of American economic growth after the Civil War. These trusts invested in mortgages, railroads, and industrial companies. Stateside investment trusts based on the English model were soon formed by bankers and brokers who foresaw the need to make professional financial management available to investors of modest means. The trusts were the forerunners of today's closed-end funds—investment companies that issue a fixed number of shares, which are then bought and sold on a stock exchange or over the counter.

The first open-end investment company was the Massachusetts Investors Trust, founded in 1924. An open-end fund is a true mutual fund. It creates new shares as needed to meet the demand and buys them back when investors wish to redeem their investment. This arrangement makes mutual fund shares highly liquid, meaning they can easily be converted into cash. Despite the added liquidity advantage, open-end funds were slow to win over investors accustomed to the then-conventional closed-end format. The Securities and Exchange Commission (SEC) estimates that by the end of 1929, shortly after the precarious peak of that decade's seemingly endless bull market in stocks, the public had poured more than $7 billion into investment companies, mostly closed-end funds. Massachusetts Investors Trust and other early mutual funds accounted for a mere $140 million, or about 2% of the total.

Although the market crash of October 1929 hit all investment companies hard, it was devastating for the many closed-end funds that aggressively used leverage, or money borrowed from banks or brokerage houses, to jack up the size of their portfolios and potential profits. By the end of 1937, according to the SEC, the average dollar invested in July 1929 in leveraged funds was worth only 5¢, compared with the 48¢ that a dollar invested in unleveraged funds was worth. Chastened by that fall, small investors increasingly shunned closed-end funds in favor of their open-end brethren in the decades following the Great Depression.

In 1936 the SEC began a regulatory review of investment companies that culminated in the federal Investment Company Act of 1940, which established the basic statutory guidelines all funds must comply with today. The law's provisions eliminated numerous fund abuses of the 1920s by prohibiting excessive leverage, self-dealing, and other conflicts of interest and by providing for the safekeeping of fund assets by an independent custodian such as a bank. And all shares sold publicly, including those of mutual funds, are subject to the Securities Act of 1933 and the Securities Exchange Act of 1934. These laws require, among other things, that a fund be registered with the SEC and provide prospective investors with a prospectus that contains detailed disclosures about the fund's management, investment policies, and objectives. In addition to the federal laws, almost every state has adopted its own regulations governing mutual funds.

While these federal and state statutes serve to safeguard the interests of investors, no amount of regulation can ensure that fund shareholders will not lose money when the market turns against them. One of the most painful reminders of this caveat still haunts many fund managers and shareholders who participated in the bull market of the late 1960s. Then the prices of so-called glamour stocks— Coca-Cola, IBM, McDonald's, and others, collectively dubbed the Nifty Fifty—rose to towering levels on widely shared expectations that these mighty companies would continue to grow steadily, more or less oblivious to the economy's periodic downturns. This unbridled optimism carried over to stock funds, which in 1968 accounted for 92% of the $52.6 billion in assets held by about 220 funds.

Some of the most popular stock portfolios were headed by market gurus known as go-go managers or gunslingers because they made quick-trigger decisions based on instinct as much as research. These managers actively courted the press. The publicity was partly responsible for prompting tens of thousands of investors to flock to their high-flying funds just before growth stocks stalled, then nosedived, in

1969. The result was a double whammy of plunging portfolio values and massive shareholder redemptions, especially during the decidedly unglamorous recession that began in 1973. Stock fund total assets dropped from $49 billion in 1968 to $26.5 billion in 1974, causing such resentment that many investors swore off stock funds for the remainder of the 1970s. Indeed, in that decade mutual fund redemptions exceeded sales by about $5.4 billion.

The hemorrhage of capital would have been much more pronounced had it not been for the November 1972 introduction of money-market funds, which soon became a big hit with savers as well as investors. This innovative concept permitted small shareholders to partake in the fairly high interest rates then paid by short-term—and thus virtually riskless—corporate and government debt securities previously available only to those with $100,000 or more to invest. Moreover, withdrawals from a money-market fund

FIGURE 3. Percent Distribution of Total Net Assets by Type of Fund

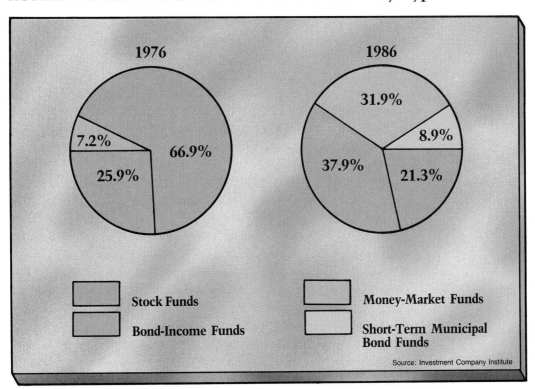

1976

7.2%
25.9%
66.9%

1986

31.9%
8.9%
37.9%
21.3%

Stock Funds   Money-Market Funds

Bond-Income Funds   Short-Term Municipal
                     Bond Funds

Source: Investment Company Institute

could be made anytime at a predictable per-share value,
often by simply writing a check drawn against the fund.

Sparked by double-digit inflation and interest rates, total
assets of money funds soared during their first 10 years of
operation, topping $232 billion in November 1982. By 1986,
assets dropped to 31.9% of all assets in mutual funds, but
still exceeded those in stock funds. (See figure 3.) With the
introductions of tax-exempt municipal bond funds in 1976
and government bond funds around 1980, the stage was set
for the decline in inflation and interest rates that touched
off this decade's market-driven surge in the number,
variety, and total assets of mutual funds overall.

HOW YOU PROFIT

The money-market funds that introduced many savers to
this new world of mutual funds offer variable interest rates,
but the per-share value is fixed at $1. The value of stock and
bond fund shares, on the other hand, often fluctuates daily
in response to changing market and economic trends.
Whether you are buying shares or redeeming them, the
shares' price—known as the net asset value—is set by the
fund on the day that you trade them. Funds calculate their
net asset value by totaling the value of their cash and
securities and dividing by the number of shares owned by
investors.

Even if a fund invests in corners of the market where
securities are thinly traded—as is often the case with over-
the-counter stocks—you can always buy or redeem your
shares at net asset value. By contrast, if you buy an infre-
quently traded over-the-counter stock yourself, as much as
20% of the price you pay for the stock goes to cover transaction costs. Of course, when you buy shares in a fund, you
hope that the net asset value will rise and you can eventually redeem your shares for a profit. But this is just one of
the ways you can make money.

A fund will periodically sell some of its securities for
capital gains, and if the fund holds bonds or dividend-paying
stocks, the portfolio will also generate interest and dividend
income. Almost all funds distribute their capital gains and

income to shareholders at least annually. Depending on your instructions, the fund will either send you a check for the amount of a distribution or reinvest the money in additional shares. The fund incurs no tax liability on its distributions. Instead, you owe taxes on capital gains and income received from the fund as though you had invested in the securities yourself without the fund acting as an intermediary.

You can buy fund shares in one of two ways: directly from a fund by mail or phone, or through a salesman. Many funds sell shares directly to the public with no sales charge, or load, or at most a low one. Other funds rely on brokers, financial planners, or insurance agents to help you select the fund that balances your desire for returns with your stomach for risk. These load funds pay their sales forces commissions, typically 8.5%. The fee is deducted from your purchase before you are issued your shares. The higher the front-end load, the harder it is for you to turn a profit, because this cost reduces your gain (or increases your loss) when you eventually sell your shares. A few funds may even levy a small exit fee or back-end load when you redeem shares. (For a breakdown of how fund fees add up over time, see table 2, page 82, and table 3, page 84.)

This information is explained in the prospectus, a fact-filled document that the fund must supply to prospective shareholders. The prospectus outlines the fund's fees and investment objectives, assesses the degree of risk involved, and presents statistics on the fund's past performance. A corollary document, usually referred to as Part B, or the statement of additional information, describes in detail the fees that the fund charges. Once you become a shareholder, you will also receive regular statements that report on the fund's progress, any expenses incurred, and changes in the securities that make up its portfolio.

THE MANAGEMENT TEAM

The duties of operating a fund, from answering phone calls to deciding what to invest in, are conducted by its management company or adviser. This firm is retained by, and answerable to, the fund's board of directors, which is elected by shareholders the same way corporate board members are voted on by holders of a company's stock. In most cases, the management company founded the fund and framed its investment policies. The company generally is paid a percentage of the assets of each fund it manages. Management fees typically range from 0.5% to 0.75% annually, out of which the adviser pays fund-related operating costs such as rent, advertising, and the salaries of specialists who manage the portfolios.

These specialists, the mutual fund managers, may or may not be identified in the literature a fund sends you. But they are the individuals primarily responsible for making the investment decisions for funds. What type of person is this individual likely to be?

Today's fund manager, contrary to much popular belief, is not 25 years old and fresh out of Harvard. According to a poll of 150 stock and bond fund managers commissioned by *Money* magazine in 1986, he is male (96% are), white (94%), and in his forties (40%). Moreover, he probably was a liberal arts major in college (62%) and attended graduate school (80%), most likely picking up a master's degree in business administration (70%).

The poll, the first to survey such a large sample of fund managers, also revealed the following characteristics.

• Roughly half of the fund managers work in the Northeast, and about the same percentage grew up there. About a fifth of the managers have undergraduate degrees from the eight Ivy League schools; at least a third earned their M.B.A.'s from one of these. But the typical fund manager pays his dues, having been with his present company for an average of 11 years. Most managers have worked their way up from securities analyst, bond trader, or assistant portfolio manager.

• The fund managers have profited in the mutual fund boom along with their investors. Fully 65% of the managers polled said they earned more than $100,000 a year. A quarter of them made $200,000 or more. Stock fund managers earn more, on average, than do managers of bond fund portfolios.

● Although some mutual fund managers work in committees, the majority choose which securities to buy or sell on their own. They often say their fund's performance would be hurt if they could make trades only after receiving approval from colleagues or superiors.

● Competitiveness is so deeply ingrained that it manifests itself in the simplest daily routines. Many managers start each workday by turning to the *Wall Street Journal*'s mutual fund tables and comparing their fund's performance on the previous day with the records of other funds having similar objectives. This preoccupation with one's day-to-day standing involves more than professional pride. Most managers are paid a salary plus an annual bonus based on their performance relative to that of their fund's principal competitors. Yet, somewhat surprisingly, *Money*'s poll found almost no correlation between a fund manager's income and his age or experience.

● Still more surprising, there is no discernible relationship between a fund's long-term performance and the investment philosophy of its manager. For example, some stock fund managers rely on what is known as the top-down approach. They first determine the major forces controlling the economy and investment markets—such as interest rates, consumer spending, and the dollar's value abroad— and then look for stocks that, in response, will benefit by rising in price or yielding above-average dividends.

Other managers favor a bottom-up approach. By doing detailed research on particular companies, such managers hunt for undervalued stocks of firms that seem poised for a turnaround because of, say, corporate restructuring or improving profit margins. Each approach has its proponents, but *Money*'s study found no indication that one approach is consistently more successful than the other.

● Investment strategies aside, most fund managers could be characterized as information addicts. The more information the managers can absorb, they reason, the more astute their decisions will be. The managers polled said that stock and bond research reports are their most important sources of investment ideas, followed by investment periodicals and meetings with executives of companies. Indeed, Peter Lynch, manager of Fidelity's much-admired Magellan Fund in Boston, attributes a good deal of his stock fund's success to his 400 or so annual powwows with corporate chiefs.

Also cited as important by some 37% of the managers are tips or leads supplied by professional associates, friends, and family members. Binkley Shorts, the Boston-based portfolio manager of the venerable Over-the-Counter Securities Fund in Fort Washington, Pennsylvania, credits his daughter with alerting him to a stock that became the fund's biggest winner in years. In 1982, Shorts noticed that many of his daughter's classmates in nursery school were wearing playpants made by Oshkosh B'Gosh, a Wisconsin firm that for nearly a century has made overalls for farmers and railroad men. So he wrote the company for its annual report. On the cover was an innocuous picture of a child in overalls, but the numbers inside made Shorts's eyes pop.

He bought as many shares of Oshkosh as he could, though not as many as he would have liked initially. The stock, then selling at around $100 a share, was closely held by corporate insiders. It was not long, however, before scores of other investors noted the company's robust sales of children's wear and began to bid up the price of its scarce shares. The stock started climbing rapidly, and the shares Shorts bought in 1982 have since split twenty-for-one and increased in value fourteenfold.

Although a fund manager is always on the alert for tips and leads, he also has to filter out information that does not pertain to his fund's investment objectives. The objective—growth, income, or a combination of the two—is a matter of policy for each fund and determines the kinds of securities a manager can buy and sell. Your job as an investor is to choose the fund or funds whose objectives match your own. The first step in that direction is to define your own approach to investing.

TWO

Finding the Right Strategy

Investing in mutual funds is like buying designer-label clothes off the rack instead of going to a tailor: you can easily find something to suit your personal style, and at a much more affordable price than if you were to seek the individualized attentions of a professional. But first you need to come to terms with what your style is. What kind of investor are you and what goals do you hope to attain with your investments?

For example, are you a young single person who is trying to amass capital as quickly as possible? Are you a middle-aged worker aiming to supplement a corporate pension?

Can you afford to take some risks while looking for higher returns, or is preservation of your capital absolutely essential? You must weigh your future financial prospects against anticipated commitments such as college costs, retirement income, or other necessities. You will also have to determine how long your money is likely to stay invested and make an honest assessment of how much risk you are willing to take. Your choice of fund—or collection of funds—will ultimately hinge on such issues.

DEFINING YOUR GOALS

Financial planners emphasize that your first priority should be to establish an emergency reserve equal to three to six months' expenses. Stash it in a liquid, safe money-market fund or account, such as those offered by federally insured banks and savings and loans. Then you can set your sights on what you hope to achieve with your investments. For some, the challenge of second-guessing the market and watching their money grow is reason enough to invest. For other people, specific goals make it easier to forgo some of life's frills while they are putting their money to work.

Begin by listing your goals. Be as specific as possible so that you can calculate roughly how much money you will need to accumulate. For example, if you want to set up a fund to pay for your child's education, try to project how much it could cost for room, board, and tuition. If your goal is to start your own business in a few years, do some homework now on all possible costs involved, from manufacturing to marketing. Price tags for more immediate goals—a vacation in Europe, say, or the down payment on a home—are easier to predict. In every instance, targeting the amount of money you need will help you to determine whether you should aim primarily for growth, income, or a blend of both.

Your investment choices also will be influenced by the importance you attach to particular goals and the deadlines you set for reaching them. Assigning priorities may require trade-offs, because few people can afford two concentrated uses of their resources at once.

WEIGHING THE RISKS

Establishing your objectives also requires that you do some soul searching on the all-important issue of risk. Assessing your willingness to take chances with your money is invariably the toughest task, because everyone wants a whale of a return at a minnow-sized risk.

You will need to weigh several kinds of risk. The first is the likelihood that you could permanently lose some or all of the money you put into a fund. Not to worry: the possibility that your principal will be wiped out or greatly eroded in a fund is extremely remote. Federal law requires funds to carry insurance to protect shareholders against losses due to fraud. And although there is no guarantee that your fund will not sink because of the manager's inept investment decisions, no fund has gone under in the history of the fund business.

You face a greater possibility of loss over time from the impact of inflation. Because inflation steadily erodes the purchasing power of the dollar, even ostensibly safe investments cannot completely protect your principal. That is why financial planners generally recommend that at least part of your portfolio include growth investments, which usually outpace inflation over time.

More nettlesome is the risk associated with a fund's volatility, or how often and how sharply the value of its shares rises and falls relative to the price swings of stocks and bonds in general. The price of a stock traditionally is based on investors' expectations of the company's future earnings. The greater the expectations, the more investors are willing to pay for a share of the company's growth. Conversely, as growing numbers of investors become disenchanted with a company's prospects, the price of its stock will slump.

The prices of bonds generally move up or down in the opposite direction of interest rates. As interest rates fall, older bonds become more attractive relative to new ones because the interest they pay is fixed at the older, higher rate. As interest rates rise, bond prices fall to make them competitive with newer bonds offering higher returns.

All stock and bond funds are of course subject to some volatility and losses, however brief. In the five-year period to April 1987, while most fund shareholders reveled in the longest bull market of the postwar era, some stock funds lost ground or barely broke even because of big losses suffered in the interim. Notable examples are 44 Wall Street, down 48.4%; American Heritage, down 14.4%; and Industry Fund of America, up 0.5%.

Yet it is reassuring to note that investors who have been willing to ride out the stock market's ups and downs historically have been rewarded with much higher returns than investors who played it safe with bonds backed by the full faith and credit of the U.S. Treasury. Over the past 60 years or so, common stocks have produced an average compounded total return—dividends plus price appreciation—of nearly 10% a year, or about six percentage points more than the comparable return for essentially riskless short-term Treasury bills.

GAUGING YOUR TOLERANCE FOR RISK

In terms of willingness to accept the possibility of loss, investors generally fall into one of three categories: conservative, moderate, or aggressive. For conservative investors, safety and income are paramount. They prefer a modest but guaranteed return in exchange for the sense of security that comes with preserving capital. Liquidity may be important because they feel more comfortable knowing that they can get at their money readily.

Moderate investors are willing to assume some risk in the hope of higher rewards. They aim primarily for growth but may also keep some assets in relatively steady income-producing holdings.

Aggressive investors go for maximum growth. They are risk takers by nature and are prepared to suffer periodic—and sometimes prodigious—losses in pursuit of the highest possible returns. They tend to be confident decision-makers and to handle stress well.

Another clue to your risk tolerance is whether you have the time or inclination needed to monitor volatile funds.

Aggressive stock funds may top the performance charts one year and sink to the bottom for the next three or more. These somewhat speculative portfolios are best used by investors who try to stay abreast of the market and the economic trends that might affect the funds. That way they may be able to cash in their shares before the market peaks and begins a big slide.

If you cannot spend an hour or more per week overseeing your fund investments, you should probably forswear the most aggressive stock funds. Instead, consider those growth-minded stock funds that have produced above-average returns in both rising and declining markets, such as the 10 all-weather funds profiled in chapter 9. This type of fund may never make the year's list of top 10 performers, but it can provide consistent profits over time.

Also try to determine the maximum decline in share value you could suffer and still sleep at night. Even if you are in your thirties and know you will not need your money for 20 years, you might not be able to stand a 40% drop in the value of your fund shares, however temporary. Many investors who buy into a risky fund and vow to hang on no matter what are among the first to panic and sell at the

FIGURE 4. Balancing Risks, Rewards, and Objectives

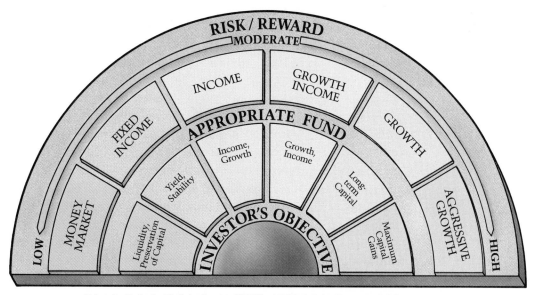

Redrawn from *The Handbook for No-Load Investors, 1986 Edition,* © 1986 by the No-Load Fund Investor, P.O. Box 283, Hastings-on-Hudson, New York 10706

market bottom, defeating their buy-and-hold strategy. They would probably be better off in a more conservative growth and income fund whose generous dividends help to cushion falling share values—and quell investors' jittery nerves—during bear markets.

Shareholders in bond funds can face similar stomach-churning decisions. When you invest in bond funds, you are buying shares of loans to corporations or to state or local governments. If some of the borrowers go bankrupt, they may default on their loans or pay off only part of them. If the thought that borrowers may not be able to pay you back makes you anxious, choose funds that invest in only the highest grade corporate or municipal bonds.

Of course, your willingness to accept risk is only part of the issue. You must also decide whether you can afford it. A retiree relying on investments for income obviously should lean toward safety, with low-risk funds that pay interest, dividends, or both. But safety could be just as important for a young couple struggling to get established financially. You should venture into the riskiest investments only with money you can afford to lose.

PUTTING IT ALL TOGETHER

Your time frame will also affect the amount of risk you can take and the kinds of funds you choose. In general, money for short-term goals—ones that you hope to achieve in five years or less—should be highly liquid. Both money-market funds and short-term bond funds hold investments that keep pace with inflation, and withdrawals can be made anytime at a predictable per-share value.

If your time horizon is five years or more, you can afford to aim for the greater returns available in stock funds. That is because the stock market moves in cycles, usually going through a complete bull and bear market cycle within four to six years. If you can hold your shares that long, you can generally be sure of outlasting periodic market downturns.

Say that you have just realized a $50,000 after-tax profit from the sale of a vacation home, and you want the money to earn enough to pay for your child's college expenses over the next four years. Because a reliable stream of dividends is of paramount importance, you should consider a fund that aims for steady income and preservation of capital.

Your safest investment would be a money-market fund, which invests in short-term debt securities issued by corporations, banks, and governments—federal, state, or local. Unfortunately, your annual return from a money-market fund would likely fall short of today's typical college costs. So you will probably need to consider the higher returns, and corresponding risks, of income-oriented funds that buy corporate and U.S. government bonds and, in many instances, high-dividend stocks—all of which seesaw in value with fluctuations in interest rates and the stock market. If you are in the top federal tax bracket, it may pay to invest instead in a tax-exempt municipal bond fund, whose earnings are off-limits to the Internal Revenue Service.

Then again, say you have accumulated $1,000 in a savings account that you would like to invest for a higher return. If you know you will not need access to the money for the next five to ten years and you want to make that sum increase as much as possible in that time, you can afford to invest for growth. You will find a wide choice of funds to serve your purpose. For example, aggressive growth funds strive for maximum capital gains by buying high-risk stocks that the fund managers believe are headed for rapid increases in price. Long-term growth funds, on the other hand, tend to concentrate on stocks of established companies known for their consistent growth in earnings and share prices over time. And international funds look for foreign growth stocks that are expected to profit handsomely from changes in the dollar's value abroad.

Or perhaps you have just inherited $10,000 you want to invest conservatively for a rainy day. If you would like the principal to grow fast enough to offset inflation, your best investment choice might well be growth and income funds, commonly called total-return funds. These portfolios aim for reliable, above-average returns by holding a mix of bonds and stocks of dividend-paying companies that offer some prospects for capital gains.

As these examples illustrate, choosing the appropriate financial objectives is the result of some dexterous juggling on your part to strike a balance between your goals, risk tolerance, and time frame. Once you have achieved that balance, however, choosing the right fund or group of funds becomes much easier.

MIXING AND MATCHING FOR SAFETY

In the same way that a fund manager selects a portfolio of stocks or bonds to achieve a specific objective, you can design a portfolio of funds to meet your objectives—to strive boldly for capital gains, to achieve above-average returns in down markets as well as up, or to generate steady tax-exempt income. Whatever your strategy, your first move is to determine whether you have enough money to diversify your fund holdings. Investment advisers generally recommend that you have at least $5,000 available. With less than that, it is difficult to diversify effectively, because of the impact of multiple management fees. But if you have that much or more, you can benefit from dividing the portion of your money devoted to stocks among several funds with different investment styles. This holds true whether you are an invest-and-forget shareholder or one who tries to time the market, switching back and forth between stock funds and money-market funds in an attempt to catch major rallies and avoid severe market slumps. (For advice on market-timing, see pages 108-10.)

Spreading your money among fund managers allows you to pick a combination of funds that will do well at different points in economic and stock market cycles. With your assets thus deployed, you have a better chance that at least one of your fund managers will be doing the right thing at any given moment. Fortified with at least some success, you are more likely to remain level-headed and make careful decisions, whether about the market's future direction or the fate of an underperforming fund in your portfolio.

The model portfolios depicted on the pages that follow suggest how five different investors might apportion their cash among various types of funds to match their objectives and tolerance of risk. In addition to studying the models, consider these guidelines for putting together your own portfolio of funds.

Diversify for balance and risk reduction. Your aim is to include in your portfolio funds with different objectives or investment philosophies. If one fund is performing badly, your loss may well be offset by gains in another fund that is thriving. If you plan to invest in more than one fund with the same objectives, choose funds that take different approaches, because one is likely to be in favor when others are not.

Among maximum-capital-gains funds, for instance, some portfolio managers will move as much as 80% of their fund's assets out of stocks and into cash to weather anticipated market declines, while others will always remain fully invested in stocks. By investing in a fund that relies on the first approach, you could feel reasonably protected from a major market downturn. At the same time, keeping some money in a fund that uses the second approach would ensure that you would get in on the ground floor of the next rally whenever it begins. Or you might divide your cash between an aggressive fund that invests in undervalued stocks of established companies and another aggressive fund that buys stocks of small, fast-growing companies, which tend to shine brightest in the late stages of bull markets.

Build inflation protection into your portfolio. Even if your sole objective is income, you should allocate part of your portfolio to funds with capital-gains potential so that inflation will not erode your principal. Over the past 60 years, inflation has run at an average annual rate of 3.1%. The average annual return for long-term government bonds over the same period was 4.1%, translating into a real, or inflation-adjusted, return of only 1%. The real return for capital-gains-producing investments, represented by the Standard & Poor's 500-stock index, was 6.7%. Thus your best choice might be a growth fund with a 10-year record of steady gains.

Gold and other precious metals are also proven inflation hedges. But gold's price is highly volatile and its lows often last longer than bear markets in stocks. Dividends from funds that invest mostly in gold-mining shares could make the wait less onerous, but not enough to justify allocating more than 10% of your portfolio to such funds.

Move into the market gradually. Investing a portion of your cash at regular intervals reduces your risk of buying fund shares at peak prices. One method of doing this is called dollar-cost averaging (see pages 106-7). Investment adviser Gerald Perritt, editor of *The Mutual Fund Letter*, suggests another strategy when you are investing in stock funds. At the outset, put in 20% of the total amount you plan to invest. Six months later or when the market declines by 10%, whichever occurs first, invest 10% more. Repeat every six months until you are fully invested. This strategy lets you take advantage of low prices during market declines, to get more shares for your money.

Adjust your fund mix as your financial circumstances change. As your children approach college age, for example, or as you reach retirement, you may want to move from growth-oriented funds to less volatile total-return or income funds. When you are five years away from drawing cash from your portfolio, you should move a higher percentage of it into liquid, predictable-value investments such as short-term bond funds or money-market funds. That way, you will not run the risk of having to redeem your shares just as stock prices—and the net asset value of your fund shares—are dropping.

THREE GROWTH PORTFOLIOS

How should you apportion your fund investments if growth is your primary goal? The answer will depend on your objectives and tolerance for risk, as well as your age and time frame. The three sample portfolios that follow were designed with the help of investment adviser Gerald Perritt, who assumed that projected returns on the Standard & Poor's 500-stock index would grow at 10% to 11% a year and that money-market rates would hover at around 6%. The Standard & Poor's index is used as a guide to measure performance because it represents the aggregate market value of a broad range of stocks, including those of financial institutions and industrial, transportation, and utility companies.

LOW RISK

Goal: You seek respectable and, above all, steady capital appreciation in case you have to withdraw your money in a hurry. Regular income is an important secondary objective.

Portfolio: Long-term growth funds, which invest mainly in stocks of established companies, will give you reasonably certain capital gains over time, though they could lose value in a market downturn. Growth and income funds also invest in well-known growth stocks, but they balance their portfolios with conservative income-producing stocks and bonds. Money-market funds invest in issues that come due in less than a year and will give you regular income in addition to providing the safety you seek. This mix should generate an average total return of about 12% a year after inflation. Based on the riskiness of the securities generally held by these types of funds, the portfolio is about 30% less volatile than the S&P 500-stock index.

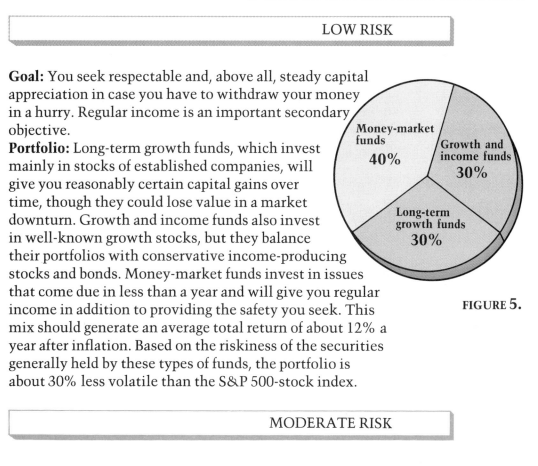

FIGURE 5.

MODERATE RISK

Goal: You want fairly rapid appreciation without risking heavy losses during sudden market downdrafts. You do not plan on withdrawing your money for at least three years.

Portfolio: By putting half your assets into long-term growth funds, you will increase your potential inflation-adjusted returns. But you will also take sizable risks by committing 20% of your cash to aggressive stock funds, which are particularly sensitive to the market's periodic ups and downs. The most volatile are maximum-capital-gains funds, which often seek out stocks of small growth companies. International funds, because they are affected by shifts in both exchange rates and foreign stock and bond markets, also can rise and fall quickly. You can expect an average total return of about 16% a year after inflation. The portfolio's volatility is about equal to that of the S&P 500-stock index.

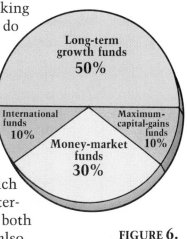

FIGURE 6.

HIGH RISK

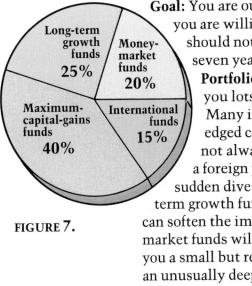

FIGURE 7.

Goal: You are out to make substantial capital gains, and you are willing to take big risks to achieve them. You should not expect to tap your portfolio for at least seven years.

Portfolio: Maximum-capital-gains funds will give you lots of growth potential—and lots of risk. Many international funds offer the same double-edged combination. But since overseas stocks do not always move in tandem with the U.S. market, a foreign portfolio could reduce your exposure to a sudden dive in the values of stateside stocks. Long-term growth funds, which rise and fall less precipitously, can soften the impact of abrupt market swings. Money-market funds will also provide a safety cushion and give you a small but reliable return should high-flying funds hit an unusually deep air pocket. Over a period of five years or so, the total return for this mix of funds averages about 20% a year after inflation. But there could be some wild gyrations in the interim: the portfolio is 30% more volatile than the S&P 500-stock index.

TWO INCOME PORTFOLIOS

These models are for investors who are primarily interested in a steady stream of income. One portfolio generates income of about 7% annually, based on the average payouts of bonds and dividend stocks in recent years. The income from this portfolio is taxable. The other portfolio produces income of about 6.6% a year free from federal taxes. Both of these portfolios are heavily weighted with intermediate-term bond funds, which generally hold bonds that mature—that is, repay investors' principal—in less than 10 years. Such bonds generally offer lower yields than do long-term bonds, which usually have maturities ranging from 10 to 30 years. But prices of intermediate-term bonds are less vulnerable to rising interest rates than are those of long-term bonds, so you assume less risk with them.

TAXABLE

Goal: You want preservation of capital and steady returns, perhaps to supplement other sources of retirement income or to meet periodic payments such as child-care expenses. Growth of capital is a secondary concern.

Portfolio: Put half of your money in intermediate-term bond funds. U.S. Treasury issues held to maturity will give you absolute protection against the possible loss of your principal. Funds that buy bonds issued by financially solid companies produce slightly higher returns at only slightly more risk. To protect yourself in the event that interest rates rise, causing a drop in the value of bonds in the fund, put 30% of your portfolio into a money-market fund. The rest of your cash should go into growth and income funds. They should pay you regular dividend income plus offer you an opportunity for capital gains that will outpace inflation over time.

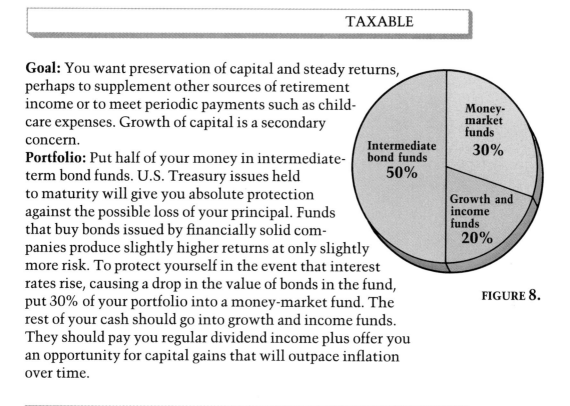

FIGURE **8.**

TAX-EXEMPT

Goal: You seek income exempt from federal taxes to supplement an existing portfolio that contains taxable growth-oriented investments.

Portfolio: Municipal bond funds holding medium-term issues with average maturities of about five years will reduce your risk should interest rates rise sharply. What is more, these bonds pay almost as much interest income as munis with longer maturities. Money-market funds will also limit the damage caused by rising interest rates. Funds holding long-term bonds serve as a hedge; their shares will rise sharply in value if interest rates fall. If you live in California, Connecticut, New York, or other states with high state income tax rates, you might consider funds that invest exclusively in munis issued within your state. That income is exempt from your state and sometimes local taxes, as well as from federal taxes.

FIGURE **9.**

SPECIAL STRATEGIES FOR IRAS

The virtues of mutual funds as diversified and professionally managed portfolios make them ideally suited for Individual Retirement Accounts. True, changes in federal tax law have reduced or eliminated some of the tax-sheltering benefits of an IRA. But many investors who bemoan their loss of the IRA deduction have overlooked the fact that the account's most important benefit has survived: long-term, tax-deferred compounding of their retirement funds. While you may no longer be eligible for the deduction, you will still be able to contribute $2,000 a year and defer taxes on your IRA's earnings.

Figuring out whether you can still deduct your IRA contribution is fairly simple. If neither you nor your spouse is covered by a company pension or profit-sharing plan, you can invest and deduct up to $2,000 a year for yourself and an additional $250 for a nonworking spouse, regardless of your income. If you are single and covered by a company plan—even if you are not yet vested—you rate a full deduction only if your adjusted gross income is $25,000 or less. Your allowable deduction drops $10 for each $50 you earn above $25,000 until you hit $35,000, when the deduction phases out entirely. Married couples filing jointly, with either spouse covered by a company plan, get the full deduction only if their adjusted gross income is $40,000 or less. Their deduction also disappears in $10 increments for each additional $50 in income up to $50,000, when the deduction vanishes.

When plotting your IRA strategy—with or without the deduction—you should follow the same general guidelines that you would for any fund investment. For example, an IRA that you plan to tap within five years should be invested conservatively in income or money-market funds, while cash that you will not need to touch for many years can be invested for growth in stock funds. If you have a substantial non-IRA portfolio of funds, however, you probably should avoid putting aggressive growth funds in your retirement account. The reason is that in an IRA, losses from a volatile fund cannot be used to offset capital gains from other funds, as is the case with gains and losses realized on investments outside your IRA.

In addition, there are three main points to keep in mind when you are choosing a mutual fund for your IRA.

How does the IRA fit into your retirement nest egg? You should determine what other retirement assets you have and how the funds you are considering for your IRA help to diversify those assets. If your other retirement money is invested in, say, company stock and a profit-sharing plan that also is primarily in stocks, then perhaps you should tilt the balance in your IRA toward income funds. Conversely, if you can count on a sizable pension payout from a retirement plan that is conservatively invested in fixed-income securities, you might want to be more venturesome with your Individual Retirement Account.

How much money is in your IRA? Concentrate your cash in only one or two funds if you have less than $10,000 to invest. That is because most funds charge annual IRA administrative fees ranging from $5 to $15 per account. Spreading your IRA money among several funds can cause fees to take an unacceptably large bite out of your annual contributions. If you divide $2,000 among four funds, for instance, you could easily pay $60 in annual maintenance fees, or 3% of your total investment, in addition to the usual management fees and expenses or internal assessments that are deducted each year by the funds.

How hefty are the fund's sales charge and operating expenses? If other factors such as long-term performance and level of risk are more or less equal, the lowest-cost fund among those you are considering will allow the tax-sheltered earnings in your IRA to compound to their fullest. Take two funds, both of which return 10% a year on their investments for the next 30 years. One is a no-load, and the expenses incurred by its manager cost you 1% of your assets each year. The other is a load fund that deducts an 8.5% sales charge from each contribution, and its expense ratio is 2%. If you put $2,000 a year in IRAs in each fund for 30 years, you would amass $320,201 in the low-cost no-load fund and $237,248 in the high-expense load fund.

Finally, do not automatically rule out funds that seem at first glance to be out of your reach. Some of the funds that have been top performers over time are closed to new investors but not to those opening retirement accounts. And many funds with minimum initial investments that you might find prohibitive offer lower minimums for IRAs. Take, for example, the Gabelli Asset Fund, a no-load growth-oriented portfolio run by noted money manager Mario Gabelli. It is excluded from the fund listing in chapter 10 because of its high minimum investment of $25,000. But you can open an Individual Retirement Account at Gabelli with as little as $2,000.

THREE

The Many Flavors of Diversified Funds

You have determined your investment goals, decided how much risk you can stand, and considered ways to deploy your money in a portfolio of mutual funds that matches your financial objectives. Now you need to take a closer look at the types of funds that best suit your tastes as an investor. The task could seem daunting—there are more kinds of mutual funds than flavors in an ice cream parlor. But the situation is less confusing than it appears. Most funds belong to one of three basic types of broadly diversified funds, which can be described in terms of their objective: income, growth, or total return.

INCOME FUNDS FOR STEADY RETURNS

The goal of an income fund is to pay regular, generous dividends. That is the principal reason why such funds are so attractive to retirees and other people who depend on investment earnings for a large portion of their everyday living expenses. Many growth-oriented investors also own income funds to help diversify their holdings and lower the risks inherent in fairly aggressive portfolios.

Most income funds invest primarily in bonds, which obligate the issuing company or government to pay interest, usually at regular intervals, and to repay the face value of the bond at maturity. Some of these funds seek capital gains as a secondary goal by supplementing their bond holdings with high-dividend stocks or convertible securities. Convertibles are hybrids—issued either as bonds or as preferred stock—that pay fixed income the way bonds do but can be exchanged for shares of the issuing company's common stock at a specified price. A growing number of funds provide tax-exempt income by investing exclusively in municipal bonds issued by city and state governments.

The most popular yardstick of an income fund's performance is yield—the fund's annual dividend divided by the current price of its shares. When comparing yields, keep in mind that funds with nearly identical objectives do not necessarily calculate their yields in a uniform manner. Different funds measure earnings over different periods, and some try to fatten their dividends with income from options they sell on the securities in their portfolios. Prodded by the SEC, funds are expected to adopt a standard method of computing yields using only interest and dividends earned over the previous month. Meanwhile, you can easily compare current yields by consulting the fund rankings that are published regularly in *Money*, which calculates all yields on a uniform basis.

Also remember that unlike, say, a bank certificate of deposit, an income fund's payout is not guaranteed. Your total return from a fund depends not only on the dividends you get but also on the price you receive when you sell your shares. The value of bonds—and of funds that own them—

appreciates when interest rates decline and falls when interest rates rise, so the price you receive when you cash in shares could be higher or lower than the price you paid for them originally.

Interest rates have been heading down for much of the 1980s, rewarding income fund shareholders with handsome total returns enhanced by capital gains. But a reversal of this trend and the resultant drop in fund share prices might come as a shock to investors who, in pursuit of secure higher yields, have migrated en masse to bond funds from money-market funds, which have fixed share values.

Contrary to popular belief, prices of bonds can and sometimes do fluctuate wildly. For example, when interest rates soared from 6.5% to 13.4% between 1977 and 1981, long-term bond prices sank more than 50%. During much of 1981, in fact, the bond market was over 1½ times more volatile than the stock market. (See figure 10.) So pay closer attention to an income fund's total return than to its yield. The total return figure, found in a fund's latest shareholder

FIGURE 10. Relative Volatility: Long-term Treasury Bond Index/S&P 500 Index

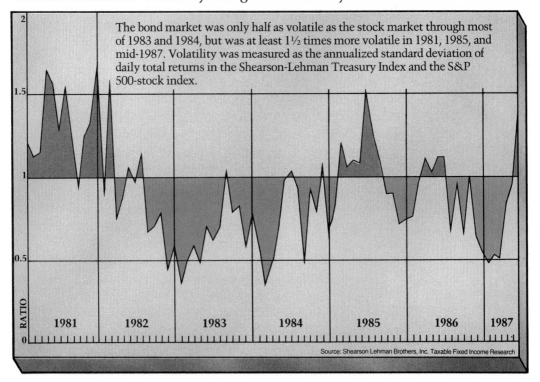

The bond market was only half as volatile as the stock market through most of 1983 and 1984, but was at least 1½ times more volatile in 1981, 1985, and mid-1987. Volatility was measured as the annualized standard deviation of daily total returns in the Shearson-Lehman Treasury Index and the S&P 500-stock index.

RATIO

1981   1982   1983   1984   1985   1986   1987

Source: Shearson Lehman Brothers, Inc. Taxable Fixed Income Research

report, takes into account both the past year's dividends paid and the change in share value.

Generally speaking, the higher a bond fund's yield, the greater the overall credit risk, maturity, and volatility of the bonds the fund holds. There is no credit risk, or likelihood of a bond issuer's defaulting on its interest or principal payments, among those funds that invest exclusively in bonds or mortgage-backed securities that are guaranteed by the federal government. Nor should there be any concerns for the safety of funds whose bond holdings have the highest credit ratings awarded by Standard & Poor's or Moody's, which grade companies and municipalities from AAA (tops) to D (in default).

Financially solid, A-rated issuers pay the least to borrow money, so you get lower yields from their bonds. To produce higher income, some funds concentrate on poorer-quality issues, commonly called junk bonds. These are rated below investment grade, B or lower. Though relatively few junk bonds have defaulted over time, they are the ones investors dump first in anticipation of recession, causing their prices to fall faster and further than those of more creditworthy issuers.

Moreover, long-term bonds—those not maturing for 10 years or more—almost always yield more than bonds of shorter maturities because their prices are the most sensitive to fluctuations in interest rates. (See figure 11.) If rates were to rise by just one percentage point, the value of recently issued twenty-year Treasury bonds would fall about 9%, while three-year Treasury notes would drop only 2.5%. So if you think interest rates are going to rise, consider funds that restrict their holdings to short- or intermediate-term bonds coming due in less than 10 years. If you expect rates to fall, favor long-term bond funds. Each fund generally keeps its holdings' maturities within a range that is specified in the prospectus. To find out a fund's current average maturity, you must call the fund.

The most common kinds of income funds include the following, in descending order of volatility.

Equity income funds. These portfolios emphasize high-dividend stocks and convertibles as well as bonds. As a result, equity income funds tend to generate lower yields

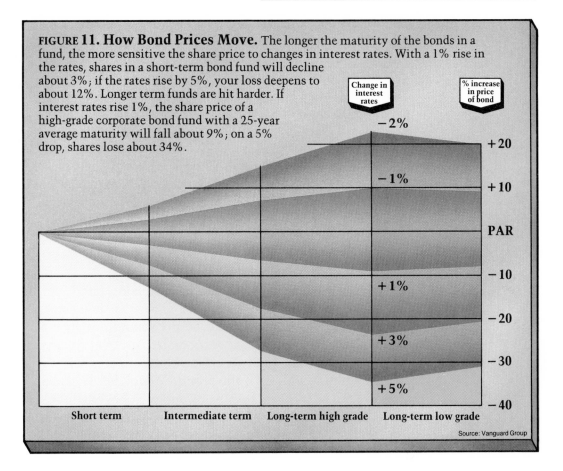

FIGURE **11. How Bond Prices Move.** The longer the maturity of the bonds in a fund, the more sensitive the share price to changes in interest rates. With a 1% rise in the rates, shares in a short-term bond fund will decline about 3%; if the rates rise by 5%, your loss deepens to about 12%. Longer term funds are hit harder. If interest rates rise 1%, the share price of a high-grade corporate bond fund with a 25-year average maturity will fall about 9%; on a 5% drop, shares lose about 34%.

Change in interest rates

% increase in price of bond

−2%

+20

−1%

+10

PAR

−10

+1%

−20

+3%

−30

+5%

−40

Short term   Intermediate term   Long-term high grade   Long-term low grade

Source: Vanguard Group

and to fluctuate in price more than do income funds that mainly buy bonds. But over the long term these stock-and-bond portfolios should give you much higher total returns because of their greater potential for capital gains. For example, Fidelity Equity-Income yielded 5.3% for the year ending in April 1987, about three percentage points below that of the average bond fund. But its 10-year total return of 617% smartly outpaced the 176% total return for bond funds as a group. To understand what that return means in dollars, consider that an initial investment of $1,000 made 10 years ago in Fidelity Equity-Income would have since multiplied 6.17 times. Adding the principle back in, the investment would be worth $7,170 today. Although equity income funds overall fell short of Fidelity Equity-Income's stellar performance, they still did considerably better than bond funds, posting an average 10-year return of 389%.

High-yield corporate bond funds. They invest largely in junk bonds. In 1986 about 3.7% of all junk bonds defaulted, compared with the negligible default rate for investment-grade bonds. To compensate investors for accepting the greater risk of default, junk bonds pay yields that typically are three to four percentage points higher than those of high-quality corporate and government bonds. Although junk bonds are risky, a fund that holds a large number of them—most own 100 or more—will be only slightly affected if one issue defaults. So look for funds with no more than 3% of their holdings in any one issue. A fund's latest shareholder report has a list of the bonds it holds and the size of its investment in each.

High-grade corporate bond funds. They buy bonds issued by well-established, financially secure companies rated A or higher. These funds take few risks and thus yield considerably less than junk bond portfolios and about one percentage point more than funds that specialize in government bonds. But the high-grade funds may outperform their higher-yielding siblings if the economy declines, because they are not as likely to be hurt by defaults. For example, Vanguard Investment-Grade Portfolio weathered recessionary 1980 with a 3% decline in share price and a total return of 8%, while its more daring sister, Vanguard High-Yield Portfolio, dropped 8% in price and finished the year with a 5% total return.

Option income funds. These funds, which trade options on securities in their portfolios to fatten the payouts to shareholders, deliver only when the stock market is as flat as a lake on a breezeless day. But such calm conditions have been notably scarce in the bullish 1980s. Partly as a consequence, option-trading income funds turned in their fifth sub-par year in a row in 1986, rewarding investors with a mere 8.2% total return on average, compared with an average of 13.9% for all income funds and 18.7% for the Standard & Poor's 500-stock index with dividends reinvested.

At the heart of the sales pitch for these funds is a flawed and misleading claim: specifically, that the funds' sophisticated options strategies generate *income* of 12% to 15%, compared with the single-digit yields commonplace among ordinary income funds. Simultaneously, the funds are said to reduce risk to a minimum by trading options to hedge—or offset potential losses—on the securities they hold.

The funds' basic strategy is to invest in widely held stocks—some of which pay attractive dividends—and sell call options against these shares. A call option is the right to buy a block of stock by a certain date at a specified price. In return, the call buyer pays the fund a fee, called a premium. The premiums—which are actually short-term gains, not income—are then used to plump up distributions to shareholders.

If the price of an optioned stock remains stable, the premiums leave the fund richer than if it had simply bought and held the stock. If the optioned stock rises above the specified price, the option buyer will exercise the right to buy the fund's shares for less than the going rate. The fund does keep the premium but misses out on what could be a much larger gain. Conversely, if the stock slips, the option buyer will not exercise the right, and call-selling profits can help offset the fund's loss.

But the strategy protects you only marginally against a strong downturn. Thus in anything but a listless market, you get a hedge of the most perverse kind—one that keeps you from reaping lofty gains but leaves you vulnerable to hefty losses.

For instance, suppose that a stock against which a fund has sold a call option plunges in price. In that case, the fund is left with a realized gain—from option premiums—and an unrealized loss on the stock. This puts the fund manager in a bind. By law, funds must pay out to shareholders all realized gains left after subtracting *realized* losses. Thus if the manager does not sell the loser, he gets to pay out the full premium to shareholders. The unrealized loss on the stock, however, reduces the fund's net asset value. If the manager sells the stock and takes the loss, it must be offset against the gain from the premium. That preserves net asset value but cuts into the cash that is available to pay out to shareholders.

Rather than sacrifice their fund's prime selling point, most option income fund managers would rather hold on to their losers and let net asset value slide. Share values in

First Investors Option Fund, for example, dropped from $6.63 at the end of 1981 to $4.68 at the end of 1986—which explains how the fund could have returned only 45% over five mostly bullish years.

Government bond funds. Their portfolios contain super-secure bonds issued by the U.S. government or its agencies. The government guarantees interest and principal payments on Treasury bonds and other obligations such as Ginnie Maes, which are mortgage-backed securities issued by the Government National Mortgage Association. (In the rankings in chapter 10, funds that invest in these securities are designated as either U.S. government or mortgage-backed bond funds.) Government bond funds are not totally riskless, however, because the Treasury protects only against default, not against price declines caused by rising interest rates.

What is more, in recent years investors in Ginnie Mae funds have had to worry about another kind of risk: early return, or prepayment, of principal. Because mortgage rates have been on the decline, large numbers of homeowners have refinanced their loans at cheaper rates and paid off their old high-rate mortgages. So funds that hold the high-interest Ginnie Maes get back big chunks of capital that they must reinvest at lower rates, driving the funds' yields down. A fund may even lose capital if its Ginnie Maes are trading for higher than face value when the unwanted prepayments occur, which is usually the case. To play it safe, you should avoid funds that are heavily invested in Ginnie Maes paying more than two percentage points over current mortgage rates. You will find a list of a fund's investments in its most recent quarterly report.

A growing number of government bond funds also trade options. Among the largest funds employing this strategy are American Capital Government Securities, Colonial Government Securities Plus, Paine Webber GNMA, and Van Kampen Merritt U.S. Government Fund. As a result, some of these funds have achieved impressive yields, but often at the expense of appreciation in their share prices.

The impact of this strategy on total return can be dramatic. In mid-1986, for example, the YES Fund, which sells call options on Treasury securities it owns, claimed a 12%

yield at a time when the average government bond fund
yielded 9.6%. But the YES Fund's 12-month total return
was an anemic 1.6%, a little more than one-seventh of the
total return for all government bond funds during the same
period. When bond prices are flat or declining, however, the
YES Fund's total return may top that of other government
bond funds because of the income generated from option
premiums.

Target funds. In recent years sold only by the Benham and
Scudder mutual fund families, target funds buy bonds that
all mature in the same year. The purpose is to give long-
term investors a predictable stream of income or a clear
idea of what their investment will be worth on a specific
date—say, upon retirement. Target funds hold corporate or
government bonds, municipal bonds, or zero-coupon Treasuries. Zero-coupon bonds pay no interest but are issued at
deep discounts to their face value and are redeemed at face
value upon maturity.

   As with any mutual fund, you can cash in your target
fund shares at any time. But if you do so before the bonds in
the portfolio mature, you risk losing part of your principal.
Like all bond portfolios, the value of a target fund's shares
will fluctuate as interest rates rise or fall. Zero target funds
are particularly volatile, as are targets with distant maturity
dates—for instance, 15 years or more. So unless you are
willing to gamble on an interest-rate decline, avoid these
target funds if you think you may have to get at your
principal before maturity.

MUNI BOND FUNDS FOR TAX-EXEMPT EARNINGS

The problem with investing for income is that you usually
have to share your annual earnings with the Internal Revenue Service. But you can cut the federal tax man out of the
action by investing in funds that buy bonds issued by
municipalities and states. The interest they pay is exempt
from federal taxes and, if you live in the state where the
bonds were issued, the interest is exempt from state and
sometimes local taxes as well.

Changes in federal tax laws in 1986 left income from municipal bonds largely untouched, with two notable exceptions. Interest from a few kinds of bonds—those issued to pay for sports stadiums and convention centers, for example—is now fully taxable. Income from another category, which includes water and sewer bonds and airport bonds, is taxable too, but only to fairly wealthy taxpayers subject to the alternative minimum tax. However, all municipal bonds issued before August 8, 1986, and most of those issued since then, remain completely exempt from federal taxes.

As for municipal bond fund yields, the lower tax brackets that went into effect in 1987 make tax-exempt income only slightly less attractive than before. Most muni funds still make sense for investors in the 28% tax bracket or higher. You are in that bracket if you are married, filing jointly, and have taxable 1988 income of more than $29,750 a year, or are single and have taxable income of more than $17,850 a year. In that bracket, a taxable 20-year utility bond yielding, say, 9% would return about 6.5% after federal taxes. Comparable munis would yield nearly a percentage point more. For help with calculating and comparing after-tax returns of the different types of bond funds, see appendix A.

Tax-exempt funds can be divided into four major categories, depending on the types of bonds they buy.

High-yield muni funds. Investors can expect the share values of these funds to swing as vertiginously as high-yield corporate funds that specialize in junk bonds. High-yield munis invest in low-grade bonds (those rated B or lower), which pay above-average returns to holders who are comfortable with the bonds' greater risk of default. On average, these funds yield only about a third of a percentage point more than high-grade muni funds—not much of an enticement for the added risk. For example, investors may have lost the better part of $2.25 billion when the Washington Public Power Supply System defaulted on several nuclear power plant projects in 1983. In selecting a high-yield muni fund, check its prospectus to see how it did in periods such as 1981, when rising interest rates pushed muni fund total returns down 5.7% on average. Be wary of funds that did worse than that.

High-grade muni funds. These funds invest in long-term municipal bonds rated A or better. Many high-grade funds buy only bonds guaranteed against default by private insurers. Since insurance costs the fund—and you—between a quarter and a half of a percentage point in yield, and since issuers of high-grade bonds rarely default, most bond analysts think you are better off investing in funds that concentrate on uninsured issues. You usually can determine whether a fund favors insured issuers from its name—for example, Colonial Tax Exempt Insured—or from its statement of investment objectives in the prospectus.

Single-state muni funds. They invest only in the issues of a particular state, especially high-tax states such as California, Michigan, Minnesota, New York, and Ohio. Single-state funds generally yield a quarter to a half of a percentage point less than national municipal funds, so do not automatically assume that a single-state portfolio will give you the best after-tax yield. Also remember that a dollar you save on state taxes (and therefore do not deduct on your federal tax return) will be partly offset by a corresponding increase in your federal tax bill.

Intermediate-term muni funds. Their portfolios hold only high-grade munis that usually mature in less than 10 years, making them suitable for conservative investors. Such funds fluctuate less in price than do long-term muni funds but also yield one to three percentage points less. Intermediate portfolios vary widely in their average maturities, however. For example, Fidelity Limited Term Municipals Bond Fund maintains an average maturity of about 10 years. By contrast, Calvert Tax-Free Reserves Limited Term Portfolio restricts the average maturity of its portfolio to three years or less. A fund's policy is listed in its prospectus.

GOING FOR GAINS WITH GROWTH FUNDS

If seeing the value of your fund shares rise is more important to you than getting regular payments for dividends or interest, you have the makings of a growth fund investor.

Growth funds generate returns primarily by buying and selling stocks. You profit principally from increases in the value of your fund's stock portfolio and the resulting boost in the price of the fund's shares.

All growth funds carry varying degrees of risk associated with volatility, or the degree and frequency of a fund's price fluctuations relative to those of stocks in general. When the stock market enters a bear phase, most growth funds suffer as share prices fall across the board. Conversely, when investors turn bullish, most growth funds are buoyed by the tide of rising prices. Thus no matter how astutely your money is managed in a stock fund, your shares will periodically and unpredictably bob in value with the ebb and flow of the stock market. Since the market moves in cycles of four to six years, you probably should not use growth funds for money you expect to need within that time span. Otherwise you run the risk of a downdraft in stock prices just when you need to cash in your shares.

Growth funds fall into two categories: long-term growth funds, which aim for steady increases in share value, and more aggressive maximum-capital-gains funds, which undertake greater risks for heftier profits.

Long-term growth funds. They tend to focus on stocks of established, brand-name companies such as AT&T, IBM, or McDonald's, with histories of consistent earnings growth and appreciation in share prices. Many of these stocks also pay regular dividends. This income, combined with interest earned on the funds' cash reserves—usually 6% to 12% of total assets—produces an average annual yield of about 2%. The growth rate for these funds is much more impressive. In the 10 years to April 1987, long-term growth funds achieved an average total return of 461%, assuming that dividends and capital-gains distributions were reinvested. That is significantly better than the 380% total return for the Standard & Poor's 500-stock index of mostly blue chip companies.

Such profitable results over time make these funds particularly appealing to buy-and-hold shareholders with ample resources and the resolve to ride out market slumps. Based on the performance of all no-load funds between 1982 and 1985, Sheldon Jacobs, head of No-Load Investor in

Hastings-on-Hudson, New York, has calculated that long-term growth funds are about 12% less volatile than the Standard & Poor's 500-stock index. These funds generally outperform the index when prices are rising and nearly match it when stocks plummet.

To help shore up their share values during periods of market uncertainty or decline, some growth funds shift heavily into cash in anticipation of lower stock prices. A notable example is the top-performing Nicholas Fund, a Milwaukee-based fund with $1.3 billion in assets under management. When the S&P 500 dropped 9.5% during the first seven months of 1982—one of the steepest declines this decade—Nicholas slipped just 3.4%.

Maximum-capital-gains funds. These portfolios invest in high risk/reward stocks that their managers believe are headed for rapid price run-ups. Such stocks are often those of small or fledgling growth companies. (In the rankings in chapter 10, portfolios that specialize in these stocks are designated as small-company growth funds.) Or they could be issues of advanced technology firms, takeover targets, and any other shares that fund managers anticipate will be Wall Street's next hot stocks. When—and if—the stocks do take off, the managers try to sell them before they flame out and fall from favor. Since maximum-gains portfolios are heavily weighted with young or other non-dividend-paying companies, they generally yield only 1% or less annually. But over time these funds can reward patient shareholders handsomely for the extra risks they take. As a group they compiled an average total return of 548% over the 10 years to April 1987.

Because the stocks that maximum-gains funds hold are most sensitive to market movements, the funds tend to be hit harder than long-term growth funds in bear markets and to outperform them in bull phases. According to Jacobs, maximum-capital-gains funds are considerably more volatile than the S&P 500, appreciating two or three times as much as the index in rising markets and falling twice as much as the index in declining ones.

While the unpredictable stocks favored by maximum-capital-gains funds are primarily responsible for the high volatility of their portfolios, the fund manager's trading strategy may also be a contributing factor. Unlike long-term growth funds, maximum-gains funds sometimes use speculative techniques such as buying stocks on margin—that is, using money borrowed from brokers. This practice boosts a fund's buying power during bull markets but heightens its losses when stocks dive.

Moreover, at least half of all of these aggressive funds always remain fully invested in stocks, accepting losses of 50% or more during bear markets to ensure that they benefit when stock prices take off again. But keep in mind that just to break even from a loss of 50%, a fund must gain 100% in the next bull phase. If you are a buy-and-hold investor, you might consider maximum-gains funds only for money you will not need for 10 years or more. If you are not content to buy and hold, you can still help minimize your risk by switching back and forth between maximum-gains funds and money-market or more conservative stock funds in an effort to capture the aggressive funds' big gains and avoid their inevitable slides.

SOOTHING PROFITS FROM TOTAL-RETURN FUNDS

Total-return funds blend the safety and income of government and corporate bonds with the growth potential of stocks. Their aim is to produce reliable long-term returns with a minimum of fluctuations along the way. This balance between risk and return makes such funds appropriate for all but the most conservative and the most daredevil investors.

In recent years, almost all total-return funds have benefited from the fall in interest rates, which boosted the value of the bonds and high-dividend stocks in their portfolios. The tax reforms of 1986 have also added to the appeal of a growth and income strategy. Consider the implications of the increase in the capital-gains tax rate to 28%, versus the previous 20% top rate, plus the elimination of the preferential rate on capital gains effective in 1988. These changes make income from dividends and interest—now taxed at the same rate as gains—just as attractive after taxes as earnings from growth. At the same time, investors will no

longer be as highly rewarded for the additional risk of
pursuing growth alone.

The easiest way to follow this strategy is to invest in
total-return funds, which tend to be staid but steady performers. Over the 10-year period to April 1987, this category of funds has grown an average of 369%. In broad-based
bull markets, they traditionally rise more slowly than funds
committed strictly to growth. In mostly bullish 1986, however, total-return funds gained on average 16.2%, compared
with the average growth fund's 13% rise. When growth
stocks take a tumble, total-return funds' income helps to
buttress their share value. In 1984, when aggressive growth
funds lost 8% on average, growth and income funds gained
4% as a group.

The comparatively sedate investment approach of total-
return funds makes them attractive to investors who wish
to build capital without enduring the boom-and-bust cycle
of growth stocks. Such investors range from retirees who
want to add a conservative growth component to a predom-
inantly income-oriented portfolio, to young families who
seek growth but are not willing to pursue it headlong. Be
aware, however, that the funds are meant to be bought and
held for a minimum of five years.

When you choose among total-return funds, be sure to
check a fund's prospectus for its record in the bear market
years of 1977 and 1981 and the flat market of 1984. To
qualify as a top candidate, the fund should have outperformed the S&P 500 index in each of those years. (See
appendix C for the S&P 500's total returns.)

It is worth noting that total-return is a middle-of-the-road
category that includes funds of widely varying approaches.
Many seek growth over income and are willing to take
sizable risks for big returns, while others play it safe. In
addition, some equity income funds, which typically give
top priority to dividends, use the term "total return" in
their names. If a fund's orientation is not clear from its
statement of investment objectives in the prospectus, you
can get a good notion of it by comparing its current yield
with that of other total-return funds. Generally, the higher
the portfolio's yield, the greater its emphasis on bonds
versus stocks—the basic distinction between the following
types of total-return funds.

Growth and income funds. They invest mostly in high-dividend stocks and convertibles such as those issued by utilities, oil companies, banks, and insurers. But at times some of these funds can be as opportunistic as growth portfolios, investing boldly in high-flying stocks or those of troubled companies long out of favor on Wall Street.

If you prefer high capital gains to steady income, you may want to consider a relatively venturesome portfolio such as Eaton Vance Total Return, which normally has most of its assets in stocks. In the three years to April 1987, the fund grew 131%, versus an average of 88% for growth and income portfolios overall.

If you would rather take lower risks, you would probably be better off with a more conservative total-return fund such as Mutual Shares, which along with its younger sister fund, Mutual Qualified Income, made the list of 10 all-weather funds (see chapter 9). Mutual Shares has consistently generated superior long-term results by seeking out troubled companies whose stocks are cheap relative to the value of their assets. In the three years to April 1987, the fund had a below-average 84% total return. But it gained 649% over the 10-year period, compared with 369% for growth and income funds as a group.

Balanced funds. They generally get their growth exclusively from stocks and their income from bonds. In fact, many balanced funds guarantee in their prospectuses to keep a minimum portion of their portfolio—from 20% to 50%, depending on the fund—always invested in bonds.

Among balanced funds, for example, Kemper Total Return stresses capital appreciation and takes some risks to achieve it. At times the fund puts as much as 80% of its portfolio in stocks—some of them in fast-growing but unpredictable industries such as biotechnology and telecommunications. Kemper also owns high-yielding corporate junk bonds. Fund shareholders have profited nicely from this strategy, which has produced a 10-year total return of 482%, as against 317% for balanced funds as a group. At the other extreme, Stein Roe Total Return is more cautious, sticking with high-grade corporate bonds and conservative, income-oriented stocks such as those of Exxon, Amoco, and Duke Power. The fund's 10-year total return was 235%.

FOUR

Adding Spice with Specialized Funds

Among the broadly diversified mutual funds described in the previous chapter you are likely to find funds that suit your objectives and investment philosophy. But what if nothing fits quite right? Say you want predictable income from most of your investments but would like to speculate with a small portion of your cash—your mad money, so to speak—in the hope of earning a big capital gain. Or perhaps you want to hedge your investments against the possibility that double-digit inflation will come back. In such cases you can custom-tailor your investments by putting most of your money in growth, income, or total-return funds and the remainder in specialized portfolios.

There is a vast and often vexing array of specialized funds to consider. For example, sector funds concentrate their holdings in stocks of a single industry, such as chemicals, computer equipment, and electric utilities, or services such as health care, retailing, and banking. International funds invest in foreign companies. Precious-metals funds buy mostly shares of gold-mining companies both in the United States and abroad. Index funds own portfolios that replicate popular stock or bond market barometers such as the Standard & Poor's 500-stock index. Closed-end funds differ from the more familiar open-end funds in that they have a fixed number of shares that trade on the stock market in the same way individual stocks do. Self-styled social conscience funds restrict their holdings to stocks of ethically responsible companies. And relatively new asset allocation funds provide one-stop shopping for all your portfolio requirements.

Investors use sector funds and, to a lesser degree, gold funds in pursuit of ultrahigh appreciation because such funds tend to experience dramatic swings in share value. Sector buyers aim to purchase the shares as they begin to rise sharply and sell them just before they turn down. You can also buy and hold certain specialized funds to counter cyclical fluctuations in the stock and bond markets. International funds, for example, can help you capture gains in foreign stock markets that happen to be flourishing while Wall Street is on the wane. They can also let you take advantage of sudden drops in the dollar's exchange rate.

THE JOYS—AND HAZARDS—OF SECTOR FUNDS

If you are willing to take big risks to get maximum capital appreciation, you might consider putting some of your money into sector funds, an increasingly popular category that had grown to more than 100 funds by mid-1987. Because such portfolios buy only shares of companies in a particular industry, a fund invested in the hottest sector invariably will outperform diversified stock funds. One reason is that diversified funds will always contain stocks

FIGURE **12. Sector Fund Volatility, 1986**

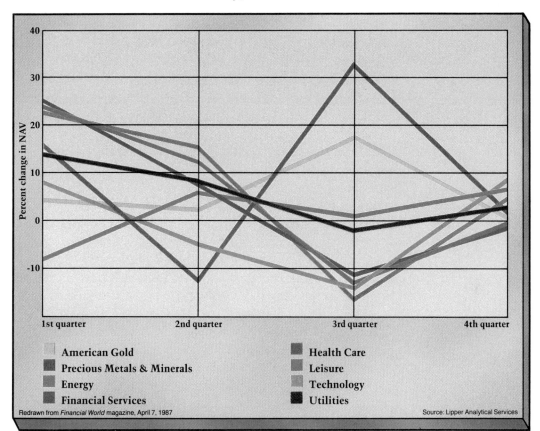

Redrawn from *Financial World* magazine, April 7, 1987

Source: Lipper Analytical Services

in weak as well as strong sectors. With sector funds, as with individual stocks, you decide which industry group is likely to be most profitable. The difference is that with a sector fund you rely on a manager to assemble and monitor a portfolio of the most promising stocks within that group.

The challenge, of course, is to pick the groups of companies that are poised to become market leaders and to avoid the pacesetters that are about to falter—sector funds tend to dominate short-term rankings of both the best- and the worst-performing portfolios. But the odds are not in your favor. In the 12 months to April 1987, for example, sector funds gained on average 23.4% including dividends, just a shade better than the average stock fund's 22% total return.

That is a fairly puny reward for accepting the added risk of owning a sector fund. With all its bets placed on the same industry, a sector fund can fall much faster than a diversified fund when market sentiment turns against its industry. This shift can be triggered by events as monumental as a nuclear accident half a world away—as was the case with electric utilities funds following the 1986 Chernobyl accident in Russia—or as prosaic as a disappointing earnings report from a top company. When a sector sours, as most do eventually, investors can quickly lose most of their gains.

Compounding the risk for investors is the fact that they cannot rely on sector fund performance records in the same way as with diversified funds. With conventional funds, a superior record reflects a manager's decisions about when to buy and sell stocks in different industries. With sector funds, recent strong performance by the industry does not mean the trend will continue. Indeed, the hotter the fund is, the greater the possibility that the industry could hit a down cycle soon. By the rules of sector fund charters, fund managers must stay mostly invested in the designated industry; managers usually can switch no more than 20% of fund assets into cash or bonds as defensive measures.

Even good news about an industry can create problems for sector fund managers and prospective shareholders. As investors' money pours in, managers must chase stocks, paying ever more as they climb. Then, often as the industry trend levels off after the spurt, the fund's sizzling recent performance continues to draw an avalanche of new investor cash. The late arrivals, however, get nothing like the soaring results that inspired their investment. That is because the fund manager cannot find an endless number of promising places to invest the new cash.

A classic example involves Fidelity Select-Technology. From June 1982 to June 1983, when stocks of small, high-tech firms shot up in frenzied buying, the fund notched a resounding 168% return, raising the price per share from $10.32 to $27.63. Meanwhile, assets grew from $2 million to $699 million, a jump of 34,950%. Yet approximately half of that asset growth came in after the fund's share price had risen to $25 in May 1983. Thus thousands of investors rode the fund upward for just a month; in June the fund and the technology stocks it held peaked and then fell 35% over the next 13 months. Not until 1987 did Select-Technology's share price work its way back to the heights of June 1983.

Mindful of the risk, you can use sector funds in two ways. One is to treat them like a maximum-capital-gains fund, riding out the fluctuations in share value in hopes of hefty gains down the line. If you choose an industry with excellent long-term prospects, you could do better over time than you would with a more diversified growth fund. As with any highly volatile fund, however, you should invest only cash that you do not expect to need for at least 10 years. Moreover, because the potential for loss is so great, many investment advisers recommend that you put no more than 20% of your portfolio into sector funds.

A second and more common use of these funds is as highly speculative short-term investments. With this approach you try to buy into a fund just as it hits bottom and sell when it reaches a peak. Since this means selecting the right industries at the right times—an impressive feat even among professional investors—this technique is best used by experienced investors as a less hazardous alternative to speculating in individual stocks. Owning a sector fund can be safer than trading a specific stock because with the latter you could correctly identify the next hot industry but still pick the one stock that fails anyway. The funds avoid that pitfall by holding 30 or more issues. And investors in Fidelity's 35 or so sector funds need not worry about losing track of their portfolios' value during an unusually hectic day of stock market trading. The offering prices—net asset value plus the funds' 2% sales charge—are updated *hourly*, as opposed to daily for all other funds.

If you plan to transfer money frequently among sectors, choose a family of funds that offers telephone switching privileges. This will facilitate quick moves. (For more on fund-switching, see pages 107-15.)

GOING GLOBAL WITH INTERNATIONAL FUNDS

Stateside investors who are eager to partake in investment opportunities abroad can buy mutual funds that invest entirely or partially outside this country. For example, international funds, which primarily buy foreign stocks and bonds, were among the most spectacular performers in the

12 months to April 1987. They gained on average 42.6% versus 26.2% for the Standard & Poor's index of 500 widely held domestic stocks.

Much of this international good fortune came from the declining dollar, which in 1986 lost 11.7% of its value against a basket of currencies from 15 other industrialized countries. When a foreign currency strengthens against the dollar, it boosts the dollar value of the funds' investments— and their profits. But shareholders in these funds probably will not see the same magnitude of profits once the dollar stabilizes in value, and they could suffer losses if the dollar rebounds strongly against other currencies. Still, owning a fund with foreign holdings can balance the risk of a portfolio dominated by stock funds that respond solely to the U.S. economy. Your choices include the following two types.

Global funds. They allow you to spread your cash among foreign and domestic stocks in a single portfolio. Globals can shift their assets between foreign and domestic markets largely as the fund managers see fit. As a group, they returned 28% on average in the 12 months to April 1987.

Most globals lately have been particularly partial to stocks on this side of the sphere, investing an increasing percentage of their assets in the United States. Consider Prudential-Bache Global, the group's top one-year performer with a 43.7% return. In the 12 months to April 1987, the fund more than doubled its relative weighting of domestic securities, from about 15% to 33% of total holdings. It allocated around 40% of its remaining assets to the Pacific Basin—a region that stretches from Japan to Australia—and 25% to Europe. The fund's manager, Wallace Wormley, says that the fund will invest even more heavily in the United States when the management sees little further scope for the dollar's decline and considers stocks in this country attractive compared with those of companies in other markets.

Each global fund has its own investment goals. You can choose a fund such as Prudential-Bache, which aims for growth and income, or a more aggressive fund such as Putnam International Equities, whose 154% total return made it the best-performing global over the three years to April 1987. Globals may also operate under restrictions, as described in their prospectuses. Prudential-Bache, for example, can put no more than two-thirds of its holdings in any one country, including the United States.

International funds. These are basically growth funds that invest almost exclusively in foreign stocks, though with differing approaches. For instance, Fidelity Overseas searches for bargains among stocks of foreign companies that the manager believes are undervalued relative to what prospective corporate acquirers would pay for the firms' assets. T. Rowe Price International, on the other hand, focuses on such fundamentals as earnings growth, interest rates, and currency trends. As a result, internationals can also differ widely in performance, depending on which approach or foreign stock market has lately been in vogue. Despite generally stellar results in recent years, their three-year total returns ranged from 59% for Alliance Canadian, which invests exclusively in Canadian stocks, to 196% for Merrill Lynch Pacific, which focuses on Japanese stocks.

If you know enough about overseas markets and currency trends, you may want to choose funds that invest all their assets in one corner of the world. Say you think Japan's yen will rise against the dollar, while other Asian currencies will not. You can buy a fund that invests only in Japan, such as Japan Fund or GT Japan Growth. Japan Fund, originally a closed-end fund, converted to an open-end one in 1987. The $8 million GT Japan Growth, founded in 1985, is too small to be included in this book's alphabetical listing. For information, call the fund toll-free at 800-824-1580.

Or you can concentrate on a larger area. Say you are impressed with the growth opportunities in South Korea, Singapore, and other rapidly industrializing Asian nations. Then you might invest in Nomura Pacific Basin, which specializes in companies based in those countries.

HEDGING YOUR BETS WITH PRECIOUS METALS

Like gold and other hard assets, precious-metals funds tend to rise rapidly in value during times of high inflation. In 1979, for example, with annual price increases well into the double digits, gold zoomed toward its all-time high of $850 an ounce. By year-end 1979, funds that specialized in the stocks of companies that mine gold, silver, and platinum achieved annual total returns of as much as 183%. Then over the next several years, inflation slowed to about 4% a year, and precious-metals funds underperformed most other investments. But in the 12 months to April 1987 gold funds rebounded sharply—gaining 85% as a group—in part because of investors' concerns over the dollar's declining value abroad. If you think the prospects for gold will continue to look good, or if you are looking for a long-term hedge against rising inflation, you may want to put a small portion of your assets—most investment advisers recommend no more than 10%—into precious-metals funds.

There are two dozen or so such funds, most of which are known as gold funds because they invest primarily in gold bullion and the stocks of gold-mining companies in Australia, North America, or South Africa. Up to 10% of their holdings are usually spread among the stocks of companies that mine silver, platinum, zinc, and other metals. When evaluating gold funds, keep in mind that some of them invest heavily in the shares of South African mines, which tap the world's largest reserves of gold and platinum. These funds, such as United Services Gold Shares and Strategic Investments, face acute and unpredictable political hazards that have depressed their share prices for many years.

You can reduce your risk by making sure you choose a gold fund that allocates its holdings among South African, North American, and Australian stocks. One example: Lexington Goldfund, whose three-year total return of 50.2% was the best among precious-metals funds. Or you might consider one of the funds that invest only in gold mines outside of South Africa, such as United Services New Prospector and USAA Gold.

If you are nervous about the gold situation, you might also consider the one mutual fund, Strategic Silver, that maintains at least 80% of its holdings in North American silver-mining companies. Silver, which is widely used in electronics and photography, is in demand by industry. As a result, the price of silver does not always decline as rapidly as that of gold when precious metals and other hard assets are out of favor.

INDEX FUNDS FOR AVERAGE RETURNS

Almost all mutual funds aim to beat the Wall Street stock indexes—and are not shy about advertising their triumphs when they do. But over the past 10 years or so, more than half of all mutual funds followed by *Money* failed to keep pace with the Standard & Poor's 500-stock index. And in the 12 months to April 1987, when the index charged ahead 26.2% including reinvested dividends, the total return for the average diversified stock fund was 18.1%.

Because so many funds have underperformed the market averages in recent years, stock-index funds have enjoyed a surge of popularity. These weighted portfolios of all the stocks in a particular index aim to replicate it in performance. Before rushing to invest in such funds, remember that their enticing returns came during a sharply rising market. If stocks turn down or stay flat, the index funds will react accordingly. By contrast, with a well-managed fund, you have a chance of substantially beating the market over time.

Investment adviser Burton Berry, editor of the *NoLoad Fund X* newsletter in San Francisco, has calculated that $10,000 invested in 1978 in Vanguard Index Trust would have been worth $32,023 through September 1986. The same amount invested in Evergreen Total Return, a top-ranked equity income fund, would have grown to $48,912.

Still, some investment advisers believe that it can make sense for conservative investors to put a small portion of their holdings—10% to 15%—into one or more index funds as insurance against losses in more aggressive funds. For example, Vanguard Index Trust tries to match the bellwether S&P 500-stock index, which represents about 70% of the total value of shares on the New York Stock Exchange. Vanguard was up 25.5% including dividends for the 12 months to April 1987, less than a percentage point shy of the S&P 500's total return.

Or you might consider funds that duplicate the S&P 100, made up of stocks for which options are listed on the Chicago Board Options Exchange. Funds following this index of widely held blue chips sell options on the index itself or on individual stocks they own in an effort to boost their income. As a result, these funds underperform the index in advancing markets and tend to outperform it when stock prices are static or falling. Two funds included in this book's alphabetical listing of 738 funds are modeled on the S&P 100: Gateway Option Income and Principal Preservation's S&P 100 Plus Portfolio.

In addition, funds tied to indexes of international stocks might appeal as a means of getting into overseas markets that may be unfamiliar to you. One such fund is Colonial's International Equity Index, which follows Morgan Stanley's EAFE—Europe, Australia, Far East—index of some 800 companies in 16 countries. Partly because of the dollar's steep decline in value abroad over the 12 months to April 1987, the EAFE was up an impressive 72.4%. Whether Colonial can keep abreast of the index remains to be seen; the fund was founded in July 1986.

CLOSED-END FUNDS FOR BARGAIN HUNTERS

Investors in search of excellent buys may find them among the 100 or so U.S. closed-end mutual funds, which you buy through brokers and pay the same commission as you would on a stock purchase. Like open-end funds, closed-ends are managed portfolios of stocks or bonds. The basic difference is that open-end funds continually sell and redeem their shares at net asset value, while closed-ends have a fixed number of shares that trade the way stocks do on exchanges or over the counter. Thus the price of a closed-end share is determined by supply and demand. Depending on the balance between the two, the price may be more or less than the fund's net asset value.

A closed-end fund can be a bargain when its shares sell at a discount to net asset value, as most of them do. Thomas Herzfeld, a South Miami investment manager who specializes in closed-end funds, notes that many closed-ends trade at as much as 20% below net asset value. One reason for the discounts is that investors tend to overlook closed-ends because they are not heavily promoted by brokers and fund managers.

What matters most to investors, of course, is performance. Surprisingly, a study conducted by *Money* reveals
that the closed-end structure seems more conducive to
success than the open-end one. In fact, the portfolios of
eight of the ten closed-end funds that *Money*'s study identified as having open-end equivalents outperformed those of
their open-end brethren by margins of 3% to 14% over a
recent three-year period. (For performance figures of widely
held closed-end portfolios, refer to appendix B.)

One explanation of the study's findings is that in open-
end funds, investors' cash tends to flow in the wrong
direction. It floods in during market advances, when stocks
get more and more pricey, and then flees as the market falls,
forcing the fund manager to sell stocks into the teeth of a
storm to cover redemptions. By contrast, shareholders who
want to bail out of a closed-end fund can sell their shares to
other investors. But the sales do not affect the fund's assets
or the manager's investment strategies.

As with any mutual fund, look for closed-end portfolios
that fit your investment goals. They should also have a
solid record of growth—in terms of net asset value and
share price—compared with the records of open-end funds
and other closed-ends with the same objectives. You can
generally determine a closed-end fund's investment philosophy by reading its annual report, which you can get from
your broker or from the fund. *Wiesenberger Investment
Companies Service* and *The Value Line Investment Survey*,
both available in most large public libraries, publish performance data for many closed-end funds. You will find more
detailed analyses of fund records in the newsletter *Investor's Guide to Closed-End Funds*. Current discounts and
premiums on closed-end stock funds appear in the *Wall
Street Journal* on Mondays (look under the heading "Publicly Traded Funds"). The *Journal* prints the same information for closed-end bond funds on Wednesdays.

The rare closed-end fund that trades well above its net
asset value should generally be avoided because this premium—usually justified by the fund's above-average dividends or some other special attribute—typically shrinks or
disappears over time. Instead, ask your broker to suggest
some candidates that are selling at wider discounts than
they normally do—and to explain why he thinks they are

bargain-priced. Historically, unusually wide discounts tend to narrow during both bull and bear markets—a boon to closed-end shareholders. When the market rises, the shrinking discount adds an extra boost to any gain in the fund's assets. If the market turns down, the fund's disappearing discount cushions the loss in net asset value.

FUNDS THAT EMPHASIZE ETHICS

If you want a fund whose investment policies do not conflict with your ethical values, you might consider putting your money into a portfolio that uses various political and social criteria when selecting stocks. You may pay a price for following your conscience, however. In the 12 months to April 1987, the seven such funds included in the alphabetical listing in chapter 10 had an average total return of 14.5%, compared with 22% for stock funds overall.

These so-called social conscience funds have investment objectives ranging from long-term growth to income. They tend to be politically liberal. For example, Calvert Social Investment Managed Growth, a growth and income fund, shuns nuclear power and defense stocks, as well as companies that operate in South Africa. Dreyfus Third Century, a growth fund, selects stocks based in part on how well the companies conserve natural resources and promote employee safety. Pax World, a balanced fund, shuns arms makers as well as alcohol, tobacco, and gambling companies. Pioneer Group is a family of three growth and income funds—Pioneer, Pioneer II, and Pioneer Three— plus one income fund, Pioneer Bond. All stay clear of alcohol and gambling companies and stocks of companies with holdings in South Africa.

ASSET ALLOCATION FUNDS

Relative newcomers to the mutual fund field, asset allocation funds combine holdings in different investment areas—putting, say, 20% of your money in international stocks, 30% in domestic stocks, 20% in precious metals, and 30% in bonds. They provide, in effect, one-stop shopping for all your portfolio requirements. Within the category, there are two principal management approaches: keeping the elements in a permanent fixed percentage and altering the mix in an effort to time the market.

Because it spreads assets over four to six investment areas, an allocator fund cannot deliver the results of a fund that puts all its eggs in one or two baskets that happen to be the right ones at the right time. With rare exceptions, allocators will generally fall behind the average stock fund in a rising market. One reason is that few asset sectors can be expected to move in tandem; even the shrewdest combinations would be weighted down—if only temporarily—by a lagging sector. Conversely, when one part of the portfolio sours, the allocation fund should not suffer the drastic declines that plague more narrowly focused funds.

Generally, asset allocators are best for defensive-minded investors who are satisfied with steady but ho-hum performance over time. The funds should help to reduce the number of fitful nights you spend wondering whether you should be in stocks, bonds, gold, or real estate. And there is always a chance that one of these super-diversified funds could be a sleeper, as was the case with USAA Cornerstone in 1986.

Founded in 1984, this San Antonio-based fund was up 40.8% in 1986, placing it third on *Money*'s list of leading diversified funds for that year. Chief portfolio manager Harry Miller divides his holdings almost equally among five investment areas: U.S. stocks, foreign stocks, non-South African gold stocks, government bonds, and real estate investment trusts. REITs, as they are called, are publicly traded companies that manage a portfolio of real estate holdings much the way mutual funds manage stocks and bonds.

In 1986, obviously, Cornerstone's fixed mix of assets was nearly perfect. Strong foreign and domestic stock markets, plus a late-fall surge in gold bullion prices, translated into fat gains. But Miller sets more modest goals for the fund over the long haul. He is not trying to outguess the market, but rather to stay close to the S&P 500 in an up market and not fall as much as the index in down markets.

Another variation on the allocator theme is Permanent Portfolio, which sticks to fixed percentages split six ways: U.S. government bonds (35%), gold (20%), real estate and natural resources (15%), U.S. stocks (15%), Swiss francs (10%), and silver (5%). Blanchard Strategic Growth employs four separate portfolio managers who specialize in U.S. stocks, foreign stocks, bonds, and precious metals. A fifth manager serves as the mixmaster, deciding the weighting of each portfolio in the main fund. (The fund, founded in 1986, is not included in this book's alphabetical listing. For information, call 800-453-4100, 212-750-0555 in New York.) And Vanguard Star is a fund of funds. Instead of splitting assets among categories of investments, Star places 60% to 70% of its cash in other Vanguard stock funds, such as the top-performing Windsor growth and income fund, and 30% to 40% in Vanguard bond funds.

As growing numbers of individual investors rush to buy mutual funds, investment companies keep devising new ways to tap the market. The result is a range of "products" to suit every type of investor, from sector funds for the speculator to asset allocators for the convenience shopper. Once you have chosen the type of fund that will most likely get you to your goals, you are ready to start narrowing down the choices to particular funds.

Money Source

> **Investor's Guide to
> Closed-End Funds**
> c/o Thomas J. Herzfeld
> Advisors
> 7800 Red Road
> South Miami, FL
> 33143
> ($200 per year,
> 12 issues)

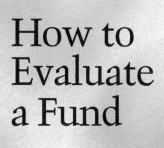

FIVE

How to
Evaluate
a Fund

If your primary objective is to invest in next year's hot mutual fund, you will probably be disappointed. Although investment pundits sometimes make claims to the contrary, there is no reliable way to predict a fund's short-term performance. More often than not, one year's star is the next year's has-been. For example, the Number 1 performer of 1983, Oppenheimer Regency, sank to 516th out of 536 funds the following year. The leader for 1984, Prudential-Bache Utility, came in 167th in 1985.

All you need to be a successful mutual fund investor is a portfolio that consistently makes money. Consider, for instance, the immensely popular Fidelity Magellan Fund, a long-term growth fund founded in 1963. Magellan has made the list of top 10 stock funds just twice in the past 10 years (1978 and 1980). Yet its first-place 1,962% total return over the 10 years to April 1987 far outdistanced that of the second place finisher in the mutual fund marathon, Twentieth Century Growth, a maximum-gains fund that grew 1,232%. Even if your fund just kept up with the Standard & Poor's 500-stock index over the 10-year period, your investment would have increased at least 380%, assuming that dividends were reinvested.

Picking the right fund—a steady performer whose objectives and style match your own—begins with a careful study of performance data. The mutual fund rankings and alphabetical listing in chapter 10 give you the basics. You will want to pay particular attention to those funds with above-average three- and ten-year records. Then weigh each fund's record against its volatility. The listing also supplies you with a fund's sales charges, total assets, and other facts that are useful in sizing up promising prospects. Here are some guidelines you can use to sort out which funds are really right for you.

THIN OUT THE THICKET OF CHOICES

Many mutual fund experts suggest you make the first cut of candidates on the basis of whether a fund has a hefty initial sales charge, or load, which is deducted from your share purchases. Since a load reduces the amount of money you have working for you in a fund, a load fund must achieve a higher rate of return than a no-load to earn you the same amount of money. For instance, a fund that charges the typical 8.5% load would have to earn 15.4% a year over a three-year period for its total return to equal that of a no-load fund that earned just 12% a year for the same period.

Paying a commission on load funds sold by brokers, financial planners, or insurance agents can make sense if the fund has had a superior long-term record. Standouts include growth-stock funds American Capital Pace, AMEV

Growth, Growth Fund of America, and New England
Growth—all of which carry hefty loads and are among the
top 25 performers over the 10 years to April 1987. A load
may also be justified if you feel more comfortable buying
through a trusted broker or adviser who will choose a fund
for you, monitor its results, and counsel you on when to sell
or switch.

Otherwise, confine your search to no-load funds or low-
load ones—those charging 3% or less—that usually sell
their shares directly to investors. That way you will start
out with more money in your account. Numerous studies
have shown that, on average, there is no difference between
the performance of load and no-load portfolios over time.
The sole advantage of investing in a load fund is to get a
salesman's advice.

FACTOR IN A FUND'S SIZE

Some advisers think another important criterion is a fund's
size, as measured by its total assets under management. A
relatively large stock fund, for example, can diversify its
holdings broadly, thereby reducing the likelihood that a few
bad stocks will pull the portfolio down. A big fund can also
get volume discounts on brokerage costs. On the other
hand, a large fund often buys and sells stocks in such big
blocks—each block represents 10,000 shares or more—that
it cannot get into or out of a company quickly without
adversely affecting the share price, pushing it up as a buyer
and knocking it down as a seller.

By contrast, a small fund has greater flexibility to take
advantage of, or reduce its exposure to, changing market
conditions. It can nimbly buy or unload securities and take
large positions in those up-and-coming companies that,
because they are newly public or have relatively few shares
outstanding, are frequently off-limits to big, block-trading
funds. If only one of these fast-growing companies takes off,
the small fund can make prodigious profits.

In mid-1986, for example, the Strong Opportunity Fund
had assets of about $17 million, compared with assets of
about $240 million for the average stock fund. In May of

that year the maximum-capital-gains fund invested 5% of its assets in the first public shares of Home Shopping Network, the Florida firm that helped to pioneer the field of selling merchandise over cable television. In its initial four months of trading on the American Stock Exchange, Home Shopping's price shot up more than 600% and propelled Strong Opportunity to the top of *Money*'s list of best performers in 1986, with a whopping 57% total return to shareholders.

Proponents of small funds maintain that ones with assets under $100 million or so have a performance edge over their larger brethren, though the evidence is far from conclusive. Being big does not seem to have been a drawback in the case of $8 billion Fidelity Magellan or $5 billion Vanguard Windsor, a growth and income fund that has been one of the most consistent performers over 10 years, gaining 594%. Yet Windsor, Quasar Associates, and several other top-performing stock funds have closed their doors to new investors primarily because the managers of these funds feared that their burgeoning assets would undermine their outstanding results.

In some cases, such as that of Windsor, the solution was to establish a clone fund—so called because it is set up to duplicate the sibling fund's objectives and strategies. The clone, $900 million Windsor II founded in 1985, was up 20.2% for the 12 months to April 1987, versus the original Windsor's 22.1% total return.

What should you do in the face of such uncertainty about size? Many respected fund watchers, including Gerald Perritt, editor of *The Mutual Fund Letter* in Chicago, recommend that investors seeking aggressive growth favor agile stock funds with portfolios smaller than $250 million. Perritt advises investors looking for conservative growth funds or reliable total-return funds to consider ones with assets of up to $500 million because these funds invest in actively traded large companies; hence the funds' sizable assets are not much of a handicap. As for giants such as Magellan and Windsor, Perritt suggests that you avoid them. If you already own them, you may want to sell at the first sign of lagging performance.

Just the opposite applies to bond funds. With them, flexibility counts for less than diversification and lower operating costs, and Perritt advises that you seek out funds with at least $500 million in assets.

STUDY THE PROSPECTUS CAREFULLY

After you have identified half a dozen or so suitable funds, phone each one to request copies of its prospectus and most recent annual and quarterly reports. Most funds have toll-free numbers, which can be found in the alphabetical listing in chapter 10. An application form is included with the documents. In the case of a load fund, you can get these documents from your broker or financial planner.

Although a mutual fund's prospectus is by design a dull read, it is full of useful facts and disclosures required by federal securities law. In general, a prospectus describes the fund's investment objectives, strategies, and risks; presents statistics on its past performance; lists the sales and management fees; and explains how you can buy and sell shares. Make sure that you are sent a copy of the statement of additional information, usually referred to as Part B. This document is important because it describes the fund's fees in detail, a subject that is usually treated cursorily in the prospectus.

The cover of the prospectus lists the fund's address and phone numbers and, in most cases, briefly summarizes the fund's objectives and states the initial sales charge, if any. Though formats vary, most prospectuses are divided into a dozen or so sections. Start your examination with the section commonly called "General Description of the Fund." Ranging in length from a few paragraphs to more than a page, this section should spell out the difference between the fund's objectives and its policies—the investment strategies and techniques it is permitted to employ to achieve its objectives. These might include buying stocks on margin (using money borrowed from brokers), trading options, or other sophisticated tactics you may not feel comfortable with. In addition, if the fund has more than 25% of its assets in one industry, or if it holds bonds rated below investment quality, these policies must be noted in the prospectus.

Pay particular attention to the table usually called "Per Share Income and Capital Changes" (see figure 13 for an example from Fidelity Magellan's 1986 prospectus). This table gives the fund's annual performance over the past 10 years—or the life of the fund if it is younger than that. It shows you whether a fund's performance has been steady or erratic, and it can be used to compare a fund's year-to-year changes in share value with those of other funds whose prospectuses you are sizing up.

For example, does the fund owe much of its long-term return to one or two lucky years, or did it consistently outperform comparable funds and market barometers such as the S&P 500 index? Many prospectuses plot the fund's performance against the S&P 500; for those that do not, you can look up the index's yearly total returns in appendix C of this book. You also will want to see how well the fund weathered the down markets of 1977 and 1981 and the flat market of 1984.

FIGURE 13. Per-Share Data from Fidelity Magellan's 1986 Prospectus

The per-share data gives information about the fund's financial history. It uses the fund's fiscal year and expresses the information in lines 1-9 in terms of a single share outstanding throughout each year.

		1986	1985	1984	1983	1982	1981	1980	1979	1978	1977
1.	Investment income	$ .76	$ 1.11	$ .63	$ .44	$ .61	$ .80	$ .66	$ .36	$ .30	$ .20
2.	Expenses	.27	.32	.26	.11	.23	.30	.22	.18	.13	.09
3.	Investment income—net	.49	.79	.37	.33	.38	.50	.44	.18	.17	.11
4.	Dividends from investment income—net	(.65)	(.37)	(.26)	(.33)	(.58)	(.39)	(.17)	(.16)	(.12)	(.08)
5.	Realized and unrealized gain (loss) on investments—net	19.59	5.75	2.73	15.80	(.02)	14.46	2.17	3.99	1.43	.71
6.	Distributions from realized gain on investments—net	(1.78)	(3.69)	(1.88)	(1.23)	(9.92)	(.13)	—	—	—	—
7.	Net increase (decrease) in net asset value	17.65	2.48	.96	14.57	(10.14)	14.44	2.44	4.01	1.48	.74
	Net asset value:										
8.	Beginning of year	37.69	35.21	34.25	19.68	29.82	15.38	12.94	8.93	7.45	6.71
9.	End of year	$55.34	$37.69	$35.21	$34.25	$19.68	$29.82	$15.38	$12.94	$8.93	$7.45
10.	Ratio of expenses to average net assets	1.08%	1.12%	1.04%	.85%	1.34%	1.23%	1.40%	1.52%	1.60%	1.49%
11.	Ratio of investment income—net to average net assets	1.95%	2.79%	1.47%	2.56%	2.39%	2.08%	2.77%	1.49%	2.03%	1.98%
12.	Portfolio turnover rate	96%†	126%†	85%	120%	194%	277%	338%	249%	238%	205%
13.	Shares outstanding at end of year (000 omitted)	109,975	62,716	45,757	23,403	5,896	1,971	2,096	2,358	2,598	2,868

*Years Ended March 31,**

* Adjusted for a 3 for 1 split paid December 19, 1980.

† In accordance with the Securities and Exchange Commission's 1985 rules amendment, the 1986 and 1985 rates include U.S. Government long-term securities which were excluded from the calculations in prior years.

Audited—See the Report from our Independent Certified Public Accountants on page 38.

In analyzing the table, note the ratio of operating expenses to average net assets, generally referred to as the expense ratio. This figure tells you how much investors are assessed annually to pay management fees and operating expenses. About 1% is average for funds overall. The ratio for stock funds is about 1.1% and for bond funds, about .9%. Be wary of any fund whose costs exceed 1.5%.

Another key figure in the table is the portfolio turnover rate, which indicates how actively the fund trades securities. Most stock and bond funds have a turnover rate of 80% to 100%. The higher the turnover, the greater the fund's brokerage costs. These costs, which are not included in the expense ratio, can cut into your return because they reduce the profits or increase the losses on securities trades. Indeed, transaction costs can siphon off as much as 4% of the value of a stock being traded. This means that rapidly changing portfolios must substantially outperform less active ones just to stay even. Bond funds, because they tend to buy and sell securities in big blocks, usually have lower transaction costs than do stock funds.

Because a prospectus is usually updated only once a year, it may or may not list the fund's securities holdings as of a specified date. For the most current accounting of a portfolio's cash and securities holdings—and the percentage of total assets each represents—turn to the fund's most recent annual and quarterly shareholder reports. Study the documents closely for clues to the fund's investment philosophy. Here are some questions to bear in mind.

● How much weight does the fund give to growth, income, and capital preservation?

● If the fund buys stocks, does it ride out market downturns more or less fully invested, or does it retreat to cash or fixed-income investments?

● Is the fund's strategy to find stocks with undervalued assets, growing earnings, or a combination of the two? Value-oriented funds such as Royce Value and Mutual Shares tend to outshine stock funds as a group when the market is unsteady, while growth-oriented funds such as Weingarten Equity often lead when stocks are on the rise.

• If the fund buys bonds, what is their average maturity? Does the fund swap long-term issues for safe shorter-term bonds when interest rates are rising?

• Is the fund holding bonds that are currently priced above face value? In that case, you may lose principal if the bonds' issuers pay them off early.

The sections of the prospectus titled "How to Purchase Shares" and "How to Redeem Shares" explain the mechanics of getting into and out of the fund, whether by mail, phone, or wire. They also tell you whether there is an initial sales charge; a minimum initial investment or a minimum for subsequent investments; a fee for switching from one fund in the same family to another; or a charge for redeeming your shares.

TABLE 1. Evaluating a Fund

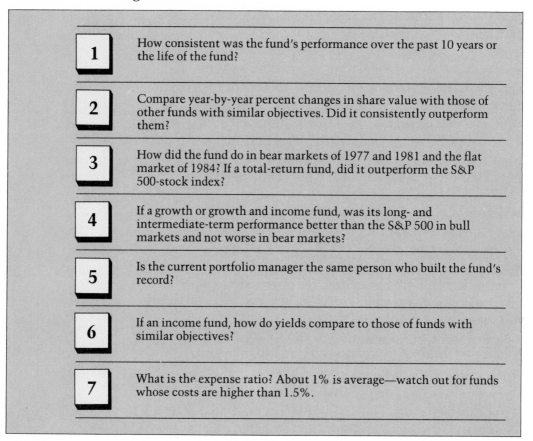

1	How consistent was the fund's performance over the past 10 years or the life of the fund?
2	Compare year-by-year percent changes in share value with those of other funds with similar objectives. Did it consistently outperform them?
3	How did the fund do in bear markets of 1977 and 1981 and the flat market of 1984? If a total-return fund, did it outperform the S&P 500-stock index?
4	If a growth or growth and income fund, was its long- and intermediate-term performance better than the S&P 500 in bull markets and not worse in bear markets?
5	Is the current portfolio manager the same person who built the fund's record?
6	If an income fund, how do yields compare to those of funds with similar objectives?
7	What is the expense ratio? About 1% is average—watch out for funds whose costs are higher than 1.5%.

CHECK OUT THE FUND MANAGER

When you put money in a mutual fund, you are not just acquiring shares in a diversified portfolio of stocks or bonds. You are also paying for high-quality management—or so you hope. Therefore, before committing your cash, you may find it worthwhile to learn as much as possible about the person or persons making the fund's day-to-day investment decisions. Managers come and go, and the hotshot stock picker who propelled a fund to the top of the charts last year may have long since left. So unless you know from reading newspapers and magazines that your fund is run by a superstar such as Peter Lynch of Fidelity Magellan or John Neff of Vanguard Windsor, you will want answers to the following questions.

How long has the manager run the fund? For all the information disclosed in a fund's prospectus and shareholder reports, you usually will not find the portfolio manager's name listed in these documents. But you can often learn it and how long he or she has been in charge by calling the fund's marketing or publicity department. Some funds will not tell you because they do not want to tie their reputations to that of an individual who might leave, causing investors to pull out their money. In that case, you can find the manager's name and longevity at the fund in the latest edition of the *Mutual Fund Sourcebook*, which you can buy quarterly or find in some large public libraries.

Compare the manager's tenure with the fund's year-by-year performance presented in the prospectus. If the manager has been at the helm since 1981—and thus was in charge during the market downturn of June 1981 to July 1982 as well as the bull market that began later in 1982—you can assume that the record shows the range of the manager's professional talents. If the manager came to the fund after 1982, those skills may not have been tested in tough times. To investigate further, you might ask the fund's marketing or publicity department to give you the name of a fund the manager ran previously, if any, and check his results at that fund.

How important is the manager to the fund's performance?
This will depend largely on the fund's objectives, size, and the way that it is operated. For example, a handful of funds have no single manager but are run instead by committees of analysts. With these funds, you should focus your attention on the team leader, if one is so designated.

In general, funds that aim for rapid capital appreciation are more apt to rely on the insights and skills of a single manager than are less aggressive stock or bond portfolios. That is because such maximum-growth funds typically try to take quick advantage of stock market movements and to latch on to small growth companies before the firms are discovered by Wall Street. To excel consistently with this approach, a manager cannot afford to wait for a cumbersome investment committee to discuss and approve which stocks the fund should buy or sell. Instead, the fund needs a decisive manager who has uncommonly good judgment and instincts.

Moreover, many relatively small stock portfolios that do not belong to a large family of funds also depend heavily on the expertise of one person—usually the entrepreneur who started the fund. Examples notable for their superior performance over the 10 years to April 1987 are the Lindner Fund (with an 875% total return under founder Kurt Lindner), Pennsylvania Mutual (up 664% under Charles Royce), and Acorn Fund (up 570% under Ralph Wanger).

With a few exceptions such as Lynch and Neff, managers of big funds and of portfolios in large families tend to be less critical to a fund's success. The principal reason is that these huge operations often make heavy use of costly computer stock-screening programs and generally have teams of experienced financial analysts feeding recommendations and economic analyses to the fund manager. Such funds are also more likely to have able assistant portfolio managers who can take charge in the event of a fund manager's temporary—or permanent—absence.

How much freedom does the manager have? Check the prospectus and the statement of additional information under the sections titled "Investment Objective and Policies." When a fund's investment strategy is quite broad, the portfolio manager's judgment and instincts become more critical. Conversely, individual expertise matters less if the fund's strategy is to invest narrowly in certain types of bonds or in specific industries. Sector funds, for example, stick mostly to stocks in their respective groups, so their fortunes fluctuate largely in tandem with those of their market sector, no matter how talented the manager is.

How should you react if the manager departs? Whether you too should consider leaving the fund will depend on just how much influence the departing manager had—and the fund's relative performance prior and subsequent to his or her leave-taking. If the value of your fund shares starts to sink while the market remains buoyant, you will obviously want to reevaluate your investment.

TAKE A HARD LOOK AT FEES

The costs of investing, administering, and marketing a mutual fund are passed along to you in the form of fees. You pay them either directly as up-front or deferred sales charges, or indirectly as annual assessments paid to the fund's management company from the portfolio's assets. Since some funds are considerably more expensive than others, it pays to study a fund's cost structure, which is explained in the prospectus and its statement of additional information. Remember, while a high-cost fund may in the end give you a better total return, it will have to perform better than a low-cost portfolio to do so.

You need to examine fees especially carefully these days because fund costs are rising and fee structures are getting more complicated. To offset higher marketing costs and to increase profits, a number of fund sponsors are adding new fees or combinations of fees, not all of them readily apparent to investors. For example, the Keystone family has abandoned front-end loads while jacking up assessments against assets and imposing new deferred sales charges, or back-end loads, that you must pay if you take your money out of the fund within four years. And some formerly no-load funds, such as Constellation Growth and those in the Strong group, now have front-end sales fees. You should

also examine the prospectus for the fund's hidden charges—
the fees that management deducts from your assets every
year. Indeed, if you plan to keep your shares for several
years, a no-load fund with high annual fees (called expenses
as a percentage of fund assets in table 2) can cost you more
than a load fund with low annual charges. The fees levied
by the four funds in the table are typical. The first line after
each fund's name shows how much you would pay in fees
the first year. The second line illustrates how those charges
add up over five years, assuming that the fees remain at
current levels.

You can expect to encounter the following types of fees
and charges as you investigate funds that interest you.

Front-end loads. The most onerous single expense is the
initial sales charge, levied by about half of the 738 funds
listed alphabetically in chapter 10. This charge, which can
be as high as 9% of your investment, is deducted before the
fund issues you shares, thereby reducing the amount of

TABLE 2. The Real Costs of Investing

	Number of years in fund	% maximum initial sales charge	% deferred sales charge	% exit fee	Expenses as percentage of assets*	Total costs as a percentage of your investment
Pennsylvania Mutual	1	None	None	1	1.03	2.02
	5	None	None	1	5.04	6.00
Hutton Special Equities	1	None	5	None	2.20	7.09
	5	None	1	None	10.53	11.42
Putnam Fund for Growth & Income	1	8½	None	None	.55	9.00
	5	8½	None	None	2.49	10.99
Fidelity Select–Energy	1	2	None	1	1.50	4.44
	5	2	None	1	7.13	10.04

*Five-year expense figure assumes that costs remain at current levels.

money you have working for you. Full loads of 4% and up
are normally imposed only by funds that sell shares through
stockbrokers, financial planners, and insurance agents; part
of the money compensates the salesman. Low-load funds,
such as those in the Fidelity group, usually sell shares
directly to investors and charge 0.5% to 3% of your investment. A few funds, including some in the IDS, Massachusetts Financial, Franklin, and Lord Abbett fund families,
deduct loads from reinvested dividends as well as from
initial and subsequent investments.

Back-end loads. Also called contingent deferred sales loads,
they are deducted by some funds when you pull your
money out. These fees start at 4% to 6% on withdrawals
during your first year in the fund and gradually decline to
zero over four to six years. Back-end loads allow the fund
groups that use them—most notably, many of the funds
affiliated with such major brokerage firms as Drexel Burnham, Dean Witter, E.F. Hutton, and Prudential-Bache—to
sell shares without front-end loads through commissioned
brokers. The fund sponsor pays the brokers from the back-
end loads and from the assessments against the fund's
assets. This combination of fees can be a bit less burden-
some than an 8.5% front-end load if you hold the shares for
less than 10 years or so. After that, even though the back-
end load disappears, the yearly accumulation of above-
average assessments may outweigh the traditional load.

Exit fees. A few funds charge exit fees either to discourage
you from making frequent trades or to recoup the administrative costs of redeeming shares. Like back-end loads,
these fees are deducted from money you take out of the
fund, but they involve much smaller amounts of money.
The fees range from a flat $2.50 per withdrawal to 1% of the
amount redeemed. With some funds the fees decline to zero
over a period of a few months or a year; with others they
remain constant. Because exit fees are so low, they should
not be a big consideration in selecting a fund.

Internal charges. These assessments against the fund's
assets include the management fee and expenses such as
accounting fees, the cost of printing and mailing reports to

TABLE 3. Comparing Loads and Fees

The worksheet and tables below, devised for *Money* by John Markese, research director for the American Association of Individual Investors, will enable you to compare all fees, including front-end loads, back-end loads, or exit fees, if any, and annual expenses. (Annual expenses, usually expressed as a percentage of the fund's total assets under "Per Share Data" in the prospectus, include management fees and 12b-1 charges.)

The key to making the conversions work is to estimate how long you will own shares in any fund you are considering. The table at left then converts front-end loads into the equivalent of fixed annual expenses. The table at right performs the same translation for back-end loads, assuming the fund grows at a 10% annually compounded rate. The worksheet makes it easy to come up with a total figure for annual expenses, expressed as a percentage of your investment.

Here is how the calculations work. Suppose you expect to hold a fund's shares for three years and want to compare the costs over that period for two funds—for example, Fidelity OTC, with a 3% front-end load and total annual expenses of 1.5%, and broker-sold Hutton Special Equities, which carries no front-end load but has total annual expenses of 2.2% and a back-end load. The charge is 5% on shares you redeem in the first year you own the fund; it declines by a percentage point each year thereafter.

OTC's 3% front-end load is equivalent to a 1% annual charge over three years (read across the row for years held until you reach its intersection with the column for a 3% front-end load). Using the worksheet, add the front-end load equivalent (line A) to the fund's 1.5% annual expense charge (line C); line B can be left blank. Total equivalent annual expense: 2.5%.

Special Equities' back-end load (3% after three years) is equivalent to an annual charge of .75% over three years. Add that figure (line B) to the fund's annual expenses of 2.2% (line C) and you get an equivalent annual expense of 2.95%. The conclusion: the Hutton fund is the higher cost fund over three years. Thus, unless you believe the assistance of a Hutton broker is worth the extra cost, or unless you expect the Hutton fund to outperform the Fidelity fund by at least 0.45% per year over the next three years, OTC is the better bet.

FIGURING YOUR FUND'S TRUE COSTS

A. Annual equivalent expense for your fund's front-end load, if any (from table at left) _____

B. Annual equivalent expense for your fund's back-end load, if any (from table at right) _____

C. Your fund's annual expenses (from fund prospectus) _____

D. Total equivalent annual expenses (add lines A, B and C) _____%

FRONT-END LOAD						BACK-END LOAD					
Years held	3%	4%	5%	6%	8.5%	Years held	1%	2%	3%	4%	5%
1	3%	4%	5%	6%	8.5%	1	0.91%	1.8%	2.7%	3.6%	4.6%
3	1.0	1.3	1.7	2.0	2.8	3	0.25	0.50	0.75	1.0	1.3
5	0.6	0.8	1.0	1.2	1.7	5	0.12	0.25	0.37	0.50	0.62
10	0.3	0.4	0.5	0.6	0.85	10	0.04	0.08	0.12	0.15	0.19

shareholders, and sometimes a marketing charge. They
range from about 0.3% to 5% of the amount you have in a
fund. In most cases these annual assessments are lumped
together in a fund's prospectus as a percentage of its net
assets, called the expense ratio. The average expense ratio is
about 1% per year, or $1 for every $100 of assets.

Expense ratios may seem insignificant compared with
loads. But they can mount up over time because the fees are
deducted from the fund's assets every year. Over 10 years, a
no-load fund with a 2% expense ratio will cost you more
than an 8% load fund with an expense ratio of 1%. Therefore you should be wary of funds with expense ratios in
excess of 1.5%, or $1.50 per $100 of assets.

12b-1 fees. About 40% of funds levy these arcanely labeled
fees named after the SEC rule that permits them. They are
most common on no-load and low-load funds, which collect the fees to pay for advertising or for commissions paid
to brokers. A few load funds—some of those in the Eaton
Vance and ABT groups, for example—also charge investors
12b-1 fees. Either way, the fees are usually included in each
fund's expense ratio. However, funds in the Keystone and
Venture families do not include all of their 12b-1 fees in
their expense ratios. This strategy makes the ratio seem
lower and the yields higher than those of otherwise comparable funds that do include these fees in their expense
ratios. Your total return will be reduced just as much as if
the fund had reported the fee in the conventional way.

TAKE THE PLUNGE

The mechanics of opening a mutual fund account are as
easy as establishing a savings account at your local bank.
You can invest in any no-load or low-load fund by complet-
ing an application form and mailing the management company a check. Or you can call a broker, financial planner, or
insurance agent. Many of them will sell you shares in
no-load or low-load funds without imposing sales charges,
but they probably will charge you an hourly consultation
fee of $75 or more.

Some load funds sold exclusively through salesmen will accept investments by mail, including those run by Merrill Lynch, the nation's largest brokerage house and fund sponsor. But you will have to pay the sales charge anyway. Some funds will even let you open an account by phone if you have money invested in another fund in the same family and promise to send in your check within seven days.

Filling out an application. Most fund applications consist of a single sheet of paper. You will have to provide basic background information, including your name, address, Social Security number (or taxpayer identification number), and birth date. You will be asked whether you want to open the account as an individual, which gives you alone the power to authorize switches and redemptions, or jointly with a spouse or friend. In that case, you or your co-owner can make investments individually, but both of you will have to sign all requests for redemptions of shares and transfers of money to another fund.

In addition, if you choose joint ownership, remember that in the event one of you dies, the other automatically owns all of the shares. If you buy them with someone else and leave your rights to the fund to a third person, you should instruct the fund on the application—often simply by checking the appropriate box—to register you and your co-owner as tenants in common. That way, if you die, the fund will transfer your rights in the fund to your designated beneficiary.

Setting up a distribution plan. Most funds require you to specify in advance what you want done with the capital gains the fund earns by trading securities in its portfolio and the dividends and interest it generates. You have three choices: 1) you can reinvest all distributions in the fund, adding to the number of shares you own; 2) you can have dividends paid to you in cash and capital-gains distributions reinvested in additional shares; or 3) you can have both dividends and capital-gains distributions paid to you in cash. Unless you are an income investor, reinvestment of all distributions is probably your best choice because the newly purchased shares then begin generating capital gains and dividends. Whatever you decide, you will owe federal taxes on the distributions unless your shares are in a tax-deferred account such as an IRA. (Capital gains earned by municipal bond funds are subject to federal taxes; the interest income is not.)

Choosing special services. You often are asked on your application whether you would like to sign up for additional services. With some funds, you may have to invest a certain amount before you qualify, but with others the services are available to all investors. Among the most common: check writing, which lets you write checks, usually of a designated minimum amount, against your fund balance; telephone switching, which enables you to transfer money among various funds in the same fund family with a telephone call; and wire-transfer privileges, which permit you to redeem shares with a phone call and have the fund wire the proceeds to your bank. This gives you access to your money the same day; by comparison, redeeming shares by mail can take more than a week.

For example, getting your money out of one of Dreyfus's stock funds can be bothersome because you normally must make your request in writing and have your signature guaranteed by a bank or broker. But you can get around this requirement with the following maneuver. Make your first investment in Dreyfus Liquid Assets, a money-market fund, and request on the application both phone-switching and bank wire-transfer privileges. There is no sign-up fee for either service. Then, once your account is open, switch your money by phone to the stock funds of your choice. To withdraw money quickly, simply transfer cash back to the money-market account by phone and instruct the fund to wire the proceeds to your bank.

Some funds charge you extra for these services, however. You may have to pay a one-time fee of $5 for check-writing privileges and up to $10 per telephone switch. In many cases you will have to fill out separate applications for each of these special services.

Buying your fund shares. Unless the fund will let you open an account by telephone, you will be required to send in your money with your application. The minimum initial investment is sometimes specified on the application; if not, you usually can find it in the prospectus in the section labeled "Purchase of Fund Shares." Funds will accept just about any form of paper payment—a personal check, certified check, or money order. Most funds will also accept money wired from your bank, but since you are required to mail in the application you might as well pay by check to avoid bank wiring fees, which can run as high as $20.

Sending a certified check or money order will not speed up the process of becoming a shareholder or affect the price you pay for your shares. With most funds, you become a shareholder the same day or the day after your application and payment are received. Therefore, you are probably better off paying with a personal check written on an interest-bearing NOW or money-market account to get the benefit of the float—the interest earned on your money until the check clears.

You should receive confirmation of your purchase within five business days. If you do not, call the fund's customer service department or the broker from whom you bought the shares. The service representative will ask for the name and Social Security number of each investor listed on the application. If all else fails, you can complain to the Securities and Exchange Commission, Office of Consumer Affairs, 450 Fifth Street N.W., Washington, DC 20549, which will call the fund and try to resolve the problem.

You will not receive share certificates upon investing in a fund unless you request them. There is no reason you need them unless you plan to use them as collateral for a bank loan. In fact, having the certificates in your possession can be an inconvenience since you will not be able to switch money to another fund or redeem shares by phone.

The price you pay for a share of a fund is its net asset value per share on the day the fund receives your application. If you are determined to get the most shares for your money, be mindful of the date on which you purchase your shares. Especially when investing in a growth-stock fund, you are better off buying shares on the day after it has declared its dividend—or gone ex-dividend—which is usually done quarterly, semiannually, or annually. Since such payments reduce the net asset value of the fund's shares, the selling price of the shares drops by the amount of the payment and your money buys more shares.

Technically, the value of your investment remains the
same; you neither lose nor gain because each share is worth
less than before the fund went ex-dividend. But by buying
in after the dividend is declared, you will avoid having to
pay taxes on that particular payout. Call the fund's customer service representative for the dates on which the
fund goes ex-dividend. Usually you can also tell when a
fund has gone ex-dividend by checking the fund performance tables in the financial pages of most daily newspapers. On the day after a fund declares a dividend payment,
an *x* appears beside the fund's net asset value.

Money Source

Mutual Fund
Sourcebook
53 West Jackson
Boulevard, Suite
1661
Chicago, IL 60604
($49.50 an issue or
$135 a year)

SIX

How to
Monitor
Your Portfolio

One of the chief benefits of investing in a mutual fund is
that you gain low-cost access to professional money management. But there is no guarantee that the fund will not
sink like a leaky canoe because of the manager's bad investment decisions or as a casualty of choppy stock and bond
markets. A wise investor, therefore, tracks his funds' performance on a regular basis. This includes examining a
fund's latest shareholder reports; analyzing its statement of
account, which most funds send out at least quarterly; and
periodically looking up the value of the fund's shares in a
newspaper's financial pages. Then, if the fund starts to

founder, you can cut your losses by moving your assets elsewhere.

A three-month checkup is probably all you need if your money is conservatively invested in a fund whose primary objective is income, long-term growth, or a combination of the two. That way you will find out about serious management problems before it is too late to do anything about them, but you will not be tempted to make mistaken changes in strategy because of short-term dips in the stock and bond markets. If you have invested in inherently volatile maximum-capital-gains or sector funds, however, you probably should turn to the financial pages for your fund's performance at least once a week or even every day. Then you will be able to respond quickly to sudden changes in the fund's fortunes.

Most investors will also want to track such economic bellwethers as the Standard & Poor's 500-stock index, yields on U.S. Treasury bills, quarterly trends in the gross national product, and changes in the Commerce Department's monthly index of leading economic indicators. This chapter tells you how to evaluate the key market indicators, which are published in the business sections of most daily newspapers. If the stock market slumps, interest rates suddenly lurch upward, or the economy turns sour, you can deftly adjust your portfolio to take advantage of these developments or to avoid the sizable losses that could result from them.

A SHORT COURSE IN MARKET ANALYSIS

For many investors, the actual value of day-to-day economic news remains elusive because the connection between the economy and securities prices is so indirect. Stocks can falter when splendid economic statistics are reported, and a bull market may begin while business conditions are terrible. If you can grasp the workings of some of these complicated interrelationships, you will be more likely to anticipate bull and bear markets and to make intelligent judgments as to which securities or sectors of the economy promise to perform best in the future.

The importance of profits. Since 1948 there has not been a single major business expansion, as measured by a large increase in the inflation-adjusted gross national product (GNP), that did not leave stock prices higher than they were when it began. Reason: a rising real GNP means that companies are selling more goods and services. As revenues rise, their total profits should grow, sending stock prices higher. Conversely, when the GNP falls in a recession—even just a little bit—corporate earnings and stock prices usually drop substantially.

Stock price movements are further complicated by the fact that they reflect the earnings that investors expect in the future, not just current profits. As a result, the stock market moves before the economy does; investment analysts call this "discounting the future." By looking at data such as the backlog of orders companies have to fill, knowledgeable investors can forecast profits fairly well for three months to a year or so into the future. This causes stock prices to start advancing anywhere from one to twelve months before the economy begins a growth phase.

The role of interest rates. After profits, interest rates are the most important influence on share prices. Buyers choose between stocks, which offer a share of a firm's future earnings, and bonds, which pay interest. When interest rates rise, so do bond yields, drawing investors away from stocks, whose future earnings look less attractive by comparison. When interest rates and bond yields fall, stock prices rise because their future earnings become more attractive to investors when compared to those slumping bond yields.

Interest rates generally begin dropping well in advance of a major economic expansion, creating an ideal environment for stocks. Falling rates and rising investor expectations of the greater profits that companies will enjoy once the expansion is under way combine to send share prices higher. As a result, bull markets are frequently most robust while businesses are feeling the lingering effects of recession, just before an economic upturn begins.

The business cycle. Interest rates and GNP growth interact to create a repeating pattern in the economy known as the business cycle. A classic cycle begins with interest rates falling. As they drop, consumers buy more homes and expensive durable goods such as automobiles because financing is cheaper. Home building and manufacturing increase, and stepped-up activity slowly spreads through the economy. As companies spend more on wages, workers can buy more.

Eventually all this business activity causes competition for credit. Businesses need to borrow to invest in more factories and equipment; home buyers want mortgages; and consumers run up their credit-card balances. Meanwhile, intensifying business activity brings marginal facilities into use and drives up labor costs, raising prices and promoting inflation. Saving suffers because so many people are spending. As a result, there is less money to lend, and interest rates ultimately rise high enough to choke off the business expansion. Then the economy cools down until rates fall once again.

This cycle, which usually takes four to six years to be completed, would occur even if the government did nothing. But since the Great Depression, the government has been an active participant in the business cycle, deliberately moving interest rates up and down through the actions of the Federal Reserve Board. In theory, the Federal Reserve is supposed to act countercyclically. The measures it takes are intended to reduce the size of the business-cycle swings by slowing down or speeding up the rate of money growth to raise or lower interest rates. In practice, however, political pressures and the difficulty of fine-tuning the economy result in the the Federal Reserve nearly always making the cycle more irregular, acting in a way that economists call pro-cyclical.

Here is how that works: right before a cycle begins, the economy is in recession. Eager to get business moving again, the Federal Reserve encourages interest rates to fall, starting the business cycle with more momentum than it would otherwise have. Like a swing given extra pushes, the business cycle eventually climbs too far. As inflation rises and the economy shows other signs of overheating, the Federal Reserve gives interest rates an extra boost to end the process and cool everything down. The economy then goes into recession and the whole pattern begins again.

Inflation. The rate of overall price rises, as measured by the government's consumer price index, has been the most important long-term economic trend in recent decades. For example, from 1965 through 1980, the level of prices rose with each business cycle. Since higher inflation tends to drive up interest rates and bond yields, it is bad news for stock and bond prices. In fact, after briefly rising above the 1000 mark in 1966, the Dow Jones industrial average did not reach 1100 until early 1983. In recent years, declining inflation has sent interest rates to lower levels, raising stock and bond prices.

KEY INDICATORS TO WATCH AND WEIGH

When the average investor opens the business pages, he or she may be overwhelmed by the growing volume of economic and market data. Some of the information is difficult to interpret; some is merely statistical data with little, if any, predictive value. You no doubt have heard numerous references to the Federal Reserve's money supply figures, designated M1 and M2. Yet even economists haggle over the figures' merits and shortcomings. Another oft-cited figure, the consumer price index, is a fairly straightforward measure of inflation. But it is best at telling you what has already happened rather than what is going to happen.

Drawing informed conclusions about the economy and the market need not be unnerving for the uninitiated. Professional investment analysts give their full attention to the following indicators, all regularly published in—and analyzed by—major newspapers.

Three-month Treasury bill rates. If you only have enough time to follow one economic statistic, your best choice would be interest rates, particularly those reflected by 90-day Treasury bills. Economists favor this figure over the prime lending rate as an indicator because the Treasury-bill rate is based on bids from investors, whereas the prime is set by banks. Banks usually lower their prime lending rates only after Treasury bills have been dropping steadily for weeks.

The Treasury-bill rate gives a weekly clue to changes in the Federal Reserve's monetary policies. To stimulate economic activity during a recession, for example, the Federal Reserve increases the amount of money in circulation. This has the effect of lowering interest rates such as those of Treasury bills. Conversely, when the economy is growing, the Federal Reserve reduces the amount of money and credit to check inflation. As a result, interest rates rise.

Because Treasury bills respond immediately to Federal Reserve action, they provide the clearest window through which to glimpse future trends in interest rates. Rising

FIGURE 14. Watching the Key Indicators

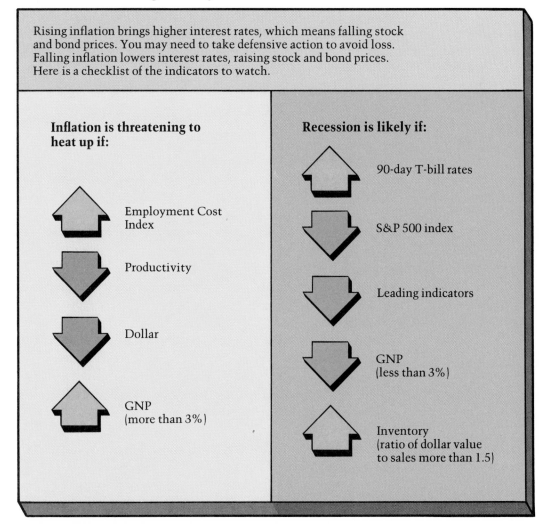

Rising inflation brings higher interest rates, which means falling stock and bond prices. You may need to take defensive action to avoid loss. Falling inflation lowers interest rates, raising stock and bond prices. Here is a checklist of the indicators to watch.

Inflation is threatening to heat up if:

Employment Cost Index

Productivity

Dollar

GNP (more than 3%)

Recession is likely if:

90-day T-bill rates

S&P 500 index

Leading indicators

GNP (less than 3%)

Inventory (ratio of dollar value to sales more than 1.5)

rates dampen corporate profits because the increased cost of borrowing reduces earnings. So sustained increases in the rates of three-month Treasury bills can foretell economic recessions and declines in the stock market. Before the disastrous 1974 recession, for instance, rates on Treasury bills doubled, climbing from 4% to 8% between early 1972 and late 1973. Falling interest rates, on the other hand, act as an immediate tonic for stock and bond prices.

The S&P 500-stock index. One of the oldest jokes on Wall Street is that the stock market has predicted nine of the last five recessions. The market may be nervous to a fault, but it is the one indicator that many economists credit with being the most prophetic. The S&P 500 is more useful than the Dow Jones industrial average because it includes 500 stocks and is therefore a broader measure than the Dow, which is limited to 30 stocks.

The stock market was one lonely bull when it charged off in August 1982 at a time when interest rates were high, corporate profits were weak, and most analysts' economic forecasts were exceedingly gloomy. About a year after the market came alive, economists agreed that the recovery was under way.

The stock market is so prescient because it responds quickly to the slightest changes in the Federal Reserve System's monetary policy. When the Federal Reserve stimulates economic health by easing credit, the stock market responds immediately with an upward move. As much as a year could pass before sustained stimulation from the Federal Reserve would have any impact on corporate profits, industrial production, or consumer sales.

On the bearish side, the market also seems to work about a year in advance. In 1932, for example, the S&P index sank to its all-time low of 4.4 from an October 1929 high of 31.3. Yet the economy still had another year to go before it hit rock bottom in the Great Depression. (As of April 1987, the S&P stood at 292.)

Leading indicators. This monthly composite of 11 indicators released by the Commerce Department's Bureau of Economic Analysis will give the best fix on where the economy will be six months from now. Since stock prices

anticipate the economy, the S&P 500 is itself one of the
leading indicators. Others include housing starts and orders
for business equipment. If a bull market has been under
way for a couple of years and the leading indicators are
down three months in a row, it is time to worry that the
business expansion may be running out of steam and that
stocks may be near a peak.

Real GNP. The Commerce Department releases both pro-
jections and retrospective numbers for each quarter's
inflation-adjusted GNP. Normally, 3% real growth is considered the optimum annual rate. A lower percentage suggests a recession might develop, while a higher one raises
the specter of increasing inflation and rising interest rates
that will choke off growth. Because stock prices already
reflect what is widely thought to be true, surprise revisions
in the GNP can trigger sharp reactions in the stock market.

Unemployment. The Labor Department's widely followed
unemployment figure is reported monthly. Perverse as it
may seem, moderately high unemployment during a period
of economic growth is considered favorable for the market.
One reason is investors' fear that the economy will grow
too fast and cause inflation and interest rates to rise.

Labor costs. When workers receive sizable raises, companies usually have to increase prices. You can get a fairly
accurate sense of the direction of inflation during the next
few years by keeping an eye on changes in wages, salaries,
and benefits. One way to do this is to follow the employment cost index, calculated quarterly by the Bureau of
Labor Statistics and reported in the *Wall Street Journal*. If
the employment cost index climbs fast, it could be a sign
that inflation is going to accelerate.

Productivity. The amount that workers can produce in an
hour also powerfully affects inflation. When productivity is
improving, as measured by this widely reported Labor Department indicator, companies can afford to pay their workers more without having to raise prices. In recent years
productivity has been fairly stagnant. Any further deteriora-
tion could warn of a revival of inflation.

Inventory. When the economy is growing fast, companies sometimes maintain too much inventory because of overly optimistic expectations of future sales. When these sales fail to materialize and the excess inventory has to be reduced, companies will buy fewer new items, thereby slowing the economy. The Commerce Department issues a ratio in the middle of each month comparing the dollar value of business inventory nationwide with sales. A ratio of more than 1.5 could indicate that an economic slowdown lies ahead.

Currency exchange rates. The dollar index, which measures the dollar's value against a group of foreign currencies, is compiled quarterly by Morgan Guaranty Trust, a New York bank, and published in the *Wall Street Journal* and *New York Times.* A strong dollar encourages cheap imports, holding inflation down but hurting certain U.S. industries that depend upon exporting. A weakening dollar helps U.S. manufacturers but may encourage inflation. From February 1981 to February 1985, the dollar soared against major foreign currencies. But since then it generally has been on the decline.

NEWSPAPER SHORTHAND EXPLAINED

In the same newspaper financial sections that cover the economic and market indicators, you will find performance data for 1,000 or so of the largest mutual funds. Here are the abbreviations, terms, and symbols used in those tables and what they mean.

NAV. The net asset value—the basic measure of a fund's performance—is what each of your shares was worth at the end of that day's trading. Each fund computes its NAV by taking the market value of the fund's assets after the stock exchanges close, subtracting all liabilities, and then dividing by the number of the fund's shares outstanding.

Offer price. Sometimes called the buy price, this is what you would pay for a share of a fund. If a fund has an initial

FIGURE 15. Mutual Fund Data in a Typical Newspaper

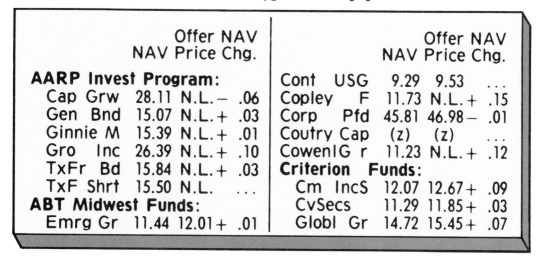

	Offer	NAV			Offer	NAV
	NAV	Price	Chg.		NAV	Price	Chg.

AARP Invest Program:

	NAV	Offer Price	Chg.
Cap Grw	28.11	N.L.	− .06
Gen Bnd	15.07	N.L.	+ .03
Ginnie M	15.39	N.L.	+ .01
Gro Inc	26.39	N.L.	+ .10
TxFr Bd	15.84	N.L.	+ .03
TxF Shrt	15.50	N.L.	...

ABT Midwest Funds:

	NAV	Offer Price	Chg.
Emrg Gr	11.44	12.01	+ .01

	NAV	Offer Price	Chg.
Cont USG	9.29	9.53	...
Copley F	11.73	N.L.	+ .15
Corp Pfd	45.81	46.98	− .01
Coutry Cap	(z)	(z)	...
CowenIG r	11.23	N.L.	+ .12

Criterion Funds:

	NAV	Offer Price	Chg.
Cm IncS	12.07	12.67	+ .09
CvSecs	11.29	11.85	+ .03
Globl Gr	14.72	15.45	+ .07

sales charge or load, the offer price equals the net asset value plus the load. A no-load fund's offer price and net asset value are the same. The abbreviation **NL** appears beside the offer price of no-load funds.

NAV Change. This is the amount, expressed in dollars and cents, that the net asset value has increased or decreased since the previous trading day. Small rises and dips in net asset value on a daily basis are normal and should not be taken as a sign that a fund is faltering. But a string of declines over several weeks during which funds with similar objectives are climbing could indicate that a fund is having trouble and that you should consider moving your money elsewhere.

Symbols. Funds that charge redemption fees when you sell your shares are identified by an *r* in newspaper listings. You will have to telephone the fund or look in its prospectus to learn the amount of the fee. An *f* next to a fund's name indicates that current share prices are not available and that the price listed is from the previous trading day. An *x* in a listing indicates that the fund has gone ex-dividend—meaning that the fund is about to distribute a dividend, a capital gain, or both to shareholders.

Often a fund that has gone ex-dividend may register a large drop in net asset value because these payments reduce the fund's assets. But such a drop in net asset value does not represent a loss to shareholders, because they will receive the distribution in cash or, if they reinvest the payment, in additional shares.

DECIPHERING YOUR FUND STATEMENT

Daily changes in a fund's net asset value are the most accessible gauge of a fund's performance. However, short-term gains and losses are of little value in determining how a fund has been doing relative to other funds with similar objectives or to the stock market overall. Nor do these figures tell you how well the fund has served you during your period of ownership.

For a better picture of your fund's performance, you will want to study the statements of account that the fund sends you—generally monthly, quarterly, or after every transaction. In addition to telling you how much your account is worth, the statement records when you bought or sold shares and what you paid for them. It also lists the interest, dividends, and capital gains your shares have earned and, if you reinvest the earnings, how many additional shares they purchased. Such information is essential for figuring the taxable gain or deductible loss when you sell shares and for gauging the performance of your fund during the time you have been a shareholder. So make sure you save enough statements to give you a complete record of your transactions.

The **beginning balance** tells how many shares you bought initially or how many were brought forward from the previous statement—in the sample statement in figure 16, 82.435. The **statement date** on the left side of the document is the day on which a transaction was recorded. You should pay closer attention to the **transaction date**, sometimes called the trade date, because it is when the transaction actually took place.

The fund's net asset value at the close of business on that date is the price that you paid for shares or received for shares that you redeemed. In the example, the shareholder invested $1,000 on January 4, 1986, buying 18.706 shares at

$53.46 each. These shares, added to the **beginning balance**, brought the **total shares owned** to 101.141.

Income and capital-gains distributions are always listed separately. On April 18, 1986, the fund recorded both types. The income distribution of 25¢ a share—amounting to $25.29—was automatically reinvested in .484 new shares, bringing the total in the account to 101.625. The 45¢-per-share distribution of short-term capital gains was paid in cash. On January 15, 1987, the shareholder withdrew $500, requiring the fund to redeem 7.564 shares at $66.10 each. This reduced the total number of shares in the account on that date to 131.345.

TRACKING YOUR FUND'S PERFORMANCE

The statement gives you a starting point for monitoring your fund's yield and total return. Current yield tells you how much dividend income your investment is generating annually as a percentage of the fund's latest net asset value. Simply add up all of the dividends paid to you in the past 12 months and divide that sum by the average price you paid for each of your shares, exclusive of sales charges.

Usually you can also find your fund's current yield in its quarterly or annual report. You can obtain the report by calling the fund's customer relations department or by referring to an independent source such as *Money*, which computes yields in the fund performance listings it publishes twice a year.

The most comprehensive, and to most investors the most useful, measure of how a fund is doing is its total return. This is the sum of all dividend and capital-gains distributions the fund has made in a given period and any increase or decrease in the portfolio's net asset value. Although some funds regularly publish their total returns in ads and brochures, many do not.

You can get an approximation of your own fund's total return for any period up to one year without going through detailed computations. Take the fund's net asset value at the end of a particular time period. Add any dividends or capital gains the fund distributed to you during the period.

FIGURE 16. A Quick Way to Figure Your Own Fund's Return

	Your fund	Example
1. The number of months for which performance is being measured (not more than two years)	_____	19
2. The value of your investment at the start of the period. The figure in the example came from multiplying total shares owned on Jan. 4, 1986, (101.141) by the share price ($53.46).	_____	$5,407
3. The value of your shares now. In the example, we multiplied shares owned on July 5, 1987, by the share price on that date.	_____	$8,837
4. Dividend income and capital-gains distributions paid to you in cash (not reinvested) during the period.	_____	$111
5. Net redemptions or investments during the period not including reinvested distributions. In the example, we subtracted the $500 redemption on Jan. 15, 1987, from the $2,000 investment on June 1, 1986.	_____	$1,500
6. Computation of your gain or loss: **Step A:** Add line 2 to half the total on line 5	_____	$6,157
Step B: Add lines 3 and 4, then subtract half the line 5 sum	_____	$8,198
Step C: Divide the step B result by the step A figure	_____	1.33
Step D: Subtract the numeral 1 from the result of step C, then multiply by 100	_____	33%
7. For your annualized return, divide 12 by the number on line 1. Multiply the result by the step D percentage, then by 100.	_____	20.8%

Your Mutual Fund Inc. 1000 Main St. New York, N.Y. 10020

Page 1 of 1
1986-87 Statement

John A. Johnson &
Joan J. Johnson
3 Oak Rd.
Mayfield, MO 63010

Account No. 98765432101

Your distribution option is

	income reinvestment	capital gains in cash

Statement Date	Transaction Date	Transaction Detail Description	Dollar Amount of Transaction	Share Price	Shares this Transaction	Total Shares Owned
		Beginning Balance				82.435
1/4/86	1/4/86	Investment	1,000.00	53.46	18.706	101.141
4/18	4/6	Income Reinvest at .250	25.29	52.25	.484	101.625
4/18	4/6	Short-term capital gain at .450	45.52	—	—	101.625
6/1	6/1	Investment	2,000.00	55.37	36.121	137.746
7/17	7/4	Income Reinvest at .250	34.44	57.04	.604	138.350
10/23	10/10	Income Reinvest at .250	34.59	61.89	.559	138.909
1/15/87	1/15/87	Redemption	500.00	66.10	-7.564	131.345
1/26	1/17	Income Reinvest at .200	26.27	66.13	.397	132.742
1/26	1/3	Short-term capital gain at .500	65.87	—	—	132.742
4/26	4/3	Income Reinvest at .300	39.82	65.88	.604	133.346
7/18	7/5	Income Reinvest at .250	33.34	66.02	.505	133.851

Divide by the net asset value at the beginning of the period. Subtract the number 1, then multiply by 100. Using the figures on the sample statement in figure 16 (and assuming the fund has no load), you would begin with the fund's net asset value on October 10 of $61.89. Add to that the payments of 75¢ in dividends and 45¢ in capital gains. Divide the sum by the beginning net asset value of $53.46, subtract 1, and multiply by 100. The approximate total return for the 10-month period was 18%.

Step 1. 61.89
       .45
   + .75 (3 distributions of a 25¢ dividend per share)
   63.09

Step 2. 63.09 ÷ 53.46 = 1.18

Step 3. 1.18 - 1.00 = .18

Step 4. .18 x 100 = 18%

To estimate your rate of return for a period of up to two years, use the worksheet in figure 16, devised with the help of John Markese, director of research at the American Association of Individual Investors in Chicago. Although it is only an estimate, the bottom line should be within two or three percentage points of your actual return. To fill in the blanks, use your most recent fund statement and one at the beginning of the period you are examining. (For simplicity, the sample statement combines two years.) If you are in a load fund, be sure the share price you use to calculate line 2 reflects any sales charges you paid. The worksheet takes account of shares you may have redeemed. If redemptions exceed investments on line 5, show the net result as a minus number.

Your fund's total return, however, gives you only half the performance picture. To find out whether that return was superior, adequate, or inferior, you need to compare it with those of funds with similar investment objectives. The rankings in chapter 10 provide one-year total returns to April 1987 for 738 funds and three- and ten-year total returns for funds that have longer-term records. To continue tracking performance on a quarterly basis for some

1,000 stock and bond funds, plus those of widely held closed-end funds, you can consult *Management Results*, from the publishers of *Wiesenberger Investment Companies Service*. Quarterly gains and losses for 515 stock funds are published by *Mutual Fund Sourcebook*. These figures will enable you to compare your fund's total returns over given periods with the averages for its category. The two references also supply total return figures for the S&P 500-stock index, which will allow you to determine whether your fund has performed better—or worse—than the market in general. The two publications are available in many large public libraries, or you may wish to buy them.

If your fund consistently underperforms the stock market average by more than a few percentage points, you should probably start looking for a portfolio with a better record.

Money Source

Management Results
1 Penn Plaza
New York, NY
  10119
($150 a year for four
  issues)

SEVEN

Managing Your Portfolio

In strong bull markets you can make money by simply buying into a swiftly rising stock fund and riding it up. But when the market sputters and starts to head down, such a buy-and-forget approach can cost you dearly. To stay ahead with most funds, you will need to monitor their performance regularly. More important, you will need to have a plan for systematically and dispassionately redeploying your portfolio as market conditions and your financial circumstances change. The following strategies should help to enhance your long-term total return without exposing you to unnecessary risk.

INVESTING BY INSTALLMENT

If you fear that you might put your cash in a mutual fund just before the market tumbles, you should consider using an installment-purchase technique called dollar-cost averaging. This strategy calls for investing a fixed amount of money at regular intervals, say, monthly or quarterly, rather than all at once. As a result, your investments buy fewer shares when prices are high and more shares when they are low. Over a full stock-market cycle, which historically means four to six years, you will accumulate most of your shares at below-average prices.

Take, for example, a hypothetical investment in Vanguard's Explorer Fund, an aggressive portfolio that has produced superior returns over time by specializing in stocks of small, advanced-technology companies. Say that instead of dollar-cost averaging you invested $2,000 in the no-load fund at the end of every year beginning in 1975. By December 1984, at the conclusion of a fairly typical 10-year period for the stock market, your total investment of $20,000 would have purchased shares with a market value of $47,680, assuming reinvestment of all dividends and capital gains in additional shares.

If you had dollar-cost averaged over the same period, investing the same $20,000 in monthly installments of $166.67, you would have shares worth $51,475 by the end of 1984—a difference of $3,795.

No-load funds are ideal for dollar-cost averaging because you can buy fractional shares without paying a sales charge. And the automatic-prepayment plans offered by many funds let you authorize your bank or employer to make your investments directly from your account or paycheck. Some funds will let you dollar average with as little as $50 a month. One fund family, Twentieth Century, has no installment minimum for six of its seven no-load funds.

Although dollar averaging should result in higher profits on the money you actually invest, it does not always produce the highest possible return for your portfolio as a whole. The reason is that you may have to park a sizable amount of your cash in a bank account or money-market fund while you are waiting to invest it in stock or bond funds. Because your cash reserve is not at risk, the relatively meager returns you earn on it may drag down your overall total return.

A SWITCH IN TIME CAN PAY OFF

To aim for the highest possible returns, you will have to pursue a more active strategy, such as fund switching. In its simplest form, fund switching involves leaping aboard a fund as it starts to soar and nimbly jumping to a safer or better-performing one when your shares begin to sink. Such switching has grown in popularity as fund companies make it easier for investors to move money from one portfolio to another in the same family, usually with only a telephone call. To get phone-switching privileges, you sign a release in advance authorizing the fund to buy and sell shares on your verbal instructions. Most large fund organizations permit unlimited switching, though in some cases you may have to pay up to $10 per telephone switch. Some major no-load families limit the number of switches you can make in a year. T. Rowe Price and Vanguard, for example, set their annual limit at six switches per fund and Financial Programs at four. If you exceed these limits, you could be asked to cash in your shares.

If you open an account with the discount broker Charles Schwab, you can easily buy, sell, or switch by phone among 250 no-load and low-load funds of different families as long as you keep your shares in your brokerage account. Thus, as stock prices started to slide, you could move your money from, say, Fidelity's aggressive OTC stock fund to Vanguard's low-risk Windsor II growth and income fund. Then, as the market turned up again, you could move to a long-term gainer such as Twentieth Century Select.

You will be charged each fund's load, if any, plus the broker's commission, which at Schwab ranges from about $30 for transactions of $2,000 to $150 for trades of $20,000 or more. As long as you are switching from fund to fund, simultaneously buying one and selling another, you pay only one brokerage fee.

Full-service brokers will also exchange your load fund shares for those of other load funds that they handle. However, high commissions of up to 9% usually make such switches uneconomical.

There are basically two types of strategies you can follow when switching funds. The first is to move your assets from an underperforming fund to another one with a similar investment objective but a better return. One such tactic, best suited to experienced investors with a high tolerance for risk, involves switching among inherently volatile sector funds. You start out by investing in a sector that you think will do well, with the idea that at its peak you will move your money to a more promising sector. This strategy requires not only strong nerves but also an almost uncanny ability to anticipate when one sector has topped out and another is about to take off.

More cautious investors can profit from switching among less risky diversified stock funds. For example, a savvy fund picker could theoretically have parlayed an initial $1,000 investment into at least $9,000 by leapfrogging from one winning fund to another over the past 10 years—twice the average stock fund's return. The challenge, of course, is to decide which funds to put your money in when stock prices take a turn in either direction. (For some candidates to consider, see table 4.)

A second approach to fund switching, known as market timing, involves shifting your money from a stock fund into a short-term bond or money-market fund when you think the stock market is about to fall. If you time your moves correctly, you can achieve astounding results. Take, for example, a hypothetical investor who started out with $1,000 in 1973. If he had put his money in a fund whose performance exactly duplicated that of the Standard & Poor's 500-stock index, he would have had $3,236 on July 1, 1986. If he had called the market's turns perfectly, however, and switched in and out of the fund accordingly, he would have roughly $11,000.

Trying to call market trends with such precision can be hazardous; no one can successfully catch each market updraft and avoid every air pocket. But you can win with market timing even if you miss the precise market turns. Retrospective studies have shown that you could have

TABLE **4. Seasoned Portfolios for Smart Switchers**

THE BEST BULL MARKET FUNDS

According to Lipper Analytical Services, the following stock funds were the top-performing mutual funds, regardless of investment objective, for the five overwhelmingly bullish years to April 1987.

Fund	% Total Return
1. Merrill Lynch Pacific	445.4
2. Fidelity Magellan	380.8
3. Loomis-Sayles Capital Development	374.4
4. Vanguard World—International	354.8
5. Alliance Technology	348.3
6. Fidelity Select—Health	327.6
7. Putnam International Equities	323.7
8. New England Growth	284.8
9. Vanguard Qualified Dividend I*	284.4
10. Fidelity Destiny I	284.0

THE BEST BEAR MARKET FUNDS

The following stock funds performed near the top of their respective investment categories over the last three down-market phases, as identified by Lipper. Additionally, all did well in the five bullish years to April 1987.

Fund	% Total Return
1. Evergreen Total Return	240.1
2. Selected American Shares	224.5
3. Mutual Shares Corp.	221.4
4. Loomis-Sayles Mutual	217.2
5. Decatur I	211.6
6. Fidelity Puritan	210.2
7. Vanguard Wellington	203.2
8. Neuberger & Berman Partners	183.8
9. Lindner Fund*	178.4
10. Vanguard Wellesley	166.2

*Closed to new investors

outperformed the market if you had 1) moved your money from a stock portfolio to a money-market fund after the market had fallen as much as 30% from its peaks and 2) moved your money back to the stock fund after the market had bounced back 30% from its subsequent bottoms. (For more on how to anticipate the stock market's next turn, see "A Short Course in Market Analysis" and "Key Indicators to Watch and Weigh," pages 91-98.)

WHEN TO SELL OR SWITCH

Deciding when to get out of a particular fund may be the most difficult task of investing in mutual funds. It is easy to be rational in evaluating a fund before you buy it. But once your money is committed, your emotions tend to come into play, alternately tempting you to hold on to winning funds long after they have peaked and to bail out of losers just before they bounce back.

To recognize the right time to sell or switch to another fund, you must continually compare the funds you own with others and with your personal financial goals. As long as your fund is meeting your objectives, hold on to it. But do not hesitate to move your money if another fund seems likely to do the job better.

Advisers say you should consider selling or switching under each of the following circumstances.

When your financial situation changes. As you get older or closer to your goals, your needs and your tolerance for risk should change. When your children near college age, for example, you should stop taking even moderate risks with your investments for their tuition because you cannot afford to lose a chunk of it in a last-minute market dip. When they are in high school you should begin switching some of the college money from growth funds to safe short-term bond and money-market funds.

When the fund itself changes. Think back to the reasons that initially led you to invest in a fund. If it no longer fits those criteria, you should consider looking for another fund to replace it. For example, your growth fund's assets may have grown so large that you fear the manager has lost the flexibility that helped him get high returns. Or your fund may have increased its annual fees beyond what you are willing to pay. You might also decide to switch if the manager responsible for the fund's past success retires or quits. Fund groups are not likely to notify investors that the manager has left. But if you notice significant changes in performance, volatility, or the fund's investment style, it could mean that a new hand is at the helm. To find out for sure, ask the fund.

When performance lags that of similar funds. Obviously, if a fund turns out to be a mediocre performer, you will want to replace it. But do not be too quick to assume a fund is a loser: in a euphoric market such as the one for small, high-technology stocks in mid-1983, a below-average performance could be a sign of a fund manager's prudence, not incompetence. In the 12 months through June 1983, the top performers were Alliance Technology (up 183%) and Twentieth Century Ultra (up 151%), both heavily invested in hot technology stocks. Warier funds such as Mutual Shares and Selected American Shares refused to gamble on those high flyers and did less well: Mutual Shares rose just 51% during that period, and Selected American Shares 42%.

Over the next 12 months, however, technology stocks crashed, devastating the funds that owned them. By June 1984, the 12-month leaders were the two former laggards—Mutual Shares, up 15%, and Selected American, up 10%—while Ultra and Alliance Technology declined 35% and 37% respectively.

Sheldon Jacobs, head of No-Load Fund Investor, suggests that you give a fund at least a year to prove itself. If you are in a conservative total-return fund, he adds, you might even give it as long as two years. After two years, though, take your money out of the fund if it still languishes in the bottom half of its group or continues to underperform the S&P 500.

When the market turns against you. Most diversified funds, whether invested in stocks or bonds, tend to rise and fall more or less in concert with the general markets. As a consequence, you can improve your return significantly if you switch into a money-market fund when stocks or bonds start slipping, then move back to more volatile funds when the bull returns. For most investors, however, successfully timing the market is too difficult. Thus your best response to a falling market is probably to hold on to your fund shares or even to buy more. After all, funds can defend themselves in a serious bear market by selling securities to raise cash.

Also, unlike an individual stock, which may stay down indefinitely, a diversified fund is almost certain to bounce back when the market regains strength. Weingarten Equity, Twentieth Century Growth, and Evergreen Fund, for instance, each rebounded from lows in 1981 and 1984 to place among the 10 best-performing funds in the decade to April 1987. If you are not sure you have the willpower to hang on to a volatile fund during a bear market, stick with a fund that has achieved steady returns in all markets, such as one of the 10 all-weather funds singled out for their consistency. (See Chapter 9.)

THE SCOOP ON ADVISORY NEWSLETTERS

Many fund shareholders have neither the time nor the skills required to master switching or timing strategies. But there are scores of investment advisers who for a fee will share their insights on how to time the market as well as when to buy, sell, and switch among selected funds. Such advisors include the writers of mutual fund newsletters. For anywhere from $50 to $300 a year, a newsletter can offer a cornucopia of information such as monthly fund performance ratings, advice on when to buy and sell fund shares, and news of management changes that could affect a fund's performance. Nearly all newsletters also publish model portfolios consisting of one to fifteen funds that they recommend.

Fund advisories commonly are characterized as either performance or market-timing newsletters. Performance letters examine a fund's past record and try to forecast its prospects. Timing letters attempt to spot stock market trends and tell you when to switch from stock and bond funds into cash or from one type of fund to another.

Performance newsletters. According to investment analysts who follow mutual fund advisories, one of the most respected performance letters is the monthly *NoLoad Fund X*. It ranks 517 funds within risk categories by their average one-year, six-month, three-month, and one-month performances. Editor Burton Berry suggests that most readers invest only in the top five funds in each category. If a fund drops out of the top five, he advises selling it and buying another top no-load fund.

Another highly regarded newsletter is the monthly *Growth Fund Guide*. In each issue, editor Walter Rouleau forecasts the performance of 40 stock funds. He also predicts how specific funds will fare in both bear and bull markets.

The monthly *No-Load Fund Investor* covers more funds but in less depth. Editor Sheldon Jacobs publishes the performances of 460 no-load and low-load funds, recommending as many as 80 an issue.

One of the newer newsletters, *Mutual Fund Forecaster*, is produced monthly by Norman Fosback and Glen King Parker, publishers of the well-known *Market Logic* stock newsletter. The *Forecaster* gives performance figures for aggressive and long-term growth funds and rates each fund according to its expected volatility for the coming year.

Market-timing newsletters. They can help you take advantage of dramatic moves in the stock, bond, and precious-metals markets. The newsletters issue buy and sell recommendations as frequently as once a month. Some offer—often at an extra charge—telephone hotlines you can call daily to get the editor's latest market advice. Since buy and sell signals can change at a moment's notice, a hotline can tip you off to an opportunity or warn of trouble so you can take quick action.

Some of these advisories forecast market shifts quite accurately. After studying buy and sell recommendations by nine market-timing newsletters from 1980 to 1985, *Hulbert Financial Digest*, a Washington, D.C., service that rates investment newsletters, found that investors who followed the advice of eight of the letters would have substantially outperformed the overall stock market.

For example, one portfolio suggested by the monthly letter *Switch Fund Advisory* more than doubled the market's record over the period. And investors could have nearly doubled their money by mimicking the market-timing moves suggested by two other monthlies, *Telephone Switch Newsletter* and *Professional Timing Service.*

The monthly *Mutual Fund Strategist* is one of the most widely read timing newsletters and among the best at anticipating market movements. Another well-regarded fund-timing letter is the monthly *Wellington's Worry-Free Investing.* In each issue, editor Bert Dohmen publishes prices at which he thinks investors ought to buy or sell the shares of 100 or so funds.

In recent years several timing letters have sprung up specializing in sector funds. These newsletters generally recommend when to shift your money among sectors and identify specific funds to buy. Two of the most popular sector timing letters are *Sector Fund Connection* and *Timer Digest.* Shareholders in one or more of the 35 sector funds in Fidelity's Select portfolios receive free of charge *Sector Trends,* a monthly newsletter prepared by Standard & Poor's but published by Fidelity.

Choose your fund advisory carefully; some of these newsletters can get carried away with their switching or timing strategies. For example, *O'Malley's Fidelity Watch,* an Ellisville, Missouri, publication that covers Fidelity sector funds, claimed that its recommended portfolio of funds produced a 22.6% total return in 1986. But to get that return you would have had to switch funds 16 times. Further, in computing the return, the letter did not deduct Fidelity's $10-per-switch fee or the 2% initial sales charge levied on its sector funds. These fees alone almost certainly would have knocked your gain well below 20%.

Equally important, the letter's performance did not take taxes into account. Every time you switch from one fund to another, the Internal Revenue Service considers the move a sale, which means that in this example you would have had 16 capital gains or losses to report. By contrast, if you had held for a year the four Fidelity funds that O'Malley began with in 1986—Financial, Utilities, Leisure, and Health

Care—your gain would have been roughly 16% and your paperwork and tax headaches minimal.

How do you determine the best newsletter for you? One way is to examine the performance of a letter's sample portfolios. To do this you can refer to another newsletter, the monthly *Hulbert Financial Digest*, which monitors the model portfolios of 25 of the best-known mutual fund newsletters. Hulbert's methodology is generally accepted in the industry. You can get a sample copy of his newsletter for $5 or consult it at a few large public libraries.

Before subscribing to a fund newsletter, examine a copy. Most newsletters will mail you a back issue free upon request. You can often get a trial subscription for a prorated amount. Or contact Select Information Exchange, 2095 Broadway, New York, NY 10023. For a small fee, this clearinghouse will arrange for each of 20 performance and timing newsletters to send you one to five sample issues.

HIRING YOUR OWN MARKET TIMER

If the potential profits of market timing appeal to you, but you have neither the inclination nor enough hours in the day to pursue such a strategy yourself, consider hiring one of the 50 or so money managers who specializes in timing the market with mutual funds and who caters to investors of fairly modest means.

These investment pros usually pick your funds or help you do it. You do not necessarily have to be rich to sign on; the firms sometimes will accept as little as $2,000 in an IRA. Entry levels for regular accounts range from $2,500 to $100,000. At the beginning of 1987, the firms managed only about $3 billion in clients' money, but that was twice the assets they controlled five years earlier.

As market timers, the managers' goal is to move your money into stocks when the market begins rising and then protect gains by switching to the safe haven of money-market funds as stocks start to head down. They are usually better at getting you out than at getting you in on time. Although few fund-switching firms have been managing money this way long enough to have documented their prowess, several who participated in a *Money* study of their clients' results succeeded admirably in taking gains near market tops.

The fees that timers charge run high—2% or more of your assets, or about twice the typical mutual fund management fee. Some companies add to your costs by using load funds with initial sales charges of 4% to 8.5%. To shed light on whether fund-switching market timers are worth their prices, *Money* sampled the actual results, after expenses, of 18 clients at nine firms that had records of clients going back five years or more and agreed to provide copies of the records for the study. Of 30 firms identified as eligible to participate, 21 either could not produce records for enough clients or declined to do so.

The period studied, from July 31, 1981, through September 30, 1986, is just a bit longer than five years so that it could begin with the collapse in stock prices that occurred from August to September 1981. Since the prime goal of a timer should be to protect you against big losses, *Money* evaluated how well the firms in the study did at preserving investors' capital in that selling spree, in which the Lipper growth-fund index of 30 such funds dropped 18.2%. The period covered also took into account the 15% correction, as measured by the Lipper index, between January and May 1984. (To compare the five-year performance of the firms, see table 5.)

Although a few of the investors did abysmally, 12 of the 18 got better results than they would have achieved if they had left their money sitting for the same period in an average growth fund. The composite result of the timers' clients was an average compounded annual return of 15.2%, compared with 13.6% for the Lipper index. The comparison, however, omitted taxes, which would be higher for a successful timer's clients because frequent fund switches create additional taxable gains.

The two clients who did best, both under the management of J.D. Reynolds Company in the Cincinnati suburb of Terrace Park, Ohio, had compounded annual returns of more than 20%. Reynolds and the other firms that showed up well in this survey chose stock funds that performed strongly while their clients' money was in them. Furthermore, clients whose accounts were successfully timed did far better than they would have if they had merely left their money in the same funds those five years.

The study bolsters the opinion of analysts that market timers do best not at matching the peak gains of bull markets but at protecting your assets when prices start to tumble. After all, if you stay in the market all the time, you can get the full gain when prices rise. If you are out, you will seldom get back in ahead of the next bullish move— and neither will a professional.

The timers whose results were analyzed vary considerably in size and methods. Their assets under management ranged from a low of $11 million at Portfolio Management Services in Mission Viejo, California, to a high of $500 million at R. Meeder & Associates in Dublin, Ohio. Some use load funds, some use only no-loads, and some use both. A few will apply their timing to almost any fund a prospective client already owns. In all cases, the client keeps the mutual fund account in his or her own name and can add or withdraw money at will. The client simply gives written authorization for the timing service to switch among stock and money-market funds at the manager's discretion.

The findings of the *Money* study, combined with the advice of specialists in mutual fund investing, suggest some points to consider in choosing a fund-switching money manager.

Weigh the tax consequences. Unless your money is in an IRA, a teachers' retirement fund, or some other tax-deferred account, any switch out of a stock fund that has risen will involve capital gains—to be taxed at a maximum of 33% beginning in 1988.

Be wary of frequent switching. Top-performing timer J.D. Reynolds averaged fewer than four moves a year, which is about average for the firms studied. But some timers hop in and out of stocks more often. There is no evidence that more frequent switching adds anything but extra taxes.

Be skeptical of timers' performance claims. Ask whether the firm you are considering achieved its record entirely with money under management or partly with imaginary assets projected backward to a time before the firm was

TABLE 5. Hire Your Own Market Timer

Working from actual client records covering a bit more than five years, *Money's* consultant, Stephen Shellans of MoniResearch Corporation in Portland, Oregon, calculated the performances achieved by the nine managers in this table, all of whom time the stock market using mutual funds. To make the results comparable, Shellans assumed that each client had $100,000 in his account at the start of the study and did not add or withdraw any money for the next 62 months. Then Shellans followed exactly the moves of the manager, switching whenever he did between the same stock funds and money-market funds.

Two-thirds of the clients got bigger gains, after paying management fees and fund loads, than they would have if they had bought one average-performing growth-stock fund and held it for the full period. While growth funds had an average compound annual return of 13.6%, the typical client made 15.2%. And in two sharp market drops, no client lost as much asset value as he would have given up by staying in a typical fund. But not every above-average client would have been a clear winner after taxes.

Investment manager	Client	Value of a $100,000 investment after the 62 months to October 1986	Compound annual return
Average result for all clients		$207,830	15.2%
Comparative result in an average mutual fund without timing		193,489	13.6‡
J.D. Reynolds Co. **706 Indian Hill Rd.** **Terrace Park, OH 45174**	1	276,612	21.8
	2	259,315	20.2
Portfolio Management Services **2700 1 E. La Paz Rd., Suite 148** **Mission Viejo, CA 92691**	1	258,211	20.1
	2	200,092	14.4
R.M. Leary & Co. **3300 E. First Ave., Suite 380** **Denver, CO 80206**	1	256,043	19.9
	2	224,044	16.9
Lincoln Investment Planning **Benson East, Suite 1000** **Jenkintown, PA 19046**	1	238,991	18.4
	2	233,173	17.8
Portfolio Timing Inc. **402 Rainier Bank Bldg.** **11th & Broadway** **Tacoma, WA 98402**	1	233,708	17.9
	2	204,363	14.8
R. Meeder & Associates **6000 Memorial Dr.** **Dublin, OH 43017**	1	232,281	17.7
	2	204,328	14.8
William Mason & Co. **22801 Ventura Blvd.** **Woodland Hills, CA 91364**	1	189,641	13.2
	2	185,747	12.7
Shoal P. Berer Associates **717 Grant St.** **Pittsburgh, PA 15230**	1	156,540	9.1
	2	152,652	8.5
Managed Advisory Services **P.O. Box 79100** **Pittsburgh, PA 15216**	1	146,717	7.7
	2	141,530	7.0

* Moved out of stock funds before the market peaked; the result shown includes earnings on cash at the Treasury bill rate.
† Compared with the Lipper growth fund index because the account was invested in many funds at the same time.
‡ Based on the Lipper index.

Return on the funds without timing	% of capital preserved by selling before two big market declines		Average number of switches per year		
	18.2% drop from August to September 1981	15.5% drop from January to May 1984		Minimum investment	Highest annual fee
	81.8%	84.5%			
9.0% 10.8	96.4	95.1	3.6	$25,000	2.0%
18.4 11.0	96.4	89.1	3.2	None	1.5
19.9 19.9	96.9	90.8	5.8	100,000	2.0
12.3 12.3	105.2*	96.8	2.4	10,000	2.3
12.5 12.5	97.1	97.2	5.2	35,000	3.0
·13.6† 13.6†	105.1*	92.5	4.8	2,500 (in the firm's own mutual fund)	0.7
7.9 10.8	96.9	94.1	4.8	10,000	2.0 plus $65
18.4 14.9	101.8*	87.2	3.6	10,000	2.0
20.8 6.7	101.5*	91.3	6.0	10,000	2.0

managing accounts. Ask if the timer can provide outside verification of its results by an independent advisory service. Switch-fund timers do not usually have their results audited. But Stephen Shellans of MoniResearch Corporation, who designed *Money's* study and did the statistical work, ranks them six times a year on the accuracy of their timing signals in his *MoniResearch Newsletter*.

Choose no-load funds whenever possible. Though some timers using load funds fared relatively well in the study, the higher the fees that are deducted from an account, the higher the return the timer must achieve to overcome the expense of those fees.

Do not expect miracles. Be satisfied if a firm can demonstrate that—after expenses—it has at least edged out average mutual fund performance. According to Robert James of *Timer Digest*, the advisory newsletter in Fort Lauderdale, what you need is for the combination of timing performance and mutual fund selection to be three or four percentage points better than average annually. In the long term, that compounded return will make a big difference to your profits.

HOW TO WITHDRAW GRACEFULLY

In promoting themselves, mutual funds often emphasize the ease with which you can invest. Their ads stress, for example, how you can put in small sums regularly or reinvest dividends and capital gains. But as people get closer to retirement, they become more concerned with how best to extract cash from their investments. Many funds will set up withdrawal programs tailored to your wishes, as long as you have at least $10,000 in the account when you start taking the money out. Indeed, with funds it is usually as easy to take money out as to put it in.

If you do not wish to make regular withdrawals of the principal in your funds, you can collect the distributions of dividends and capital gains instead of reinvesting them. In this procedure, no fund shares are sold. Funds usually pass dividends on to shareholders quarterly or semiannually. Capital gains that funds realize by selling stocks usually are paid out once a year. You often can take your distributions and still see your remaining capital grow. The reason is that in a rising market stocks not yet sold may have appreciated, and their gains boost the share price.

If you take the distributions, however, do not expect inflation-beating average returns, since you will lose the compounding effect of reinvestment. As a hedge, you might collect the dividend distributions and still keep your assets growing by plowing back the capital gains.

While fund withdrawal plans are most useful for retirement income, they can also work for individuals in other circumstances. A person taking a year's sabbatical or maternity leave could set up such a plan, then stop withdrawing when regular salary resumed. Some large fund organizations will deposit withdrawals automatically in your bank account or, in the case of a stock or bond fund, in a money-market fund.

The type of fund you used for building your capital is not necessarily the best one from which to draw income. In choosing a fund for withdrawals, people nearing retirement need to consider how much protection an investment offers from both market slides and inflation. Someone who will rely on the income to meet everyday expenses probably should invest primarily in a money-market fund, where the principal will be secure. Bond funds will pay higher interest, but an account's worth will shrink if interest rates rise and bond prices drop.

Stock funds offer the best chance of staying ahead of inflation over time. A retiree could plan to protect against inflation by taking relatively small withdrawals from a stock fund in early years while letting the bulk of his or her capital continue to grow. In the later years of retirement, he or she could make larger withdrawals to compensate for price increases.

An example worked up by the T. Rowe Price fund organization shows the advantage gained by leaving as much money as is feasible in a fund. Results were calculated for two different withdrawal plans, assuming an account of $230,000 in a fund returning an average 10% a year.

In the first case, the investor takes out a fixed payment of about $23,000 a year until the account is depleted, in 25 years. In the second plan, the withdrawal equals 1/25th of the assets in the first year—or $9,200. The fraction withdrawn increases to 1/24th the next year, 1/23rd in the year after that, and so on until the account is exhausted in the 25th year. Because more money is left to grow in the early years, the second account earns enough to produce total withdrawals of just over $1 million, while the total with the first method is about $590,000.

In the T. Rowe Price example the account is an IRA, which by law must be depleted within the number of years the investor is expected to live, based on actuarial tables. Where no IRA is involved, investors can set up any withdrawal schedule they wish. For example, investors who do not have to withdraw a fixed amount every month might set up a program that initially would pay out around 6% of the account per year—well below a typical stock fund's average long-term return. Some fund groups will pay out a percentage automatically, while with others you must provide instructions monthly. As the account grows, the percentage could be increased.

You can have a fixed amount sent to you monthly or quarterly, with the fund selling the necessary number of shares to raise that sum. Withdrawing a regular dollar amount from a stock fund should be avoided if possible, however, because it is, in effect, a reversal of dollar-cost averaging. Instead of allowing you to take profits by selling shares as their net asset value climbs and buying them as it falls, a fixed-amount withdrawal forces you to take the opposite course—redeeming more shares to raise the set sum when the market is down and selling fewer near market tops.

An alternative with some stock and bond funds is to get a regular payment based on a fixed percentage of the value of your fund assets. A percentage withdrawal tends to reduce the number of shares sold in down markets and increase them when a rising market has boosted your fund assets. Of course, with such a plan check amounts will vary. But there is a way you can smooth out the fluctuations. You can put aside in a money-market fund anything over a certain amount you receive in rising markets and then use that reserve later to supplement leaner bear-market payouts.

THE MECHANICS OF CASHING IN

Taking your money out of a fund can require as little as 24 hours or more than a week, depending mostly on how you do it. The methods available are explained in every fund's prospectus. Some companies let you cash out with a telephone call. You merely ask to redeem a certain number of shares, and the proceeds are wired directly to your bank account. But most funds make you follow a more cumbersome procedure.

Many no-load or low-load funds demand that you put your redemption requests in writing, either in a letter or a telegram to the fund's transfer agent—the organization, usually a bank, that maintains the fund's records. Load fund shareholders can write the transfer agent or call their broker or financial planner, who will instruct the fund by phone to mail a check.

When liquidating only part of your holdings, it is important for tax reasons to specify in writing exactly the shares you want to dispose of, designating those to be sold by their purchase dates. (For more on the tax implications of selling shares, see Chapter 8.) If you are requesting a redemption by letter or telegram, most funds require you to list the name of the fund, your account number, the number of shares to be sold, and the address to which the check for the proceeds is to be mailed. If you are having the money wired, you will have to provide your bank's wire number, available from the bank, and your bank account number.

To guard against fraud, most funds insist that signatures on redemption letters be guaranteed by a trust company; a commercial bank that is a member of the Federal Deposit Insurance Corporation; or a brokerage firm that is a member of the New York, American, Boston, Midwest, or Pacific stock exchanges. Commercial banks and brokerage firms provide signature guarantees at no charge for account holders. Funds generally will not accept signature guarantees from notary publics or savings and loan companies. You can avoid the bother of getting a signature guarantee by requesting the redemptions by telegram, but you will have to arrange in advance with the fund for this privilege.

It is a good idea to send your redemption letter by registered mail and ask for a return receipt. This will give you a record of the date the transfer agent received your letter so that you can make sure your shares were sold at the closing price on that day. When you send a telegram you can request a confirmation, called a report delivery, for an extra charge of about $6.

Most transfer agents send you a check or wire the proceeds to your bank on the next business day after your shares are redeemed. But Securities and Exchange Commission regulations allow funds up to seven days to make payment. For example, in its prospectuses Fidelity states that it may hold up your money "if making immediate payment could adversely affect the fund," as might happen if, say, a steep market drop prompted a flood of sell orders from shareholders. Indeed, the Fidelity family has held up payment for a few days to sector fund investors on several occasions.

You can reduce the time it takes to sell shares by signing up in advance for telephone redemption. Once you have done this, you have only to call the fund and instruct a service representative to redeem your shares, but you give up the protection of a signature guarantee. Funds usually demand an identification code such as your Social Security number. A fund may also ask other questions culled from material on your account application, such as your mother's maiden name, to verify that you are who you say you are. A caveat: some funds may not make up the losses if these safeguards fail, so be sure to ask about the fund's policy before you make a redemption this way.

The quickest method to get your money is to request that it be wired via the Federal Reserve's electronic transfer system to your bank account. You will pay up to $20 for bank wiring charges, but you should have your money within two business days after the fund receives your redemption request. You can avoid a wire fee by having your money sent to your bank account through the Automated Clearing House system, rather than through the Federal Reserve's system. But that route takes about two days longer.

Another fast way to get your money is to sign up for a fund's check-writing privileges. Money-market and income funds generally offer check writing; most stock funds do not. But if you have shares in both a stock fund and a money-market fund in a family that permits telephone switching, you can call to move money from your stock fund to your money-market fund. You then write a check for the amount that you have transferred.

Money Sources

Growth Fund Guide **Growth Fund** **Research** **Box 6600** **Rapid City, SD** **57709** **($85 a year)**	***No-Load Fund*** ***Investor*** **P.O. Box 283** **Hastings-on-Hudson,** **NY 10706** **($79 a year)**	***Telephone Switch*** ***Newsletter*** **P.O. Box 2538** **Huntington Beach,** **CA 92647** **($117 a year)**
Hulbert Financial ***Digest*** **643 South Carolina** **Avenue S.E.** **Washington, D.C.** **20003** **($135 a year)**	***NoLoad Fund X*** **235 Montgomery** **Street** **San Francisco, CA** **94104** **($95 a year)**	***Timer Digest*** **P.O. Box 030130** **Fort Lauderdale, FL** **33303** **($175 a year, 18** **issues)**
MoniResearch ***Newsletter*** **P.O. Box 19146** **Portland, OR 97219** **($90 a year)**	***Professional Timing*** ***Service*** **P.O. Box 7483** **Missoula, MT 59801** **($185 a year)**	***Wellington's*** ***Worry-Free*** ***Investing*** **733 Bishop Street,** **Suite 1800** **Honolulu, HI 98613** **($129 a year)**
Mutual Fund ***Forecaster*** **3471 North Federal** **Highway** **Fort Lauderdale, FL** **33306** **($49 a year)**	***Sector Fund*** ***Connection*** **8949 La Riviera** **Drive** **Sacramento, CA** **95826** **($79 a year, 16** **issues)**	
Mutual Fund ***Strategist*** **P.O. Box 446** **Burlington, VT** **05402** **($127 a year)**	***Switch Fund*** ***Advisory*** **8943 Shady Grove** **Court** **Gaithersburg, MD** **20877** **($140 a year)**	

EIGHT

How Tax Reform Affects Your Funds

In the case of mutual funds, the Tax Reform Act of 1986 has both given and taken away. The most notable losses are two obscure tax breaks you might never have noticed and probably will never miss—that is, until you file your returns. One loophole allowed funds to defer income for you by paying it out the year after it was earned. The other, in effect, let you automatically write off investment expenses the fund incurred. Without that deduction, you could wind up owing taxes each year on earnings that went to pay the fund's bills.

On the bright side, the new law clears the way for funds

to use sophisticated hedging techniques to protect share values in falling markets. And the law leaves intact provisions that give fund investors special latitude in calculating capital gains—the difference between what you paid for your shares and what you receive when you redeem them.

For most fund shareholders, however, the key changes are not the ones aimed specifically at funds but those that affect all investors: the reduction in tax brackets and the repeal of the preferential treatment for long-term capital gains. These revisions favor some types of investments over others, and they could lead you to consider switching funds.

THE NEW RULES FOR INVESTORS

Most significantly, the new tax code shifts its affection from racy growth-stock funds to their traditionally stodgy income-oriented cousins, which invest in bonds or high-dividend stocks. The reason is the phase-out of the distinction—as far as taxes are concerned—between income and long-term capital gains. Before January 1, 1987, if you owned any security longer than six months and sold it at a profit, only 40% of the gain was taxable. But beginning in 1987, all capital gains—not just 40%—are taxable.

For 1987 only, there is a transition rule: the maximum long-term gains rate is 28%, even for investors paying rates of 35% or 38.5% on other income. In subsequent years, capital gains and and other income such as your salary, interest, and dividends are taxed at the same rate, up to the maximum 33% rate for married couples filing jointly with taxable incomes over $71,900 (or $43,150 for single filers).

Thus, other investment considerations aside, income-producing funds look more attractive than they did formerly, relative to low-yielding growth funds. Take the case of a married couple with a taxable income of $37,980 to $49,420, which put them in the 33% tax bracket in 1986. Now the rate they pay on long-term gains has more than doubled, from 13.2% in 1986 to 28% in 1987 and thereafter. But the tax they face on their interest and dividends has dropped from 33% to 28%. As a result, the couple will net 17% less after taxes from a growth fund that appreciates exactly as much as it did in 1986. But they earn 7.5% more from an income fund that paid identical dividends in 1986.

While market analysts still expect growth funds to outperform income funds over the long haul, the after-tax advantage will narrow. Because the tax code no longer rewards you for taking the risk of investing in stock funds, you have a strong incentive to look into income funds. Moreover, what is good for income funds may be even better for total-return funds, which aim for a mix of capital gains and income. The new law may give a lift to such funds' share prices, as yield-hungry investors flock to the high-dividend stocks and convertible securities that these funds tend to hold.

What about losses? The new law makes the chore of weeding out your losing funds a lot less onerous. In the past, there was a tax incentive to hold on to losing funds in hopes that they would turn around. Not anymore. Before tax reform, you could deduct only 50% of losses on the sale of assets held for more than six months, which had the effect of encouraging investors with significant losses to hang on to their dogs. What is more, deductible losses were limited to $3,000 a year, although losses in excess of that amount could be carried over into future years. The new law lets you deduct 100% of your long-term losses, up to $3,000 annually, and carry forward excess losses. So the tax penalty for selling at a long-term loss is gone.

NEW WRINKLES FOR FUNDS

In addition to these changes, which affect all investments, the tax code introduces a number of provisions specifically aimed at mutual funds. Here are the changes that are most likely to affect fund shareholders.

Inflexible dividend distributions. A fund can generate income in either of two ways: by taking profits on appreciated stocks or bonds in its portfolio or by receiving interest or dividends from the securities it owns. The Internal Revenue Service requires most funds to pay the income to shareholders after subtracting expenses. You owe tax on these distributions in the year you receive them, as you would on interest or dividends paid by a company in which you owned stocks or bonds. If a fund has realized any capital gains, they will be included in the distributions along with interest and dividends.

Under the old law, most funds had to pass on to shareholders all the income generated during their fiscal year, within 12 months of the fiscal year-end. That often meant that shareholders automatically deferred taxes on at least some of the income until many months after the fund had received it. For instance, the Nicholas Fund, a growth fund with a fiscal year ending on March 31, did not pay out any of the income it earned between April 1985 and March 1986 until April 1986. Shareholders paid no tax on income the fund earned in the last nine months of 1985 until they filed their 1986 tax returns.

The new law slams that loophole shut. Now by December 31 funds must distribute all of the income and profits they earn during the calendar year. This tax-law change delivers a double whammy in 1987 because a fund must pay out not only all the income it earned during the year but also whatever it still owed you from that part of 1986 that fell during the fund's fiscal 1987. In the Nicholas Fund, for example, you would end up owing taxes on 21 months' worth of income on your 1987 return. Take consolation that in 1988 and subsequent years you pay tax on only one year's worth of dividends at a time.

Deductionless expenses. In the process of investing your money, a fund incurs costs; on average, administrative expenses and investment advisory fees absorb about 1% of a fund's total assets annually. Previously the fund deducted those expenses from its investment earnings before making distributions—in effect, you automatically received a deduction for investment expenses. Under the new law, investment expenses incurred by any investor are deductible only if your total miscellaneous deductions exceed 2% of your adjusted gross income.

To make sure that mutual fund investors do not automatically receive a deduction that other investors might not get, the new law changes how funds report their distributions. For example, in its 1986 fiscal year, the Nicholas

Fund yielded $1.07 a share before expenses. If you owned 300 shares—about $9,000 worth—your portion of the gross income would have been $321. Your share of fund expenses would have been $57, and so your net income would have been $264. The fund would have distributed that amount to you in April 1986, and you would pay taxes on it when you filed your 1986 taxes.

In 1987 and thereafter, you would still receive only $264 but would have to report all $321 as income. You could include the $57 of expenses with your miscellaneous deductions. Unless the total exceeds 2% of your income, however, you lose all $57 of the deduction, and you would owe tax on all $321. The revamped Form 1099 your fund must send you in January 1988 lists both the gross dividends you must report and the expenses you can deduct.

The provision hits some funds harder than others. Dividends paid by municipal bond funds get off scot-free; their shareholders need to report only the interest they receive (and, of course, they still pay no federal taxes on it). But growth funds, which tend to run up relatively high expenses and earn little interest or dividend income, get stung. Shareholders in some of these funds may find they owe more in taxes than they receive in dividends.

Income from short-term hedges. The old tax code permitted a fund to earn no more than 30% of its total income from investments held less than three months. That limited a fund manager's freedom to protect his portfolio by hedging—using short-term defensive transactions to offset possible losses. The new law relaxes the rule. Now a gain on a short-term transaction undertaken specifically as a hedge can be offset by a loss in the part of the portfolio being hedged. For example, a fund manager, concerned that a stock in his portfolio might decline, might buy an option that would increase in value if the price of his stock drops within the next three months. If the loss on the stock and the gain on the option are equal, then none of the income from that transaction counts toward the 30% limit. That means the fund manager is free to continue hedging against portfolio losses without running over his limit.

Several fairly new funds, including Dreyfus Strategic Income and Dreyfus Strategic Investing, both launched in late 1986, are designed to take advantage of the revamped rule. They trade options on the securities in their portfolios to boost income and help hold share prices steady.

WAYS TO FIGURE YOUR CAPITAL GAINS

When you take your profits on shares of a mutual fund, you must pay tax on your capital gain. The tax code lets you use any of four methods to calculate the shares' cost, so you can choose the one that results in the smallest tax. Whatever technique you choose, remember to subtract from your gain the value of shares purchased with reinvested dividends or capital-gains distributions. You paid taxes on them in the year they were made.

Once you decide on a method, you must use it every time you sell shares from that fund. Note that if you sell all your shares in the same year, the total gain you report will be the same no matter what method you use to calculate it. But if you sell over a period of years, the different methods let you control when you will recognize different parts of the gain. Here are the four methods and how they work.

Specific identification method. This one gives you the most control over the results, but as a practical matter it is the most difficult to apply. When instructing a fund to sell, you must identify the shares in your sell order by the date you bought them and the price you paid for them. For example, to minimize your gain you could simply instruct the fund to sell the shares you paid the most for. To stand up to IRS scrutiny, however, you need confirmation that the specified shares were indeed sold, and few funds' transaction statements describe which shares were redeemed. If you bought the shares through a broker, he or she can generally confirm that the order was filled as you requested. But if you bought shares directly from a fund, you run the risk that your calculation will be disallowed in an IRS audit.

FIFO method. This method is likely to be useful only through 1987, while the transitional maximum tax on long-term gains is still in effect. If you do not specifically identify the shares you redeem, the IRS assumes that you sell shares in the order you purchased them. If your fund's shares have risen fairly steadily, this first-in, first-out (or FIFO) method will generally give you the largest gain. Normally you would want to report as small a gain as possible. But if you sell shares in 1987 that you have held longer than six months, you might prefer to use FIFO for this tax year to make sure the ones you sell qualify for the 28% rate on long-term gains. After 1987, gains are taxed up to 33% no matter how long you have owned the shares.

Single-category and double-category methods. Instead of calculating a different gain for each block of shares you bought, you can figure an average cost for shares you sell. You can use either of two averaging methods. With *single category* you simply calculate an average cost for all the shares you own, which can result in a bigger tax bill than the previously cited methods.

Or you can choose *double category*, in which you calculate one average for shares you have held longer than six months and a separate average for shares you bought more recently. Then when you file your taxes, you designate the shares you have sold as coming from one category or the other. Opting for the double category—and selling shares from the long-term portion of it—is particularly advantageous for 1987 if you are in the 35% bracket or higher. That is because you benefit from the favorable rates on long-term gains. After 1987, the sole rationale for shareholders committing to the double category is the hope that the next round of tax reforms will reinstate the preferential rates on long-term gains.

NINE

Ten
All-Weather
Funds

It is an all-too-familiar dilemma for long-term investors.
One week the Dow Jones industrial average is hitting
record highs, and the next week the market tumbles 80
points. Some investment sages contend that stocks are
headed for a big fall, while others say there is plenty of room
to grow. You, meanwhile, have more than enough to worry
about without having to size up the market's every wave
and trough. The ideal solution would be a mutual fund that
guards the value of your shares during market gales but lets
you steam ahead under clear skies. In short, you need an
all-weather fund.

This chapter serves to introduce you to 10 such steady performers and the sure-handed managers who chart their courses. Each of these funds has found a way to provide superior returns while taking comparatively limited risks, according to a statistical study conducted by *Money*. Their defining characteristic is not flashy results; only one of them, Fidelity Magellan, ranks among the top 10 funds in total return over the five years to April 1987. Nor did all of the funds outperform the Standard & Poor's 500-stock index, which soared 224% including dividends over the corresponding period. What sets the all-weather funds apart from the mutual fund pack is their combination of impressive long-term gains—each would have at least tripled your money since 1982—and relatively smooth rides through varying market conditions. That makes them eminently suitable for investors who are seeking both solid profits and peace of mind.

To compile its list of the top all-weather funds, *Money* asked the mutual fund research firm Lipper Analytical Services to rank 262 large and widely available diversified domestic stock funds by their five-year risk-adjusted performance to April 1987. (By contrast, each fund's volatility and performance in the alphabetical listing in chapter 10 is relative only to other funds with the same objectives.) The study used a formula developed by Stanford University finance professor William Sharpe. At the heart of the calculation is a measure of risk known as standard deviation, which in this case compares how much a fund's returns vary month-by-month from its average monthly return.

In Sharpe's calculation, a high return increases a fund's score, but high volatility reduces it. Thus if two funds deliver the same total return over time, the less volatile fund would receive the higher rating. Excluded from the study are bond funds, whose unusually robust appreciation was mainly due to five consecutive years of falling interest rates. Also omitted from the study were those funds that invest heavily in foreign securities, which were given an extra boost by the dollar's declining value abroad in recent years. Stock funds that were closed to new investors as of April 1987 were culled from the analysis as well.

Although all of the all-weather funds scored exceptionally well by Sharpe's measure, they are hardly carbon copies of each other. Some, such as Phoenix Growth, target the flighty shares of fast-growing firms. Others in the group, including Evergreen Total Return, Fidelity Puritan, and Strong Investment, temper the riskiness of their stockholdings with income-paying convertibles and conventional bonds. Thus a fund's appearance on the all-weather list does not absolve you of responsibility to evaluate carefully its goals and strategies before you invest. Make sure that the fund's investment objectives—for example, toward income rather than growth—match your goals, and that the fund's appetite for risk does not exceed your ability to absorb short-term losses.

The following profiles of the all-weather funds cite the funds' five-year total return, compounded annual gain, volatility rating, and initial sales charge, if any. The graph accompanying each fund charts growth in net asset value. For additional facts on a fund's performance over different periods, the fees it charges, and where to call to obtain more information, refer to the fund listing in chapter 10.

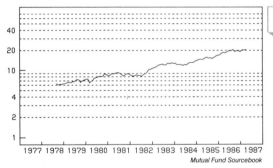

Mutual Fund Sourcebook

EVERGREEN TOTAL RETURN

Five-year total return: 240%
Compounded annual gain: 25.2%
Volatility: Very low
Load: None

Evergreen Total Return, based in the New York City suburb of Harrison, New York, is co-managed by Stephen Lieber, 61, and Nola Maddox Falcone, 47. The two place equal emphasis on income and capital appreciation. That policy draws the $1.6 billion equity income fund down two different investment paths. One leads to high-yielding stocks and convertibles of banks and utilities, which tend to suffer less during down markets because of their generous dividends. The other leads to potential takeover candidates among mostly blue chip stocks that Lieber and Falcone view as undervalued in relation to the per-share price an acquiring company might pay for the business. In either case, the managers follow a strict discipline in their selection of stocks: the yield and anticipated appreciation must add up to at least 20% a year.

Yield and value both proved to be stock market trump cards over the five years analyzed. During that period, falling interest rates greatly enhanced investors' demand for high-yielding securities, and stocks of many established companies jumped in price as soon as corporate suitors declared their merger or takeover intentions. Fifty-two of Evergreen Total Return's value stocks have been involved in mergers and acquisitions since the fund's inception in 1978, resulting in price run-ups that produced fat profits for the fund.

Managers Lieber and Falcone have lately been betting heavily on regional banks—a market sector they expect to continue sailing on the winds of deregulation of the banking and financial services industries. In the resolutely bullish first three months of 1987, though, the fund was relatively becalmed: it gained only 7.6% compared with 21.4% for the S&P 500. But one laggard quarter does not faze Lieber. "You don't have to win every race to win the regatta," he says.

FIDELITY PURITAN

Five-year total return: 210%
Compounded annual gain: 23.3%
Volatility: Low
Load: 2%

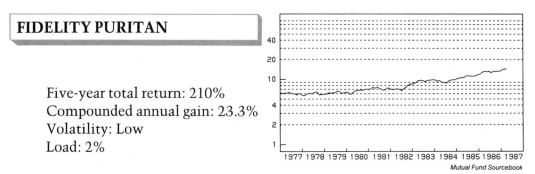

1977 1978 1979 1980 1981 1982 1983 1984 1985 1986 1987
Mutual Fund Sourcebook

Boston-bred Fidelity Puritan is the only all-weather fund with current income as its primary investment goal. Appropriately, its 6.2% yield is the highest of the group. For most of the five-year period, Puritan was run by Francis Cabour, 64. In March 1987, however, after recovering from a heart attack, Cabour ceded stewardship of the $4 billion fund to Richard Fentin, 31, former manager of Fidelity Growth Company, a $182 million aggressive growth fund. Cabour took a less demanding job as manager of Fidelity Balanced, which has $165 million under management.

Although Puritan traditionally is classified as an equity

income fund, it more closely resembles a balanced fund with an approximately three-to-two split between stocks and bonds. To maintain the fund's high yield, Puritan favors bonds rated below investment grade and high-dividend stocks, such as those of energy or utilities companies. Another fund staple is convertible bonds, which lately have averaged about 10% of the portfolio. A sizable percentage of the fund's stocks and bonds are foreign. Says Cabour: "Puritan's strength is its great flexibility. The manager can literally invest in just about anything in the world he wants."

The fund's high income and wide diversification give it a cushion against abrupt moves in share price; the fund gained a mere 10% in the first quarter of 1987. But hot bull market performance has never been Puritan's goal. For further protection from market fluctuations, the fund had nearly 15% of its assets parked in cash in April 1987. "This fund is for people who want to sleep nights and do not want to have to check the paper every day," observes Cabour. "It's not for the traders, the greedy ones, or the nervous nellies."

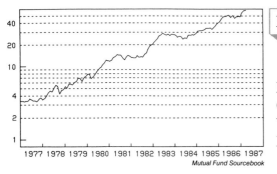

1977 1978 1979 1980 1981 1982 1983 1984 1985 1986 1987

Mutual Fund Sourcebook

FIDELITY MAGELLAN

Five-year total return: 381%
Compounded annual gain: 32.7%
Volatility: High
Load: 3%

Fidelity Magellan, also in Boston, is the largest stock fund in the country, and its captain, Peter Lynch, 42, is perhaps the best-known and best-paid portfolio manager in the business—his base salary exceeds $1 million a year. And who is to quibble? Magellan easily outperformed all other funds over the past 10 years with a total return to April 1987 of 1,962%, compared with 449% for the average stock fund and 380% for the S&P 500. At the same time, the long-term growth fund grew from $21.4 million in assets to $9.8 billion, an increase of 45,700%.

Lynch's fame and prodigious portfolio have not changed

his folksy demeanor and straightforward approach to picking winning stocks. For instance, he does not make market forecasts, saying only, "I expect the market to be up six points every day I come to work." He also dismisses the value of broad, macroeconomic analysis with the quip, "Nobody called to tell me about the recession in 1980 and 1981." Instead, Lynch prefers to concentrate on individual companies and their prospects.

Growth stocks, including small, emerging growth companies, make up about 40% of Magellan's holdings. Other portions of the portfolio are invested more conservatively in resurgent industrial giants, such as Ford Motors and Chrysler, or high-yielding electric utilities, savings and loans, and banks. Because Magellan's portfolio is almost exclusively invested in stocks, the fund is much more prone to wide swings in price than are the other all-weather funds. On average, Magellan rises and falls 9% more than does the market; Evergreen Total Return, by contrast, fluctuates in value little more than half as much. But the market's ups and downs are of little concern to Lynch, who simply says, "When the market goes down, I can put more money in."

In the past, Magellan's stupendous performance has more than compensated investors for enduring these fluctuations. As Lynch himself admits, however, the fund's mega-size makes a reprise of the past unlikely. The fund's portfolio contains more than a thousand stocks, compared with 43 in 1977, and big gains by a dozen or even a hundred stocks can easily be lost in the crowd. As a result, Lynch now aims to beat the S&P 500 index by one or two percentage points a year instead of the four to five he shot for previously.

MUTUAL QUALIFIED INCOME

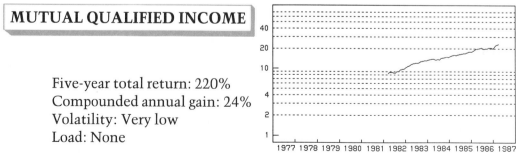

Five-year total return: 220%
Compounded annual gain: 24%
Volatility: Very low
Load: None

40
20
10

4

2

1

1977 1978 1979 1980 1981 1982 1983 1984 1985 1986 1987

Mutual Fund Sourcebook

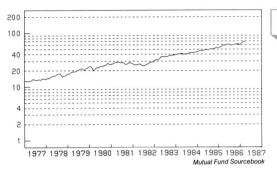

1977 1978 1979 1980 1981 1982 1983 1984 1985 1986 1987
Mutual Fund Sourcebook

MUTUAL SHARES

Five-year total return: 221%
Compounded annual gain: 24%
Volatility: Very low
Load: None

These two growth and income funds share more than a
first name, a New York City address, and virtually identical
results. Run by Max Heine, 76, and Michael Price, 35,
$1.9 billion Mutual Shares and $700 million Mutual Qualified Income are essentially the same fund. They follow the
same low-volatility, value-oriented investment approach
and own most of the same securities. "I don't play the
market," says Heine. "I buy stocks based on their individual merit." Both funds turned in a quintessential all-
weather performance over the five-year period: they ranked
in the top 15% of all diversified stock funds in total return
and in the bottom 5% for volatility.

Heine's and Price's search for bargain-priced stocks and
bonds often lands them in so-called special situations—a
Wall Street term for those dimly lit corners of the market
where less intrepid fund managers rarely tread. As of April
1987, for example, roughly 35% of each fund was invested
in securities of bankrupt, liquidating, merging, or restructuring companies whose financial circumstances typically
defy the standard measures of valuing stocks and bonds.
The two funds also held 5% of the shares outstanding in
Alexander's, a land-rich New York City retailer long
coveted by real estate developer Donald Trump.

The managers attribute the funds' enviable steadiness to
their predilection for such special situations: downtrodden
stocks of companies involved in bankruptcies or corporate
restructurings generally do not fluctuate in value as much
as the market overall, Price points out. To excel consistently with such a value-minded approach requires patience
as well as strong convictions. Years could pass before other
investors recognize a company's hidden asset value and bid
up the stock's price. Yet, Price says, bargains abound even
as the market hits new highs, as it did in early 1987.

PHOENIX BALANCED

Five-year total return: 219%
Compounded annual gain: 23.9%
Volatility: Low
Load: 8.5%

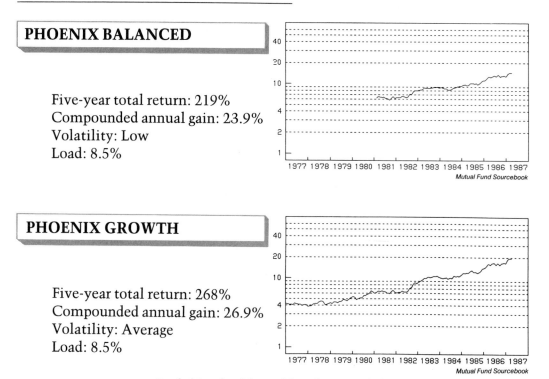

Mutual Fund Sourcebook

PHOENIX GROWTH

Five-year total return: 268%
Compounded annual gain: 26.9%
Volatility: Average
Load: 8.5%

Mutual Fund Sourcebook

Both Hartford-based funds proved their all-weather seaworthiness with manager Robert Chesek, 52, at the helms. The principal difference between the long-term growth fund and the balanced one is that Phoenix Balanced is required by its charter to keep at least 25% of the portfolio in bonds. The bond income—the major contributor to the fund's 4.1% yield—helped make Balanced about a fifth less volatile than its sister fund over the five-year period.

In 1986, however, Chesek chose to concentrate on his stock funds and turned over the $289 million Phoenix Balanced to Patricia Bannan. Although she is only 25, she has been a Phoenix stock analyst since 1982. Bannan relies on the same earnings-growth approach to stock picking that Chesek continues to use in the $450 million Phoenix Growth.

By scrutinizing earnings forecasts from stock analysts and the companies themselves, Chesek tries to anticipate which firms will grow fastest over the next five years. "If you can figure out the stocks that will have the best growth in the future," he says, "you'll end up getting top dollar." The tricky part of this strategy is to pick up the stocks before that potential is reflected in their prices.

While the payoff has been high, this can be a fairly risky way to choose stocks. One reason is that earnings predictions are notoriously optimistic. When a company's annual or quarterly results fall short of these rosy forecasts, institutions and other large shareholders are quick to hit the sell button. Chesek tries to limit his downside risk by being one of the quickest. "The difference between an amateur investor and a professional," he jokes, "is that the pro panics first."

Chesek's hunt for earnings growth led him in 1987 to invest heavily in computer stocks such as Digital Equipment and retailers such as J.C. Penney. He also had a large holding of so-called interest-sensitive stocks, such as those of telephone companies and regional banks, which benefit from declining interest rates.

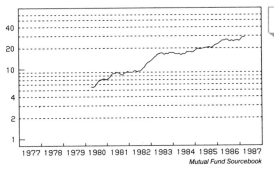

1977 1978 1979 1980 1981 1982 1983 1984 1985 1986 1987
Mutual Fund Sourcebook

QUEST FOR VALUE

Five-year total return: 237%
Compounded annual gain: 25.1%
Volatility: Low
Load: None

True to its name, this Manhattan-based maximum-gains fund has profited handsomely by investing in stocks that its manager, Paul Blaustein, 39, believes are appealingly underpriced relative to the companies' assets or earnings potential. Such bargains were plentiful before the start of the bull market in 1982, when many stocks were selling for slightly more—and sometimes less—than the firms' book value, or net worth per share. Five years later the S&P 500 had more than tripled; the stocks in the index commanded, on average, prices of nearly two and one-half times book value; and Blaustein's quest for companies priced below their intrinsic worth had become increasingly more difficult.

Undeterred, Blaustein in recent years has set his sights on firms selling for less than the per-share price he thinks they are worth in terms of their underlying assets. "I look for assets with an established market value," he explains. "For example, an airline's planes have a readily marketable value, as do individual hotels in a hotel chain."

Unsettled by the market's increasingly sharp gyrations, Blaustein has begun to employ a strategy called portfolio insurance, which allows him to hedge against a stock sell-off by buying options against the S&P 500 index. Should the market drop sharply, the resultant profits on those options would cushion the fund's losses. "This wasn't a concern in the less volatile market five years ago," he observes. "But in today's market I could see a 20% decline easily. Portfolio insurance is a way to protect against that loss."

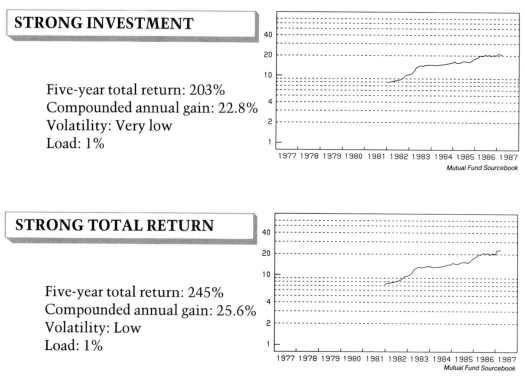

STRONG INVESTMENT

Five-year total return: 203%
Compounded annual gain: 22.8%
Volatility: Very low
Load: 1%

1977 1978 1979 1980 1981 1982 1983 1984 1985 1986 1987
Mutual Fund Sourcebook

STRONG TOTAL RETURN

Five-year total return: 245%
Compounded annual gain: 25.6%
Volatility: Low
Load: 1%

1977 1978 1979 1980 1981 1982 1983 1984 1985 1986 1987
Mutual Fund Sourcebook

Strong Total Return, which in spite of its name is a maximum-growth portfolio, and Strong Investment, which is a balanced fund, were launched in 1981 with the seemingly modest goal of outpacing inflation by an average of 5% a year. "We are in an unusually profitable period of the financial market's history," explains William Corneliuson, 44, who co-manages the Milwaukee-based funds with founder Richard Strong, 45. "But somewhere along the line the markets will run into trouble. An annual 5% real return is what is doable over the long term."

Corneliuson and Strong far exceeded their goal over the five years to April 1987, with both funds beating inflation by an average of 20 percentage points a year. One reason is that the funds' charters give their managers plenty of flexibility to preserve shareholders' capital by redeploying assets among stocks, bonds, or cash in the proportions they judge suitable to prevailing business and market conditions. Says Strong: "Our success depends largely on making the right macroeconomic call." The only constraint is that Strong Investment must remain at least 35% invested in fixed-income securities and must avoid bonds rated below investment grade.

For example, Strong Total Return adroitly bailed out of stocks in June 1983 and stayed primarily in cash for the next 12—mostly bearish—months in which the average aggressive stock fund lost 18.7% versus a 3.6% gain for Strong's. Then, later in 1984, both funds loaded up on shares of depressed property and casualty insurance companies, betting correctly that this interest-sensitive sector would rebound smartly as rates fell. By the end of the first quarter of 1987, the funds were taking their profits in insurance and other interest-driven stocks and buying shares in chemical, paper, and computer companies, which Corneliuson and Strong believed would show stronger export sales because of the weaker dollar abroad.

The managers were also raising cash to shore up the funds' assets in the event of a market slump; Total Return, with $815 million in assets, had about 15% in cash and Investment, with $330 million, about 25%. "In volatile markets cash is strength," notes Strong. "The last thing we want to do is lose all the money we have made for people."

TEN

The Mutual Fund Rankings

When you choose a mutual fund or weigh whether to stick with the ones already in your portfolio, the most important—though not the sole—criterion is past performance. In the rankings and alphabetical listing that follow, each fund is ranked according to how well its three-year total return compared with that of other funds having the same objectives.

The performance figures were prepared for *Money* by Lipper Analytical Services. To be included in the rankings, a fund must be at least one year old, have $10 million or more in assets, require a minimum initial investment of no more than $10,000, and be available to the general public in at least 25 states. In calculating the funds' performances, it was assumed that all dividends and capital gains distributions were reinvested, but any sales charges the fund may impose were not taken into account.

The fund's primary objective is indicated under the heading **Type**. (See figure 17 for the key to abbreviations and a comparison of the average gain in each group of funds over the three years to April 1, 1987.)

To compare funds that are not among the top performers, check the **three-year performance rank within type** in the alphabetical list. The first number gives the fund's ranking; the second, the number of funds in its category with three-year performance records. (A dash denotes those funds in business for less than three years.)

The rating for **volatility** will give you an idea whether a fund has been hyperactive or catatonic compared with other funds of the same type over the three-year period analyzed. A highly volatile fund can be highly profitable if you get in and out at the right time. But it may not make sense for you if you are uncomfortable with unexpected— and often pronounced—swings in share value.

When evaluating a fund's **percent gain (or loss) to April 1, 1987**, keep in mind that the performance figures do not take into account any sales charges levied by the fund. To estimate the effect of various fund fees, see table 3 on page 84. Also note that the one-year and three-year columns show performance during an unprecedented surge in the stock market. Funds with superior 10-year records have demonstrated that they can produce consistent results over a full, bull-and-bear market cycle.

To see how much a top-ranked fund profited from the bull market that began in 1982, refer to the figure for **percent five-year compounded annual return**, which breaks the five-year total return into an annualized number. The figure for **percent current yield** shows how much income a fund produced in the 12 months to April 1987.

When you buy fund shares from a broker, financial planner, or insurance agent, you may have to pay a commission, or front-end load, listed under **percent maximum initial sales charge**. In some cases—say, when you are investing $10,000 or more—the load may be lower than the one indicated. Funds with an initial charge of 7.25% or less may also levy their load on reinvested dividends (you can find out by calling the fund). Low-load funds, which charge 3% or less, usually sell shares directly to investors just the way no-load funds do. The heading **percent maximum deferred sales charge** refers to the fee some funds charge when you leave the fund. These fees generally start at 5% or 6% and decline by one percentage point each year until they disappear altogether.

Another important consideration is a fund's **expenses per $100**. This is how much a fund subtracted from assets in the past 12 months to pay management and operating costs, including 12b-1 fees. The lower the figure, the better. The average for stock funds is $1.10 for every $100 in fund assets. The average bond fund has an expense ratio of about 90¢ for every $100.

Most funds have a **minimum initial investment** of $1,000 but many will let you invest for less. The **IRA minimum initial investment** is usually $500 or less. Be prepared to pay an **IRA annual fee** of $2.50 to $25 and a one-time start-up fee of $5 to $20.

If you think that big funds are too sluggish to make nimble market moves, you might want to check the column headed **assets as of February 27, 1987**. Although a big fund can spread its expenses over a large base, large funds may have trouble finding enough promising issues to invest in. Also, large funds buy and sell stocks in such huge quantities that their trades alone can bump up—or knock down—the securities' prices. Thus some highly successful stock funds have been closed to new investors. With bond funds, however, bigger is often better because they buy issues in great volume and thus pay less for their bonds than do smaller funds.

If you want to move your money easily among funds within a family, check to see whether the group has **phone switch** privileges. These enable you to maneuver your cash in a flash by making a phone call. Funds may charge up to $10 per switch or limit you to three or four switches a year. Before investing, of course, phone and ask for the prospectus and annual report. Study both carefully.

FIGURE 17. Three-Year Performance to April 1, 1987, of 17 Fund Groups

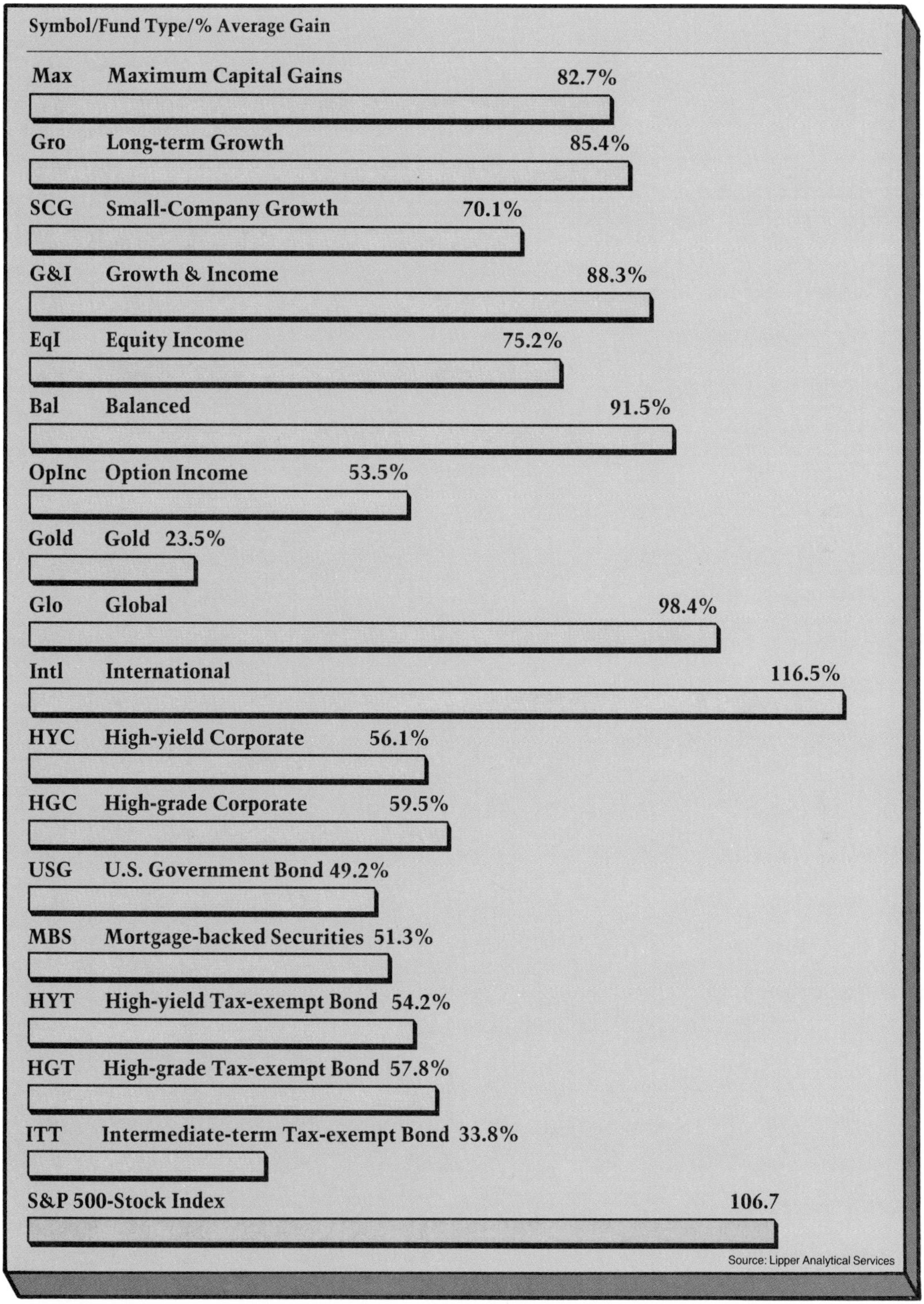

Symbol/Fund Type/% Average Gain

Max	Maximum Capital Gains	82.7%
Gro	Long-term Growth	85.4%
SCG	Small-Company Growth	70.1%
G&I	Growth & Income	88.3%
EqI	Equity Income	75.2%
Bal	Balanced	91.5%
OpInc	Option Income	53.5%
Gold	Gold	23.5%
Glo	Global	98.4%
Intl	International	116.5%
HYC	High-yield Corporate	56.1%
HGC	High-grade Corporate	59.5%
USG	U.S. Government Bond	49.2%
MBS	Mortgage-backed Securities	51.3%
HYT	High-yield Tax-exempt Bond	54.2%
HGT	High-grade Tax-exempt Bond	57.8%
ITT	Intermediate-term Tax-exempt Bond	33.8%
	S&P 500-Stock Index	106.7

Source: Lipper Analytical Services

(Note: The performances of sector funds, abbreviated Sec in the tables, are too wide-ranging for a group average to be meaningful.)

Top-Performing Stock Funds Ranked by 3-year Performance	Volatility (within Type)				
	Percent Compounded Annual Return (5 years to April 1, 1987)				
	Percent Gain (or Loss) to April 1, 1987				
		One Year	Three Years	Ten Years	Percent Current Yield
Standard & Poor's 500-Stock Index		**26.2**	**106.7**	**380.0**	
MAXIMUM CAPITAL GAINS					
1 Pacific Horizon Agg. Growth	High	—	38.0	208.5	—	0.1
2 ABT Emerging Growth	High	—	28.1	133.8	—	0.0
3 Constellation Growth	High	25.6	43.7	129.8	830.2	0.0
4 Weingarten Equity	Average	27.8	28.6	128.2	1,025.8	0.7
5 Putnam Voyager	Average	24.9	27.6	124.8	613.3	0.6
6 Shearson Aggressive Growth	High	—	40.9	118.0	—	0.0
7 Twentieth Century Vista	High	—	44.8	117.4	—	0.0
8 Neuberger & Berman Manhatttan	Average	26.5	21.9	116.8	530.4	0.8
9 Fidelity Special Situations	Average	—	19.0	113.4	—	0.5
10 Twentieth Century Growth	High	23.6	33.4	111.3	1,232.2	0.4
11 AMEV Growth	High	24.7	28.8	107.0	942.0	0.2
12 Investors Research	High	26.3	28.5	106.0	649.6	0.4
13 Sigma Capital Shares	Average	25.1	16.7	105.6	566.2	1.5
14 Omega Fund	Average	19.1	20.3	105.3	287.6	1.3
15 Oppenheimer Time	Average	25.4	26.3	105.0	727.3	1.1
16 Princor Capital Accum.	Average	25.1	23.2	104.7	412.4	1.8
17 Phoenix Stock Series	Average	26.7	22.0	104.4	893.1	1.5
18 Fidelity Freedom Fund*	Average	—	18.8	103.3	—	0.7
19 Fairmont Fund	Average	27.5	19.9	102.5	—	0.5
20 Value Line Leveraged Growth	Average	17.6	25.1	102.3	745.8	0.5

*Open to IRA investors only.

Top-Performing Stock Funds Ranked by 3-year Performance	Volatility (within Type)					
	Percent Compounded Annual Return (5 years to April 1, 1987)					
	Percent Gain (or Loss) to April 1, 1987					
			One Year	Three Years	Ten Years	Percent Current Yield
Standard & Poor's 500-Stock Index			26.2	106.7	380.0	
GROWTH						
1 Loomis-Sayles Cap. Develop.**	High	32.4	40.0	160.7	1,149.5	0.3
2 Fidelity Magellan	High	32.7	24.3	135.5	1,962.3	0.8
3 Franklin Equity	High	24.5	24.8	133.7	507.1	1.0
4 Guardian Park Avenue	High	27.5	22.4	128.9	632.3	1.3
5 Northeast Investors Growth	High	21.7	26.6	125.2	—	0.4
6 New England Growth	High	27.9	33.8	122.1	935.8	0.4
7 Quasar Associates**	High	26.6	19.0	119.3	1,161.1	0.0
8 Thomson McKinnon Growth	Average	—	31.2	116.8	—	1.9
9 Boston Co. Cap. Appreciation	Average	24.1	22.0	115.2	386.8	2.1
10 IDS New Dimensions	High	25.0	28.9	114.7	704.3	1.5
11 Nationwide Growth	Average	25.7	21.0	114.7	488.8	2.8
12 T. Rowe Price Growth Stock	Average	21.0	24.4	114.4	272.3	1.4
13 New York Venture	Average	25.4	19.7	113.9	733.7	0.9
14 Pilgrim MagnaCap	Average	22.8	17.0	113.0	432.5	2.3
15 Phoenix Growth Series	Average	26.9	22.0	110.7	687.2	1.6
16 Twentieth Century Select	High	27.0	23.7	108.4	1,198.2	0.9
17 Shearson Appreciation	Average	23.4	24.1	106.9	660.4	1.3
18 New Economy	Average	—	19.7	106.9	—	1.6
19 Fidelity Destiny—Port. I	High	27.8	20.6	106.9	761.0	1.9
20 SoGen International	Average	25.4	31.3	106.1	601.5	2.8

** Fund closed to new investors.

Top-Performing Stock Funds Ranked by 3-year Performance	Volatility (within Type)					
		Percent Compounded Annual Return (5 years to April 1, 1987)				
		Percent Gain (or Loss) to April 1, 1987				
			One Year	Three Years	Ten Years	Percent Current Yield
Standard & Poor's 500-Stock Index			26.2	106.7	380.0	
GROWTH AND INCOME						
1 Eaton Vance Total Return	High	22.9	18.2	131.1	—	4.9
2 New England Retirement Equity*	High	23.1	27.5	117.4	525.5	0.9
3 Sentinel Common Stock	High	24.6	24.7	114.8	442.4	3.3
4 Fundamental Investors	High	25.7	25.5	113.1	408.1	2.3
5 Seligman Common Stock	High	24.7	22.7	112.7	425.7	3.0
6 Selected American Shares	Average	24.3	21.2	111.1	345.0	2.7
7 Investment Co. of America	Average	24.7	23.4	109.0	469.3	2.8
8 Washington Mutual Investors	Average	25.4	21.3	108.6	461.0	3.7
9 Vanguard Windsor**	Average	26.1	22.1	108.6	593.5	4.9
10 Sovereign Investors	Average	21.8	17.3	108.1	365.5	3.9
11 Nationwide Fund	Average	22.0	22.8	107.2	267.8	2.3
12 Sigma Investment Shares	Average	22.5	24.0	107.1	379.7	2.5
13 AMEV Capital	High	24.2	25.6	105.2	649.8	0.7
14 Vanguard Index Trust	Average	23.8	25.5	103.9	355.6	2.9
15 Alliance Dividend Shares	Average	23.4	21.4	103.6	325.9	2.9
16 Affiliated Fund	Average	23.9	23.9	103.5	395.8	4.3
17 Drexel Burnham	Average	21.2	21.3	103.1	399.1	3.2
18 ABT Growth & Income Trust	Average	20.8	28.8	102.6	327.7	3.0
19 Merrill Lynch Capital	Average	22.2	18.5	99.6	476.4	1.6
20 Safeco Equity Fund	Average	21.2	21.6	99.5	372.7	2.1

*Open to IRA investors only. ** Fund closed to new investors.

Top-Performing Stock Funds Ranked by 3-year Performance	Volatility (within Type)	Percent Compounded Annual Return (5 years to April 1, 1987)			
		Percent Gain (or Loss) to April 1, 1987			
		One Year	Three Years	Ten Years	Percent Current Yield
Standard & Poor's 500-Stock Index		26.2	106.7	380.0	
EQUITY INCOME					
1 United Income	High	26.5	17.7	118.5	379.9	2.3
2 Vanguard Qual. Div. Port. I**	Average	27.9	20.9	117.7	616.0	6.7
3 Evergreen Total Return	Average	25.2	17.3	103.6	—	5.5
4 Safeco Income	Average	24.2	19.7	101.5	415.6	4.3
5 Venture Ret. Plan of Am.—Equity	High	21.0	19.6	100.9	—	0.2
6 Financial Industrial Income	High	23.4	17.7	98.9	394.8	4.1
7 Decatur I	High	23.4	25.4	98.1	434.4	3.9
8 National Total Income	High	21.7	16.6	94.2	366.9	5.3
9 Fidelity Puritan	Average	23.3	17.7	92.7	404.6	6.2
10 Fidelity Equity-Income	Average	24.4	17.2	91.7	616.5	5.3
11 Bull & Bear Equity-Income	Average	18.6	16.7	89.1	289.5	2.8
12 Oppenheimer Equity Income	Average	24.6	19.3	87.3	434.2	4.8
13 National Total Return	Average	21.6	15.6	86.3	391.9	4.7
14 Vanguard Qual. Div. Port. II	Average	19.1	14.6	83.9	189.4	8.5
15 Income Fund of America	Average	21.2	12.6	83.2	316.6	6.8
16 Putnam Convertible Inc. & Gro.	Average	19.6	16.3	82.5	416.4	5.4
17 Franklin Income Series	Average	20.5	19.3	82.1	418.2	8.7
18 Vanguard Wellesley Income	Average	20.1	12.5	80.8	275.4	7.9
19 Dreyfus Convertible Sec.	High	20.7	22.2	79.7	285.8	5.3
20 Keystone K-1	Average	20.0	17.5	77.1	269.9	5.3

** Fund closed to new investors.

Top-Performing Stock Funds Ranked by 3-year Performance	Volatility (within Type)					
		Percent Compounded Annual Return (5 years to April 1, 1987)				
		Percent Gain (or Loss) to April 1, 1987				
			One Year	Three Years	Ten Years	Percent Current Yield
Standard & Poor's 500-Stock Index			26.2	106.7	380.0	
BALANCED						
1 Loomis-Sayles Mutual	High	23.8	23.3	119.3	364.0	3.0
2 Axe-Houghton Fund B	High	21.9	23.1	113.5	309.6	4.8
3 United Continental Income	High	25.2	14.6	107.5	369.3	3.6
4 Alliance Balanced Shares	Average	22.8	18.5	107.3	294.4	4.2
5 Phoenix Balanced	Average	23.9	19.3	102.6	406.3	4.1
6 Mass. Fin. Total Return Trust	Average	22.3	19.6	97.7	320.7	4.8
7 Sentinel Balanced	Average	22.0	16.0	95.1	303.3	5.5
8 Vanguard Wellington Fund	Average	22.8	21.0	92.4	345.5	5.2
9 IDS Mutual	Average	22.0	20.9	92.3	298.7	5.6
10 Kemper Total Return	Average	21.6	24.2	90.1	482.2	2.9
OPTION INCOME						
1 Pru-Bache Option Growth	High	—	18.4	82.8	—	1.6
2 Putnam Option Income	Average	17.1	18.4	63.4	—	1.1
3 Franklin Option	Average	16.6	10.2	58.9	304.8	1.9
4 Colonial Diversified Income	Average	16.2	15.8	56.6	—	1.3
5 ABT Security Income	Low	—	15.7	54.9	—	1.3
6 Oppenheimer Premium Income	High	14.3	20.0	50.4	—	3.5
7 Gateway Option Income	Low	12.8	12.7	44.6	—	2.6
8 Kemper Option Income	Average	14.0	13.3	43.2	—	9.0
9 Hutton Inv. Series-Option Inc.	Average	—	11.8	42.1	—	2.4
10 First Investors Option	Average	11.2	15.3	37.7	211.9	1.8

Top-Performing Stock Funds Ranked by 3-year Performance	Volatility (within Type)					
		Percent Compounded Annual Return (5 years to April 1, 1987)				
			Percent Gain (or Loss) to April 1, 1987			
			One Year	Three Years	Ten Years	Percent Current Yield
Standard & Poor's 500-Stock Index			26.2	106.7	380.0	
SMALL-COMPANY GROWTH						
1 Putnam OTC Emerging Growth	High	—	27.5	129.7	—	0.0
2 Nicholas II	Average	—	22.4	116.5	—	2.1
3 GIT Equity Trust Special Growth	High	—	11.1	104.5	—	0.6
4 Acorn Fund	Low	22.6	20.8	99.6	570.4	1.1
5 Babson Enterprise	Average	—	14.8	93.2	—	0.4
6 Mass. Fin. Emerging Growth	High	25.5	19.8	86.5	—	0.0
7 Gradison Opportunity Growth	Average	—	11.0	84.6	—	0.3
8 Stein Roe Discovery	High	—	8.5	83.2	—	0.3
9 Fairfield Fund	Average	20.0	15.8	80.4	369.0	0.8
10 United New Concepts	High	—	19.4	76.9	—	0.9
SECTORS						
1 Fidelity Select Health Care	High	30.1	31.0	170.0	—	0.0
2 Pru-Bache Utility	Average	24.8	17.2	154.2	—	5.3
3 Financial Strategic Health	High	—	42.3	140.5	—	0.0
4 Alliance Technology	High	31.2	64.8	125.4	—	0.0
5 Putnam Health Sciences Trust	Average	—	26.6	118.3	—	0.9
6 Seligman Commun. & Info.	Average	—	32.2	115.6	—	0.0
7 Fidelity Select—Financial Svc.	High	25.9	1.4	114.5	—	0.6
8 Fidelity Select—Utilities	Average	22.0	11.5	108.7	—	0.8
9 Stratton Monthly Div. Shares	Average	20.6	8.7	105.5	242.5	7.4
10 Medical Technology	High	19.9	23.0	94.8	—	1.1

Top-Performing Stock Funds Ranked by 3-year Performance	Volatility (within Type)					
		Percent Compounded Annual Return (5 years to April 1, 1987)				
		Percent Gain (or Loss) to April 1, 1987				
			One Year	Three Years	Ten Years	Percent Current Yield
Standard & Poor's 500-Stock Index			26.2	106.7	380.0	
GOLD AND PRECIOUS METALS						
1 Lexington Goldfund	Average	19.9	73.2	50.2	—	0.5
2 Bull & Bear Golconda Investors	Low	14.2	77.3	40.6	378.0	0.2
3 International Investors	Average	23.0	85.4	38.7	1,122.4	2.2
4 Oppenheimer Gold & Sp. Min.	Low	—	76.5	28.5	—	1.1
5 Keystone Precious Metals	High	18.1	88.6	25.3	591.4	1.8
6 Franklin Gold	Average	20.3	83.1	24.3	928.4	2.2
7 Financial Strategic—Gold	High	—	97.1	22.4	—	0.9
8 Fidelity Select—Precious Metals	Average	20.4	77.9	21.1	—	0.6
9 United Services Prospector**	Average	—	96.5	19.1	—	0.0
10 United Services Gold Shares	Average	18.5	88.6	1.3	907.0	4.9
GLOBAL						
1 Putnam International Equities	Average	29.9	29.3	153.6	646.7	0.5
2 Paine Webber Atlas	High	—	35.8	151.4	—	5.0
3 New Perspective	Average	24.3	34.3	99.2	549.0	1.8
4 Oppenheimer Global	High	25.0	35.9	99.1	646.6	0.3
5 Dean Witter World Wide	Average	—	28.0	93.8	—	0.5
6 Templeton World	Average	24.4	19.6	90.4	—	2.5
7 Templeton Global I**	Low	26.1	20.6	86.2	—	2.3
8 Mass. Fin. Intl. Trust-Bond	Average	18.3	27.6	85.0	—	6.2
9 Templeton Growth	Low	22.5	20.6	83.4	515.0	2.7
10 Templeton Global II	Average	—	9.6	67.6	—	2.2

** Fund closed to new investors.

Top-Performing Stock Funds Ranked by 3-year Performance	Volatility (within Type)					
		Percent Compounded Annual Return (5 years to April 1, 1987)				
		Percent Gain (or Loss) to April 1, 1987				
			One Year	Three Years	Ten Years	Percent Current Yield
Standard & Poor's 500-Stock Index			26.2	106.7	380.0	
INTERNATIONAL						
1 Merrill Lynch Pacific	High	35.4	74.5	195.9	867.7	0.4
2 Vanguard World Intl. Growth	Average	31.5	37.3	139.3	—	0.6
3 Financial Strategic Pacific Basin	High	—	71.2	128.7	—	0.2
4 T. Rowe Price International	Average	27.4	45.7	128.3	—	0.6
5 Scudder International	Average	27.2	40.5	125.1	501.3	1.1
6 Keystone International	Average	23.9	54.1	123.7	370.4	0.7
7 Alliance International	Average	26.5	25.4	123.0	—	0.1
8 Transatlantic Growth	High	24.5	43.0	122.7	427.4	0.0
9 Kemper International	Average	24.4	30.6	104.4	—	1.2
10 United International Growth	Low	24.5	28.7	96.8	521.5	0.9

Top-Performing Bond Funds Ranked by 3-year Performance	Volatility (within Type)					
		Percent Compounded Annual Return (5 years to April 1, 1987)				
			Percent Gain (or Loss) to April 1, 1987			
			One Year	Three Years	Ten Years	Percent Current Yield
Standard & Poor's 500-Stock Index			26.2	106.7	380.0	
HIGH-YIELD CORPORATES						
1 Pacific Horizon High Yield	Average	—	12.8	82.2	—	10.7
2 Fin. Bond Shares—High Yield	Average	—	13.9	74.7	—	11.1
3 Fidelity High Income	Average	20.9	15.3	71.6	—	10.7
4 Kemper High Yield	Average	20.7	19.7	70.4	—	10.5
5 Delchester Bond	Average	19.2	17.0	68.1	193.6	11.9
6 Investment Port.—High Yield	Average	—	19.6	66.9	—	8.3
7 IDS Bond	High	19.1	11.7	65.6	200.7	8.6
8 United High Income**	Average	18.7	15.3	64.5	—	11.8
9 Cigna High Yield	Average	19.5	14.3	64.4	—	11.2
10 Vanguard Fixed Inc.—High Yield	Low	17.4	16.2	63.0	—	11.1
HIGH-GRADE CORPORATES						
1 Axe-Houghton Income	High	18.3	12.2	81.8	207.8	8.7
2 Hutton Bond & Income Series	High	17.2	7.1	76.6	—	8.7
3 Sigma Income Shares	Average	18.2	11.2	72.0	164.5	8.1
4 United Bond	High	18.8	10.2	70.7	171.0	8.2
5 Bond Fund of America	Average	17.8	10.7	69.4	200.1	9.8
6 Alliance Bond—Monthly Income Port.	Average	18.6	10.2	67.0	152.9	8.9
7 Mass. Financial Bond	Average	17.6	10.9	66.2	178.8	8.8
8 Hancock (John) Bond	Average	16.8	9.5	65.4	144.3	9.3
9 Investment Quality Interest	High	16.4	6.4	64.4	—	10.9
10 IDS Selective	Average	19.2	11.3	63.5	194.6	8.5

** Fund closed to new investors.

Top-Performing Bond Funds Ranked by 3-year Performance	Volatility (within Type)					
		Percent Compounded Annual Return (5 years to April 1, 1987)				
			Percent Gain (or Loss) to April 1, 1987			
			One Year	Three Years	Ten Years	Percent Current Yield
Standard & Poor's 500-Stock Index			26.2	106.7	380.0	
U.S. GOVERNMENT BONDS						
1 Lord Abbett U.S. Gov. Sec.	Average	16.2	9.1	60.6	189.4	10.6
2 Hancock (John)—U.S. Gov. Sec.	Average	13.9	7.6	56.4	151.2	8.3
3 Value Line U.S. Gov. Sec.	High	15.6	8.7	56.1	—	10.1
4 Carnegie Gov. Sec.—High Yield	Average	—	8.5	53.5	—	7.0
5 AMEV U.S. Gov. Securities	Average	14.4	8.1	53.3	161.7	9.5
6 Capital Pres. Treasury Note	High	13.1	6.6	52.4	—	6.4
7 Pru-Bache Gov.—Intermed. Term	Low	—	8.2	51.8	—	8.6
8 Fidelity Gov. Securities	Average	13.8	7.4	51.0	—	8.5
9 Mutual of Omaha America	Average	11.1	5.9	46.8	135.8	8.5
10 Hutton Inv. Series—Gov. Sec.	Average	—	7.3	45.0	—	10.4
MORTGAGE-BACKED SECURITIES						
1 Kemper U.S. Gov. Sec.	High	16.2	8.6	60.3	—	10.5
2 Vanguard Fixed Inc.—GNMA	Average	15.9	10.2	55.5	—	9.4
3 Franklin U.S. Gov. Series	Average	15.3	9.5	53.9	115.4	10.7
4 Alliance Mortgage Sec. Inc.	Average	—	9.3	51.0	—	10.6
5 Lexington GNMA Income	Low	13.9	10.7	50.2	114.1	8.7
6 Pru-Bache GNMA	Low	12.8	8.9	48.9	—	7.5
7 Putnam U.S. Gov. Guar. Sec.	Average	—	10.3	46.3	—	10.0
8 Fund for U.S. Gov. Sec.	High	15.6	7.2	44.1	129.4	9.4

Top-Performing Bond Funds Ranked by 3-year Performance	Volatility (within Type)		Percent Compounded Annual Return (5 years to April 1, 1987)			
			Percent Gain (or Loss) to April 1, 1987			
			One Year	Three Years	Ten Years	Percent Current Yield
Standard & Poor's 500-Stock Index			26.2	106.7	380.0	
HIGH-YIELD TAX-EXEMPTS						
1 Vanguard Muni Bond—High Yield	Average	17.2	12.3	60.3	—	7.4
2 IDS High-Yield Tax-Exempt	High	18.1	11.8	60.1	—	7.4
3 Pru-Bache High Yield Muni	Average	17.3	11.2	59.9	—	6.8
4 Stein Roe High-Yield Muni	Average	—	11.8	58.9	—	7.2
5 Fidelity High-Yield Muni Bond	Average	17.2	11.8	58.7	—	7.1
6 Merrill Lynch Muni—High Yield	Average	17.3	11.9	58.5	—	7.4
7 GIT Tax-Free—High Yield	Average	—	10.4	52.4	—	7.0
8 Alliance Tax-Free Shares	Average	16.2	9.8	52.2	79.5	7.3
9 Value Line Tax Ex. High Yield	Low	—	10.9	48.8	—	8.1
10 Mass. Fin. Man. High Yd. Muni Bond**	Low	—	8.5	44.2	—	9.5
HIGH-GRADE TAX-EXEMPTS						
1 Stein Roe Managed Muni	High	19.1	11.6	69.2	125.5	6.7
2 United Municipal Bond	Average	17.5	12.7	68.0	82.1	6.9
3 DMC Tax Free Inc-USA Ser.	Average	—	13.2	67.7	—	7.5
4 Mutual of Omaha Tax-Free Inc.	High	16.9	15.8	66.8	86.1	6.9
5 Hutton National Muni Bond	Average	—	14.1	66.3	—	7.3
6 Financial Tax-Free Inc. Shares	High	16.8	12.1	65.5	—	7.1
7 Seligman Tax-Exempt-National	Average	—	13.4	64.8	—	7.1
8 New England Tax-Exempt Income	High	18.4	10.9	62.9	—	6.6
9 National Sec. Tax-Exempt	Average	17.3	12.2	61.8	87.3	7.2
10 Cigna Municipal Bond	High	16.7	10.8	61.8	96.3	6.7

** Fund closed to new investors.

Top-Performing Bond Funds Ranked by 3-year Performance	Volatility (within Type)	Percent Compounded Annual Return (5 years to April 1, 1987)			
		Percent Gain (or Loss) to April 1, 1987			
		One Year	Three Years	Ten Years	Percent Current Yield
Standard & Poor's 500-Stock Index		26.2	106.7	380.0	
INTERMEDIATE-TERM TAX-EXEMPTS					
1 Scudder Tax-Free Target—1990	High	—	7.8	49.3	—	5.6
2 Vanguard Muni Bond—Intermed.	High	14.2	11.1	49.2	—	6.9
3 Fidelity Limited Term Muni Bond	High	14.0	10.8	47.6	—	6.2
4 Dreyfus Intermed. Tax-Ex. Bond	Average	—	11.2	44.7	—	7.0
5 Scudder Tax-Free Target—1993	Average	—	9.8	41.8	—	5.9
6 USAA Tax Ex.—Intermed.-Term	Average	12.4	8.3	41.6	—	7.1
7 Scudder Tax-Free Target—1987**	Average	—	6.1	36.0	—	5.2
8 Babson Tax-Free Inc.—Short-Term	Average	9.7	8.9	33.2	—	6.0
9 T. Rowe Price Tax-Free Sh. Int.	Average	—	7.5	27.9	—	5.5
10 USAA Tax Ex.—Short Term	Average	7.7	6.3	26.8	—	5.8

** Fund closed to new investors.

Alphabetical Guide to Mutual Funds	Type	3 Yr. Performance Rank within Type/No. in Category					
		Volatility (within Type)					
				Percent Gain (or Loss) to April 1, 1987			
				One Year	Three Years	Ten Years	Percent Current Yield
Standard & Poor's 500-Stock Index				26.2	106.7	380.0	
ABT Emerging Growth	Max	2/66	High	28.1	133.8	—	0.0
ABT Growth & Income Trust	G&I	18/72	Average	28.8	102.6	327.7	3.0
ABT Security Income	OpInc	5/10	Low	15.7	54.9	—	1.3
ABT Utility Income	Sec	15/35	Low	9.3	85.5	—	5.7
Acorn Fund	SCG	4/25	Low	20.8	99.6	570.4	1.1
Afuture Fund	Gro	115/118	Average	(3.7)	20.6	289.2	0.0
AIM Convertible Yield Sec.	EqI	45/46	High	0.3	36.4	—	5.2
AIM Greenway	Max	43/66	Average	15.8	69.8	284.1	1.0
AIM High-Yield Sec.	HYC	37/39	Low	11.6	43.0	—	11.7
AIM Summit Investors	Gro	43/118	Average	23.1	94.5	—	0.5
Alliance Balanced Shares	Bal	4/17	Average	18.5	107.3	294.4	4.2
Alliance Bond—High Yield Port.	HYC	—	—	10.0	—	—	12.7
Alliance Bond—Monthly Income Port.	HGC	6/36	Average	10.2	67.0	152.9	8.9
Alliance Bond—U.S. Gov. Port.	USG	—	—	8.8	—	—	10.7
Alliance Canadian	Intl	13/13	Low	28.0	59.2	262.1	1.6
Alliance Convertible	EqI	—	—	15.0	—	—	5.4
Alliance Counterpoint	G&I	—	—	21.7	—	—	2.2
Alliance Dividend Shares	G&I	15/72	Average	21.4	103.6	325.9	2.9
Alliance Fund	Sec	18/35	Average	19.2	82.3	306.3	1.2
Alliance International	Intl	7/13	Average	25.4	123.0	—	0.1
Alliance Mortgage Sec. Inc.	MBS	4/8	Average	9.3	51.0	—	10.6
Alliance Surveyor	Gro	50/118	High	24.2	91.6	382.4	0.2
Alliance Tax-Free Shares	HYT	8/11	Average	9.8	52.2	79.5	7.3
Alliance Technology	Sec	4/35	High	64.8	125.4	—	0.0
Alpha Fund	Gro	72/118	High	21.4	84.3	453.9	0.7
AMA Growth—Classic Growth Port.	Gro	76/118	Average	13.6	82.5	265.8	1.0
AMA Income	HGC	32/36	Average	7.3	48.4	136.3	6.7
AMCAP Fund	Gro	69/118	Average	25.8	85.3	710.3	1.5
American Balanced	Bal	11/17	Average	16.6	87.5	299.4	5.2
American Capital Comstock	Max	51/66	Low	21.2	65.5	700.3	2.1

Percent Maximum Initial Sales Charge	Percent Maximum Deferred Sales Charge	Expenses per $100	Minimum Initial Investment	IRA Minimum Initial Investment/Annual Fee	Assets as of Feb. 27, 1987 (in millions)	Phone Switch	Toll-free (800) + In State	Telephone
4¾	None	$1.65	$1,000	$250/$10	$ 48.1	Yes	354-0436	800-582-7396 (Ohio)
4¾	None	1.35	1,000	250/10	135.2	Yes	354-0436	800-582-7396 (Ohio)
4¾	None	1.97	1,000	250/10	18.3	Yes	354-0436	800-582-7396 (Ohio)
4¾	None	1.25	1,000	250/10	145.1	Yes	354-0436	800-582-7396 (Ohio)
None	None	.79	4,000	200/5	502.4	Yes	—	312-621-0630
None	None	1.40	500	500/10	17.5	No	523-7594	215-565-3131 (Pa.)
4¾	None	1.50	1,000	100/5	24.7	Yes	231-0803	800-392-9681 (Texas)
4¾	None	1.78	1,000	100/5	20.7	Yes	231-0803	800-392-9681 (Texas)
4¾	None	1.06	1,000	100/5	87.3	Yes	231-0803	800-392-9681 (Texas)
8½†	None	1.16	50	50/10	97.3	No	231-0803	800-392-9681 (Texas)
5½	None	.99	250	250/15	104.9	Yes	221-5672	—
5½	None	1.21	250	250/15	299.5	Yes	221-5672	—
5½	None	1.08	250	250/15	45.3	Yes	221-5672	—
5½	None	1.01	250	250/15	308.3	Yes	221-5672	—
5½	None	1.19	250	250/15	25.0	Yes	221-5672	—
5½	None	1.25	250	250/15	105.0	Yes	221-5672	—
5½	None	1.55	250	250/15	47.7	Yes	221-5672	—
5½	None	.81	250	250/15	389.1	Yes	221-5672	—
5½	None	.61	250	250/15	778.7	Yes	221-5672	—
5½	None	1.29	250	250/15	196.2	Yes	221-5672	—
5½	None	1.00	250	250/15	772.1	Yes	221-5672	—
5½	None	1.22	250	250/15	103.3	Yes	221-5672	—
4	None	.86	250	—/—	119.5	Yes	221-5672	—
5½	None	1.13	250	250/15	214.1	Yes	221-5672	—
8½	None	1.50	200	200/10	31.4	Yes	367-6535	404-521-6412 (Ga.)
None	None	1.34	1,000	500/None	47.1	Yes	262-3863	—
None	None	1.39	1,000	500/None	37.8	Yes	262-3863	—
8½	None	.54	1,000	250/10	1,791.2	Yes	421-9900	213-486-9651 (Calif.)
8½	None	.67	500	250/10	187.7	Yes	421-9900	213-486-9651 (Calif.)
8½	None	.60	500	50/10	1,106.7	Yes	847-5636	—

†Fund may impose an exit fee.

Alphabetical Guide to Mutual Funds	Type	3 Yr. Performance Rank within Type/No. in Category					
		Volatility (within Type)		Percent Gain (or Loss) to April 1, 1987			
				One Year	Three Years	Ten Years	Percent Current Yield
Standard & Poor's 500-Stock Index				26.2	106.7	380.0	
American Capital Corp. Bond	HGC	17/36	Average	9.4	59.8	147.5	10.9
American Capital Enterprise	Gro	79/118	Average	14.8	81.5	553.7	1.6
American Capital Gov. Sec.	USG	—	—	8.6	—	—	7.0
American Capital Harbor	EqI	42/46	Average	14.4	55.4	400.2	5.4
American Capital High Yield Inv.	HYC	24/39	High	6.8	54.0	—	13.0
American Capital Muni Bond	HGT	22/40	High	5.7	57.8	90.5	7.3
American Capital OTC Sec.	SCG	21/25	Average	0.8	38.6		0.1
American Capital Pace	Max	45/66	Low	21.0	69.3	1,054.5	2.3
American Capital Tax-Ex.—High Yield	HYT	—	—	5.4	—		8.4
American Capital Tax-Ex.—Insured	HGT	—	—	7.0	—	—	6.9
American Capital Venture	Max	59/66	Average	13.2	46.7	716.9	1.3
American Growth	Gro	111/118	Low	10.6	36.3	383.8	3.0
American Investors Growth	Gro	116/118	Average	1.4	19.3	120.9	0.0
American Investors Income	HYC	39/39	High	7.1	31.3	167.2	11.9
American Leaders	G&I	28/72	Low	18.4	95.8	362.4	3.2
American Mutual	G&I	33/72	Average	16.8	91.3	477.5	3.7
American National Growth	Gro	78/118	Average	23.0	82.0	503.3	1.0
American National Income	EqI	32/46	Average	19.7	63.6	434.9	3.1
AMEV Capital	G&I	13/72	High	25.6	105.2	649.8	0.7
AMEV Growth	Max	11/66	High	28.8	107.0	942.0	0.2
AMEV U.S. Gov. Securities	USG	5/13	Average	8.1	53.3	161.7	9.5
Axe-Houghton Fund B	Bal	2/17	High	23.1	113.5	309.6	4.8
Axe-Houghton Income	HGC	1/36	High	12.2	81.8	207.8	8.7
Axe-Houghton Stock	Gro	41/118	High	31.1	95.1	352.2	0.0
Babson Bond Trust	HGC	24/36	Low	9.6	57.7	158.7	9.2
Babson Enterprise	SCG	5/25	Average	14.8	93.2	—	0.4
Babson Growth	Gro	32/118	Average	29.1	101.1	298.1	2.1
Babson Tax-Free Inc.—Long-Term	HGT	28/40	Average	10.8	55.7	—	6.7
Babson Tax-Free Inc.—Short-Term	ITT	8/15	Average	8.9	33.2	—	6.0
Bartlett Basic Value	G&I	61/72	Low	11.4	69.1	—	3.7

Percent Maximum Initial Sales Charge								
	Percent Maximum Deferred Sales Charge							
		Expenses per $100						
			Minimum Initial Investment					
				IRA Minimum Initial Investment/Annual Fee				
					Assets as of Feb. 27, 1987 (in millions)			
						Phone Switch		
							Toll-free (800) +	Telephone
							In State	
8½	None	$ .37	$ 500	$50/$10	$ 141.1	Yes	847-5636	—
8½	None	.60	500	50/10	743.8	Yes	847-5636	—
6¾	None	.60	500	50/10	9,490.9	Yes	847-5636	—
8½	None	.64	500	50/10	380.5	Yes	847-5636	—
6¾	None	.35	500	50/10	619.4	Yes	847-5636	—
4¾	None	.31	500	—/—	197.2	Yes	847-5636	—
8½	None	.58	500	50/10	106.2	Yes	847-5636	—
8½	None	.32	500	50/10	2,710.7	Yes	847-5636	—
4¾	None	.50	500	—/—	184.0	Yes	847-5636	—
4¾	None	.58	500	—/—	35.0	Yes	847-5636	—
8½	None	.40	500	50/10	347.2	Yes	847-5636	—
8½	None	1.30	500	100/20	72.5	No	525-2406	303-623-6137 (Colo.)
None	None	1.40	400	400/5	73.1	Yes	243-5353	203-531-5000 (Conn.)
None	None	1.41	400	400/5	23.9	Yes	243-5353	203-531-5000 (Conn.)
4½	None	1.09	500	50/None	149.3	Yes	245-4770	—
8½	None	.45	250	250/10	2,495.1	Yes	421-9900	213-486-9651 (Calif.)
8½	None	.97	20	20/5	113.1	Yes	231-4639	800-392-9753 (Texas)
8½	None	.99	100	20/5	75.4	Yes	231-4639	800-392-9753 (Texas)
8½	None	1.06	500	500/10	140.5	Yes	872-2638	800-328-1001 (Minn.)
8½	None	1.00	500	500/10	218.2	Yes	872-2638	800-328-1001 (Minn.)
4½	None	1.00	500	500/10	99.3	Yes	872-2638	800-328-1001 (Minn.)
None	None	.98	1,000	25/10	202.9	Yes	431-1030	914-631-8131 (N.Y.)
None	None	1.37	1,000	25/10	54.2	Yes	431-1030	914-631-8131 (N.Y.)
None	None	1.28	1,000	25/10	122.7	Yes	431-1030	914-631-8131 (N.Y.)
None	None	.97	1,000	250/10	75.8	Yes	821-5591	816-471-5200 (Mo.)
None	None	1.37	1,000	250/10	56.8	Yes	821-5591	816-471-5200 (Mo.)
None	None	.75	1,000	250/10	281.2	Yes	821-5591	816-471-5200 (Mo.)
None	None	1.00	1,000	—/—	26.1	Yes	821-5591	816-471-5200 (Mo.)
None	None	1.00	1,000	—/—	16.5	Yes	821-5591	816-471-5200 (Mo.)
None	None	1.23	5,000	250/10	89.4	Yes	543-0863	800-327-4363 (Ohio)

Alphabetical Guide to Mutual Funds	Type	3 Yr. Performance Rank within Type/No. in Category					
		Volatility (within Type)					
			Percent Gain (or Loss) to April 1, 1987				
				One Year	Three Years	Ten Years	Percent Current Yield
Standard & Poor's 500-Stock Index				26.2	106.7	380.0	
Benham Gov.—GNMA Inc.	MBS	—	—	9.5	—	—	9.1
Benham Nat. Tax-Free—Intermed.	ITT	—	—	10.3	—	—	6.2
Benham Nat. Tax-Free—Long-Term	HGT	—	—	10.8	—	—	7.0
Bond Fund of America	HGC	5/36	Average	10.7	69.4	200.1	9.8
Boston Co. Cap. Appreciation	Gro	9/118	Average	22.0	115.2	386.8	2.1
Boston Co. Managed Income	HYC	11/39	Average	11.7	61.2	—	9.8
Boston Co. Special Growth	Gro	98/118	Average	6.2	65.9	—	1.3
Bull & Bear Capital Growth	Gro	100/118	Average	6.6	64.9	347.4	0.0
Bull & Bear Equity-Income	EqI	11/46	Average	16.7	89.1	289.5	2.8
Bull & Bear Golconda Investors	Gold	2/11	Low	77.3	40.6	378.0	0.2
Bull & Bear High Yield	HYC	38/39	High	4.4	42.9	—	13.0
Bull & Bear Tax-Free Income	HGT	16/40	Average	10.5	60.1	—	7.0
Calvert Income	HGC	16/36	High	3.5	61.1	—	8.5
Calvert Social Inv.—Managed Gro.	G&I	53/72	Average	14.5	82.0	—	3.2
Calvert Tax-Free Res. Limited	ITT	11/15	Average	6.4	25.3	—	5.8
Capital Pres. Treasury Note	USG	6/13	High	6.6	52.4	—	6.4
Cardinal Fund	Gro	31/118	Low	17.8	101.3	461.0	2.1
Carnegie Cappiello—Growth Ser.	Gro	71/118	Low	16.0	85.0	—	1.0
Carnegie Gov. Sec.—High Yield	USG	4/13	Average	8.5	53.5	—	7.0
Carnegie Cappiello Total Return	G&I	—	—	15.9	—	—	3.6
Century Shares Trust	Sec	12/35	High	0.3	92.6	408.1	2.5
Charter Fund	Max	31/66	Average	24.9	85.2	559.3	1.6
Cigna Aggressive Growth	SCG	—	—	13.7	—	—	0.1
Cigna Growth	Gro	82/118	Low	20.8	78.9	354.4	1.6
Cigna High Yield	HYC	9/39	Average	14.3	64.4	—	11.2
Cigna Income	EqI	31/46	Average	9.0	66.0	175.5	8.4
Cigna Municipal Bond	HGT	10/40	High	10.8	61.8	96.3	6.7
Cigna Value	G&I	—	—	17.1	—	—	2.4
Colonial Adv. Strategies Gold	Gold	—	—	92.7	—	—	1.9
Colonial Diversified Income	OpInc	4/10	Average	15.8	56.6	—	1.3

Percent Maximum Initial Sales Charge									
Percent Maximum Deferred Sales Charge									
	Expenses per $100								
		Minimum Initial Investment							
			IRA Minimum Initial Investment/Annual Fee						
				Assets as of Feb. 27, 1987 (in millions)					
					Phone Switch				
						Toll-free (800) +		Telephone
							In State	
None	None	$ .75	$1,000	$100/None	$ 378.5	Yes	472-3389	800-982-6150 (Calif.)
None	None	.50	1,000	—/—	21.3	Yes	472-3389	800-982-6150 (Calif.)
None	None	.50	1,000	—/—	39.1	Yes	472-3389	800-982-6150 (Calif.)
4¾	None	.58	1,000	250/10	788.2	Yes	421-9900	213-486-9651 (Calif.)
None	None	.95	1,000	500/10	596.8	Yes	225-5267	—
None	None	.50	1,000	500/10	55.7	Yes	225-5267	—
None	None	1.31	1,000	500/10	45.3	Yes	225-5267	—
None	None	2.25	1,000	100/5	95.4	Yes	847-4200	—
None	None	3.00	1,000	100/5	15.9	Yes	847-4200	—
None	None	2.39	1,000	100/5	38.3	Yes	847-4200	—
None	None	1.37	1,000	100/5	212.7	Yes	847-4200	—
None	None	1.18	1,000	—/—	24.4	Yes	847-4200	—
4½	None	.85	2,000	1,000/10	26.8	Yes	368-2750	301-951-4800 (Md.)
4½	None	1.30	1,000	1,000/10	127.5	Yes	368-2750	301-951-4800 (Md.)
None	None	.81	2,000	—/—	216.4	Yes	368-2750	301-951-4800 (Md.)
None	None	.75	1,000	100/None	43.3	Yes	472-3389	800-982-6150 (Calif.)
8½	None	.89	250	1,000/10	114.1	No	848-7734	800-282-9446 (Ohio)
4½	None	1.50	1,000	250/2.50	58.6	Yes	321-2322	216-781-4440 (Ohio)
4½	None	1.30	1,000	250/2.50	39.5	Yes	321-2322	216-781-4440 (Ohio)
4½	None	1.80	1,000	250/2.50	85.1	Yes	321-2322	216-781-4440 (Ohio)
None	None	.77	500	500/5	162.5	No	321-1928	617-482-3060 (Mass.)
4¾	None	1.20	1,000	100/5	88.5	Yes	231-0803	800-392-9681 (Texas)
5	None	1.19	500	500/10	23.2	Yes	562-4462	—
5	None	.85	500	500/10	253.0	Yes	562-4462	—
5	None	.92	500	500/10	268.2	Yes	562-4462	—
5	None	.82	500	500/10	283.1	Yes	562-4462	—
5	None	.78	500	500/10	301.2	Yes	562-4462	—
5	None	1.04	500	500/10	56.8	Yes	562-4462	—
6¾	None	1.75	250	25/10	43.2	Yes	345-6611	—
6¾	None	.99	250	25/10	1,100.0	Yes	345-6611	—

Alphabetical Guide to Mutual Funds	Type	3 Yr. Performance Rank within Type/No. in Category					
		Volatility (within Type)					
			Percent Gain (or Loss) to April 1, 1987				
				One Year	Three Years	Ten Years	Percent Current Yield
Standard & Poor's 500-Stock Index				26.2	106.7	380.0	
Colonial Equity Income	EqI	28/46	High	13.7	72.6	—	2.1
Colonial Fund	G&I	35/72	Average	20.4	90.8	319.9	3.9
Colonial Gov. Mortgage	MBS	—	—	7.0	—	—	6.5
Colonial Gov. Sec. Plus	USG	—	—	7.7	—	—	7.1
Colonial Growth Shares	Gro	67/118	Average	20.6	85.5	381.2	0.6
Colonial High Yield Sec.	HYC	13/39	Low	14.8	60.6	201.3	11.3
Colonial Income	EqI	40/46	Low	10.2	55.9	155.7	11.2
Colonial Income Plus	OpInc	—	—	9.8	—	—	2.3
Colonial Tax-Exempt High Yield	HYT	11/11	High	10.1	41.9	—	7.6
Colonial Tax-Exempt Insured	HGT	—	—	8.6	—	—	6.6
Columbia Fixed Income Sec.	HGC	30/36	Low	10.6	53.7	—	9.0
Columbia Growth	Gro	74/118	Average	13.6	83.4	539.1	0.8
Columbia Special Fund	Max	—	—	22.6	—	—	0.0
Commerce Income Shares	EqI	27/46	Average	12.6	73.3	278.4	3.0
Constellation Growth	Max	3/66	High	43.7	129.8	830.2	0.0
Copley Tax Managed	G&I	38/72	Low	10.9	90.2	247.6	0.0
De Vegh Mutual	Gro	81/118	Average	16.0	81.2	263.2	1.6
Dean Witter Convertible Sec.	EqI	—	—	16.2	—	—	5.8
Dean Witter Developing Growth	SCG	22/25	Low	4.8	31.3	—	0.1
Dean Witter Dividend Growth Sec.	G&I	23/72	Average	20.0	97.4	—	2.5
Dean Witter High Yield Sec.	HYC	15/39	Average	14.3	59.9	—	12.5
Dean Witter Industry-Valued Sec.	Gro	87/118	Average	18.8	77.5	—	1.9
Dean Witter Nat. Resources	Sec	28/35	Average	34.4	30.6	—	1.4
Dean Witter Option Income	OpInc	—	—	8.5	—	—	6.1
Dean Witter Tax-Exempt Sec.	HGT	17/40	Average	11.3	59.8	—	7.3
Dean Witter U.S. Gov. Sec.	MBS	—	—	8.1	—	—	9.6
Dean Witter World Wide Inv.	Glo	5/11	Average	28.0	93.8	—	0.5
Decatur I	EqI	7/46	High	25.4	98.1	434.4	3.9
Delaware Fund	G&I	30/72	High	13.5	95.2	438.2	2.1
Delaware Group Gov.—GNMA	MBS	—	—	8.0	—	—	10.2

Percent Maximum Initial Sales Charge									
	Percent Maximum Deferred Sales Charge								
		Expenses per $100							
			Minimum Initial Investment						
				IRA Minimum Initial Investment/Annual Fee					
					Assets as of Feb. 27, 1987 (in millions)				
						Phone Switch			
							Toll-free (800) +		Telephone
								In State	
6¾	None	$1.50	$ 250	$25/$10	$ 14.3	Yes	345-6611	—	
6¾	None	1.06	250	25/10	216.0	Yes	345-6611	—	
4¾	None	1.24	250	25/10	42.4	Yes	345-6611	—	
6¾	None	1.10	250	25/10	3,998.3	Yes	345-6611	—	
6¾	None	1.25	250	25/10	92.4	Yes	345-6611	—	
4¾	None	1.11	250	25/10	478.3	Yes	345-6611	—	
4¾	None	1.11	250	25/10	174.8	Yes	345-6611	—	
6¾	None	1.04	250	25/10	215.8	Yes	345-6611	—	
4¾	None	1.05	250	—/—	1,500.0	Yes	345-6611	—	
4¾	None	1.10	250	—/—	115.7	Yes	345-6611	—	
None	None	.81	1,000	1,000/25	131.6	Yes	547-1037	503-222-3600 (Ore.)	
None	None	1.00	1,000	1,000/25	251.0	Yes	547-1037	503-222-3600 (Ore.)	
None	None	1.54	2,000	2,000/25	26.5	Yes	547-1037	503-222-3600 (Ore.)	
4¾	None	1.12	100	100/10	84.3	Yes	—	713-751-2400	
4¾	None	1.00	1,000	100/5	153.2	Yes	231-0803	800-392-9681 (Texas)	
None	None	1.40	1,000	100/7	35.0	No	—	617-674-8459	
None	None	1.20	1,000	1,000/5	57.6	No	225-8011	—	
None	5	1.72	1,000	1,000/5	1,763.9	Yes	221-2685	212-938-4554 (N.Y.)	
None	5	1.80	1,000	1,000/5	165.9	Yes	221-2685	212-938-4554 (N.Y.)	
None	5	1.55	1,000	1,000/5	1,646.3	Yes	221-2685	212-938-4554 (N.Y.)	
5½	None	.60	1,000	1,000/5	1,932.7	Yes	221-2685	212-938-4554 (N.Y.)	
None	5	1.39	1,000	1,000/5	104.1	Yes	221-2685	212-938-4554 (N.Y.)	
None	5	1.39	1,000	1,000/5	82.8	Yes	221-2685	212-938-4554 (N.Y.)	
None	5	1.90	1,000	1,000/5	598.4	Yes	221-2685	212-938-4554 (N.Y.)	
4	None	.60	1,000	—/—	1,077.4	Yes	221-2685	212-938-4554 (N.Y.)	
None	5	1.20	1,000	1,000/5	11,666.2	Yes	221-2685	212-938-4554 (N.Y.)	
None	5	2.35	1,000	1,000/5	446.7	Yes	221-2685	212-938-4554 (N.Y.)	
8½	None	.63	25	250/15	1,464.5	Yes	523-4640	215-988-1333 (Pa.)	
8½	None	.69	25	250/15	452.6	Yes	523-4640	215-988-1333 (Pa.)	
4¾	None	.95	1,000	250/15	70.4	Yes	523-4640	215-988-1333 (Pa.)	

Alphabetical Guide to Mutual Funds	Type	3 Yr. Performance Rank within Type/No. in Category					
		Volatility (within Type)					
			Percent Gain (or Loss) to April 1, 1987				
				One Year	Three Years	Ten Years	Percent Current Yield
Standard & Poor's 500-Stock Index				26.2	106.7	380.0	
Delaware Group Gov.—U.S. Gov.	USG	—	—	7.3	—	—	9.7
Delchester Bond	HYC	5/39	Average	17.0	68.1	193.6	11.9
Delta Trend	Max	57/66	Average	13.6	58.2	467.0	0.0
DMC Tax Free Inc.—USA Ser.	HGT	3/40	Average	13.2	67.7	—	7.5
Drexel Burnham	G&I	17/72	Average	21.3	103.1	399.1	3.2
Drexel Burnham Lambert Tax-Free	ITT	15/15	Low	4.0	15.4	—	4.0
Drexel Series—Bond Debenture	HGC	—	—	8.6	—	—	8.1
Drexel Series—Emerging Growth	SCG	—	—	3.3	—	—	0.0
Drexel Series—Gov. Sec.	MBS	—	—	8.3	—	—	8.1
Drexel Series—Growth	Gro	—	—	18.2	—	—	1.9
Drexel Series—Option Inc.	OpInc	—	—	13.6	—	—	1.5
Dreyfus A Bond Plus	HGC	13/36	Average	9.3	62.8	179.0	8.6
Dreyfus Convertible Sec.	EqI	19/46	High	22.2	79.7	285.8	5.3
Dreyfus Fund	G&I	59/72	Low	15.2	71.5	381.2	3.4
Dreyfus Gen. Agg. Growth	Max	21/66	High	12.4	101.4	—	0.4
Dreyfus GNMA	MBS	—	—	8.2	—	—	8.9
Dreyfus Growth Opportunity	Gro	104/118	Average	25.0	61.5	472.8	1.5
Dreyfus Insured Tax-Exempt Bond	HGT	—	—	8.5	—	—	6.7
Dreyfus Intermed. Tax-Ex. Bond	ITT	4/15	Average	11.2	44.7	—	7.0
Dreyfus Leverage	Max	24/66	Low	20.8	97.6	509.7	2.4
Dreyfus Tax-Exempt Bond	HGT	35/40	Low	11.4	52.1	89.2	7.3
Dreyfus Third Century	Gro	102/118	Low	15.4	64.2	418.9	3.8
Eaton & Howard Stock	G&I	24/72	Average	18.0	97.2	301.6	3.6
Eaton Vance Gov. Obligations	USG	—	—	7.2	—	—	9.5
Eaton Vance Growth	Gro	46/118	Average	22.8	93.0	482.7	1.2
Eaton Vance High Yield	EqI	29/46	Low	15.1	70.8	175.0	10.9
Eaton Vance High Yield Muni	HYT	—	—	8.2	—	—	7.9
Eaton Vance Income of Boston	EqI	24/46	Low	15.8	75.3	225.5	9.8
Eaton Vance Investors	Bal	15/17	Low	13.9	71.6	307.9	4.7
Eaton Vance Muni Bond	HGT	13/40	Average	11.2	60.6	—	7.1

Percent Maximum Initial Sales Charge	Percent Maximum Deferred Sales Charge	Expenses per $100	Minimum Initial Investment	IRA Minimum Initial Investment/Annual Fee	Assets as of Feb. 27, 1987 (in millions)	Phone Switch	Toll-free (800) +	In State / Telephone
4¾	None	$ .95	$1,000	$250/$15	$ 57.3	Yes	523-4640	215-988-1333 (Pa.)
6¾	None	.84	25	250/15	333.2	Yes	523-4640	215-988-1333 (Pa.)
8½	None	1.20	25	250/15	87.5	Yes	523-4640	215-988-1333 (Pa.)
4¾	None	.80	1,000	—/—	366.5	Yes	523-4640	215-988-1333 (Pa.)
3½	None	1.00	1,000	250/10	199.0	No	272-2700	212-482-1623 (N.Y.)
1½	None	.74	1,000	—/—	103.4	No	272-2700	212-482-1623 (N.Y.)
None	5	2.39	1,000	250/10	26.2	Yes	272-2700	212-482-1623 (N.Y.)
None	5	2.35	1,000	250/10	41.1	Yes	272-2700	212-482-1623 (N.Y.)
None	5	1.87	1,000	250/10	477.0	Yes	272-2700	212-482-1623 (N.Y.)
None	5	2.28	1,000	250/10	33.9	Yes	272-2700	212-482-1623 (N.Y.)
None	5	2.26	1,000	250/10	45.1	Yes	272-2700	212-482-1623 (N.Y.)
None	None	.87	2,500	750/5	315.8	Yes	645-6561	718-895-1206 (N.Y.)
None	None	.85	2,500	750/5	228.9	Yes	645-6561	718-895-1206 (N.Y.)
None	None	.74	2,500	750/5	2,555.5	Yes	645-6561	718-895-1206 (N.Y.)
None	None	1.50	2,500	750/5	35.7	Yes	645-6561	718-895-1206 (N.Y.)
None	None	.96	2,500	750/5	2,434.9	Yes	645-6561	718-895-1206 (N.Y.)
None	None	.98	2,500	750/5	516.3	Yes	645-6561	718-895-1206 (N.Y.)
None	None	.73	2,500	—/—	225.1	Yes	645-6561	718-895-1206 (N.Y.)
None	None	.75	2,500	—/—	1,357.5	Yes	645-6561	718-895-1206 (N.Y.)
8½	None	.91	2,500	750/5	543.1	Yes	645-6561	718-895-1206 (N.Y.)
None	None	.69	2,500	—/—	4,089.9	Yes	645-6561	718-895-1206 (N.Y.)
None	None	.97	2,500	750/5	172.6	Yes	645-6561	718-895-1206 (N.Y.)
7¼	None	.86	1,000	50/10	88.5	No	225-6265	617-482-8260 (Mass.)
4¾	None	1.46	1,000	50/10	427.7	No	225-6265	617-482-8260 (Mass.)
4¾	None	.91	1,000	50/10	92.7	No	225-6265	617-482-8260 (Mass.)
4¾	None	.93	1,000	50/10	35.9	No	225-6265	617-482-8260 (Mass.)
None	6	.63	1,000	50/10	884.1	No	225-6265	617-482-8260 (Mass.)
4¾	None	1.16	1,000	50/10	47.9	No	225-6265	617-482-8260 (Mass.)
4¾	None	.86	1,000	50/10	242.0	No	225-6265	617-482-8260 (Mass.)
4¾	None	.81	1,000	50/10	58.1	No	225-6265	617-482-8260 (Mass.)

Alphabetical Guide to Mutual Funds	Type	3 Yr. Performance Rank within Type/No. in Category					
		Volatility (within Type)					
			Percent Gain (or Loss) to April 1, 1987				Percent Current Yield
				One Year	Three Years	Ten Years	
Standard & Poor's 500-Stock Index				26.2	106.7	380.0	
Eaton Vance Nautilus	Sec	33/35	Low	4.0	(2.8)	—	0.0
Eaton Vance Sanders Special	Gro	117/118	Low	3.7	16.8	355.7	0.4
Eaton Vance Special Equities	Gro	109/118	Average	4.3	50.4	430.5	0.0
Eaton Vance Total Return	G&I	1/72	High	18.2	131.1	—	4.9
Equitec Siebel Total Return	G&I	—	—	13.6	—	—	2.5
EuroPacific Growth	Intl	—	—	29.0	—	—	0.6
Evergreen Fund	Gro	39/118	Average	14.7	96.2	952.5	0.9
Evergreen Total Return	EqI	3/46	Average	17.3	103.6	—	5.5
Fairfield Fund	SCG	9/25	Average	15.8	80.4	369.0	0.8
Fairmont Fund	Max	19/66	Average	19.9	102.5	—	0.5
Farm Bureau Growth	G&I	66/72	Average	8.4	60.5	233.3	2.4
Fidelity Aggressive Tax Free	HYT	—	—	12.1	—	—	7.7
Fidelity Contrafund	Gro	63/118	Average	20.8	86.4	304.7	0.9
Fidelity Destiny—Port. I	Gro	19/118	High	20.6	106.9	761.0	1.9
Fidelity Destiny—Port. II	Gro	—	—	39.3	—	—	0.0
Fidelity Equity-Income	EqI	10/46	Average	17.2	91.7	616.5	5.3
Fidelity Flexible Bond	HGC	26/36	Average	7.3	56.4	148.1	9.3
Fidelity Freedom *	Max	18/66	Average	18.8	103.3	—	0.7
Fidelity Fund	G&I	29/72	Average	19.7	95.6	414.9	3.1
Fidelity GNMA	MBS	—	—	9.6	—	—	8.3
Fidelity Gov. Securities	USG	8/13	Average	7.4	51.0	—	8.5
Fidelity Growth & Income	G&I	—	—	25.8	—	—	1.0
Fidelity Growth Company	Gro	24/118	High	16.7	104.1	—	0.0
Fidelity High Income	HYC	3/39	Average	15.3	71.6	—	10.7
Fidelity High-Yield Muni Bond	HYT	5/11	Average	11.8	58.7	—	7.1
Fidelity Insured Tax Free	HGT	—	—	9.1	—	—	6.3
Fidelity Limited Term Muni Bond	ITT	3/15	High	10.8	47.6	—	6.2
Fidelity Magellan	Gro	2/118	High	24.3	135.5	1,962.3	0.8
Fidelity Mortgage Sec.	MBS	—	—	9.0	—	—	9.0
Fidelity Municipal Bond	HGT	24/40	Average	11.5	57.1	75.2	6.5

*Open to IRA investors only.

Percent Maximum Initial Sales Charge	Percent Maximum Deferred Sales Charge	Expenses per $100	Minimum Initial Investment	IRA Minimum Initial Investment/Annual Fee	Assets as of Feb. 27, 1987 (in millions)	Phone Switch	Toll-free (800) + In State	Telephone
4¾	None	$1.75	$1,000	$50/$10	$ 20.9	No	225-6265	617-482-8260 (Mass.)
4¾	None	.92	1,000	50/10	92.3	No	225-6265	617-482-8260 (Mass.)
7¼	None	.99	1,000	50/10	43.6	No	225-6265	617-482-8260 (Mass.)
4¾	None	1.65	1,000	50/10	676.1	No	225-6265	617-482-8260 (Mass.)
None	5	1.00	1,000	250/15	117.0	Yes	826-7194	—
8½	None	1.31	250	250/10	207.7	Yes	421-9900	213-486-9651 (Calif.)
None	None	1.04	2,000	None/10	779.1	Yes	235-0064	—
None	None	1.11	2,000	None/10	1,428.8	Yes	235-0064	—
8½	None	.95	500	250/5	57.5	Yes	223-7757	212-661-3000 (N.Y.)
None	None	1.26	10,000	10,000/30	104.3	Yes	—	502-636-5633
None	None	.99	100	None/10	54.0	Yes	247-4170	800-422-3175 (Iowa)
None	1	.65	2,500	—/—	472.0	Yes	544-6666	617-523-1919 (Mass.)
None	None	.95	1,000	500/10	120.4	Yes	544-6666	617-523-1919 (Mass.)
9	None	.60	50	50/10	1,361.7	No	225-5270	617-328-5000 (Mass.)
9	None	1.50	50	50/10	23.9	No	225-5270	617-328-5000 (Mass.)
2	None	.66	1,000	500/10	3,967.6	Yes	544-6666	617-523-1919 (Mass.)
None	None	.67	2,500	500/10	482.9	Yes	544-6666	617-523-1919 (Mass.)
None	None	1.14	500	500/10	1,172.9	Yes	544-6666	617-523-1919 (Mass.)
None	None	.66	1,000	500/10	977.6	Yes	544-6666	617-523-1919 (Mass.)
None	None	.75	1,000	500/10	1,072.7	Yes	544-6666	617-523-1919 (Mass.)
None	None	.81	1,000	500/10	816.7	Yes	544-6666	617-523-1919 (Mass.)
2	None	1.33	2,500	500/10	1,144.1	Yes	544-6666	617-523-1919 (Mass.)
3	None	1.18	1,000	500/10	212.4	Yes	544-6666	617-523-1919 (Mass.)
None	None	.83	2,500	500/10	1,972.1	Yes	544-6666	617-523-1919 (Mass.)
None	None	.56	2,500	—/—	2,604.6	Yes	544-6666	617-523-1919 (Mass.)
None	None	.60	2,500	—/—	182.3	Yes	544-6666	617-523-1919 (Mass.)
None	None	.71	2,500	—/—	660.6	Yes	544-6666	617-523-1919 (Mass.)
3	None	1.08	1,000	500/10	9,499.4	Yes	544-6666	617-523-1919 (Mass.)
None	None	.75	1,000	500/10	804.5	Yes	544-6666	617-523-1919 (Mass.)
None	None	.46	2,500	—/—	1,265.1	Yes	544-6666	617-523-1919 (Mass.)

Alphabetical Guide to Mutual Funds	Type	3 Yr. Performance Rank within Type/No. in Category					
		Volatility (within Type)					
				Percent Gain (or Loss) to April 1, 1987			
				One Year	Three Years	Ten Years	Percent Current Yield
Standard & Poor's 500-Stock Index				26.2	106.7	380.0	
Fidelity OTC	SCG	—	—	14.5	—	—	0.1
Fidelity Overseas	Intl	—	—	62.0	—	—	0.0
Fidelity Puritan	EqI	9/46	Average	17.7	92.7	404.6	6.2
Fidelity Select—Brokerage & Inv.	Sec	—	—	8.1	—	—	0.1
Fidelity Select—Chemical	Sec	—	—	32.3	—	—	0.0
Fidelity Select—Computer	Sec	—	—	34.6	—	—	0.0
Fidelity Select—Electronics	Sec	—	—	(6.6)	—	—	0.0
Fidelity Select—Energy	Sec	26/35	Average	42.2	46.4	—	0.0
Fidelity Select—Financial Svc.	Sec	7/35	High	1.4	114.5	—	0.6
Fidelity Select—Food & Agriculture	Sec	—	—	29.7	—	—	0.0
Fidelity Select—Health Care	Sec	1/35	High	31.0	170.0	—	0.0
Fidelity Select—Leisure	Sec	—	—	16.4	—	—	0.0
Fidelity Select—Precious Metals	Gold	8/11	Average	77.9	21.1	—	0.6
Fidelity Select—Software	Sec	—	—	39.6	—	—	0.0
Fidelity Select—Technology	Sec	31/35	Average	6.9	23.8	—	0.0
Fidelity Select—Telecommunications	Sec	—	—	29.7	—	—	0.0
Fidelity Select—Utilities	Sec	8/35	Average	11.5	108.7	—	0.8
Fidelity Special Situations	Max	9/66	Average	19.0	113.4	—	0.5
Fidelity Thrift Trust	HGC	25/36	Average	7.1	56.6	202.2	11.1
Fidelity Trend	Gro	61/118	Average	14.1	87.7	327.3	1.2
Fidelity Value	Max	54/66	Low	9.1	61.9	—	0.6
Fiduciary Capital Growth	SCG	17/25	Average	1.8	61.2	—	4.3
Fin. Bond Shares—High Yield	HYC	2/39	Average	13.9	74.7	—	11.1
Financial Dynamics	Max	42/66	Average	20.6	70.4	373.0	0.6
Financial Industrial	G&I	52/72	Average	15.4	82.8	353.5	1.7
Financial Industrial Income	EqI	6/46	High	17.7	98.9	394.8	4.1
Financial Bond Shares—Select Inc.	HGC	11/36	High	11.9	63.5	184.7	8.9
Financial Strategic—Gold	Gold	7/11	High	97.1	22.4	—	0.9
Financial Strategic—Health	Sec	3/35	High	42.3	140.5	—	0.0
Financial Strategic—Pacific Basin	Intl	3/13	High	71.2	128.7	—	0.2

Percent Maximum Initial Sales Charge								
	Percent Maximum Deferred Sales Charge							
		Expenses per $100						
			Minimum Initial Investment					
				IRA Minimum Initial Investment/Annual Fee				
					Assets as of Feb. 27, 1987 (in millions)			
						Phone Switch		
							Toll-free (800) +	Telephone
							In State	
3	None	$1.50	$2,500	$500/$10	$1,056.5	Yes	544-6666	617-523-1919 (Mass.)
3	None	1.63	2,500	500/10	2,265.8	Yes	544-6666	617-523-1919 (Mass.)
2	None	.60	1,000	500/10	3,643.4	Yes	544-6666	617-523-1919 (Mass.)
2	1	1.73	1,000	500/10	24.5	Yes	544-6666	617-523-1919 (Mass.)
2	1	1.61	1,000	500/10	67.9	Yes	544-6666	617-523-1919 (Mass.)
2	1	2.03	1,000	500/10	105.1	Yes	544-6666	617-523-1919 (Mass.)
2	1	1.85	1,000	500/10	28.1	Yes	544-6666	617-523-1919 (Mass.)
2	1	1.51	1,000	500/10	97.4	Yes	544-6666	617-523-1919 (Mass.)
2	1	1.58	1,000	500/10	96.8	Yes	544-6666	617-523-1919 (Mass.)
2	1	1.66	1,000	500/10	11.2	Yes	544-6666	617-523-1919 (Mass.)
2	1	1.44	1,000	500/10	407.1	Yes	544-6666	617-523-1919 (Mass.)
2	1	1.53	1,000	500/10	90.1	Yes	544-6666	617-523-1919 (Mass.)
2	1	1.51	1,000	500/10	201.9	Yes	544-6666	617-523-1919 (Mass.)
2	1	1.72	1,000	500/10	102.8	Yes	544-6666	617-523-1919 (Mass.)
2	1	1.50	1,000	500/10	409.6	Yes	544-6666	617-523-1919 (Mass.)
2	1	1.63	1,000	500/10	19.4	Yes	544-6666	617-523-1919 (Mass.)
2	1	1.34	1,000	500/10	181.0	Yes	544-6666	617-523-1919 (Mass.)
3	None	1.50	1,000	500/10	184.2	Yes	544-6666	617-523-1919 (Mass.)
None	None	.79	1,000	500/10	386.7	Yes	544-6666	617-523-1919 (Mass.)
None	None	.52	1,000	500/10	844.1	Yes	544-6666	617-523-1919 (Mass.)
None	None	1.13	1,000	500/10	130.9	Yes	544-6666	617-523-1919 (Mass.)
None	None	1.20	1,000	1,000/10	59.5	No	—	414-271-6666
None	None	.76	250	250/None	50.6	Yes	525-8085	800-525-9769 (Colo.)
None	None	.90	250	250/None	95.4	Yes	525-8085	800-525-9769 (Colo.)
None	None	.74	250	250/None	434.8	Yes	525-8085	800-525-9769 (Colo.)
None	None	.71	250	250/None	415.2	Yes	525-8085	800-525-9769 (Colo.)
None	None	.85	250	—/—	28.0	Yes	525-8085	800-525-9769 (Colo.)
None	None	1.50	250	250/None	12.2	Yes	525-8085	800-525-9769 (Colo.)
None	None	1.50	250	250/None	10.1	Yes	525-8085	800-525-9769 (Colo.)
None	None	1.50	250	250/None	32.6	Yes	525-8085	800-525-9769 (Colo.)

Alphabetical Guide to Mutual Funds	Type	3 Yr. Performance Rank within Type/No. in Category					
		Volatility (within Type)					
			Percent Gain (or Loss) to April 1, 1987				
				One Year	Three Years	Ten Years	Percent Current Yield
Standard & Poor's 500-Stock Index				26.2	106.7	380.0	
Financial Strategic—Technology	Sec	16/35	High	43.7	82.7	—	0.0
Financial Tax-Free Inc. Shares	HGT	6/40	High	12.1	65.5	—	7.1
First Investors Bond Appreciation	HYC	28/39	High	11.8	50.9	—	9.6
First Investors Discovery	SCG	25/25	Low	(0.7)	(10.5)	235.2	0.0
First Investors Fund for Growth	Gro	118/118	Average	8.9	(1.8)	210.0	0.0
First Investors Fund for Inc.	HYC	36/39	Low	12.1	43.7	159.0	12.0
First Investors Government	MBS	—	—	11.4	—	—	9.0
First Investors International Sec.	Glo	11/11	Average	55.4	59.4	—	0.2
First Investors Nat. Resources	Sec	35/35	Average	32.5	(27.5)	1.2	0.8
First Investors Option	OpInc	10/10	Average	15.3	37.7	211.9	1.8
First Investors Tax-Exempt	HGT	38/40	Low	11.5	49.9	—	7.4
Flexfund—Bond	HYC	—	—	4.8	—	—	8.8
Flexfund—Growth	Max	—	—	10.6	—	—	0.4
Flexfund Retirement Growth	Max	58/66	Average	11.7	52.0	—	0.5
44 Wall Street	Max	66/66	Average	1.8	(53.1)	21.1	0.0
44 Wall Street Equity	Max	41/66	High	41.0	72.0	—	0.0
Founders Equity Income	EqI	37/46	Average	19.6	59.4	278.0	4.6
Founders Growth	Gro	53/118	High	22.2	91.1	504.4	3.6
Founders Mutual	G&I	25/72	High	19.5	97.0	275.1	2.9
Founders Special	Max	52/66	Average	19.2	65.4	491.9	0.8
FPA Capital	Gro	75/118	Average	20.5	83.1	262.2	2.7
FPA Paramount**	G&I	58/72	Average	27.6	72.7	471.0	4.2
FPA Perennial	G&I	—	—	16.0	—	—	3.1
Franklin AGE High Income	HYC	23/39	Average	13.4	55.2	212.3	12.4
Franklin DynaTech Series	Sec	28/35	Average	12.5	41.7	398.9	0.5
Franklin Equity	Gro	3/118	High	24.8	133.7	507.1	1.0
Franklin Federal Tax-Free Inc.	HGT	20/40	Low	11.2	57.9	—	8.2
Franklin Gold	Gold	6/11	Average	83.1	24.3	928.4	2.2
Franklin Growth Series	Gro	68/118	Low	23.0	85.5	334.9	1.6
Franklin Income Series	EqI	17/46	Average	19.3	82.1	418.2	8.7

** Fund closed to new investors.

Percent Maximum Initial Sales Charge									
	Percent Maximum Deferred Sales Charge								
		Expenses per $100							
			Minimum Initial Investment						
				IRA Minimum Initial Investment/Annual Fee					
					Assets as of Feb. 27, 1987 (in millions)				
						Phone Switch			
							Toll-free (800) +		Telephone
								In State	
None	None	$1.50	$ 250	$250/None	$ 23.1	Yes	525-8085	800-525-9769 (Colo.)	
None	None	.68	250	—/—	146.4	Yes	525-8085	800-525-9769 (Colo.)	
7¼	None	1.08	1,000	1,000/None	218.6	No	423-4026	—	
8½	None	1.30	200	200/None	37.2	No	423-4026	—	
8½	None	1.07	200	200/None	62.9	No	423-4026	—	
8½	None	.98	200	200/None	1,766.1	No	423-4026	—	
7¼	None	1.22	1,000	1,000/None	300.2	No	423-4026	—	
8½	None	1.75	200	200/None	36.1	No	423-4026	—	
8½	None	1.70	200	200/None	19.5	No	423-4026	—	
7¼	None	1.01	200	200/None	218.5	No	423-4026	—	
7¼	None	1.02	2,000	—/—	771.6	No	423-4026	—	
None	None	.78	2,500	500/8	16.6	Yes	325-3539	614-766-7000 (Ohio)	
None	None	1.49	2,500	500/8	11.8	Yes	325-3539	614-766-7000 (Ohio)	
None	None	1.44	2,500	500/8	77.9	Yes	325-3539	614-766-7000 (Ohio)	
None	.25	3.26	1,000	1,000/5	24.5	Yes	221-7836	212-344-4224 (N.Y.)	
1†	None	2.41	1,000	1,000/5	18.0	No	221-7836	212-344-4224 (N.Y.)	
None	None	1.59	1,000	25/10	15.2	Yes	525-2440	800-874-6301 (Colo.)	
None	None	1.27	1,000	25/10	82.7	Yes	525-2440	800-874-6301 (Colo.)	
None	None	.74	1,000	25/10	220.3	Yes	525-2440	800-874-6301 (Colo.)	
None	None	1.02	1,000	25/10	92.7	Yes	525-2440	800-874-6301 (Colo.)	
6½	None	.90	100	100/7.50	57.7	Yes	421-4374	—	
6½	None	1.02	1,500	100/7.50	131.2	Yes	421-4374	—	
6½	None	1.14	1,500	100/7.50	67.8	Yes	421-4374	—	
4	None	.57	100	2,000/10	1,626.1	Yes††	632-2180	—	
4	None	.87	100	2,000/10	41.5	Yes	632-2180	—	
4	None	.89	100	2,000/10	217.6	Yes	632-2180	—	
4	None	.64	100	—/—	2,472.0	Yes	632-2180	—	
4	None	1.01	100	2,000/10	149.6	Yes	632-2180	—	
4	None	.87	100	2,000/10	62.5	Yes	632-2180	—	
4	None	.71	100	2,000/10	318.9	Yes	632-2180	—	

†Fund may impose an exit fee. ††Family permits switching only through brokers.

Alphabetical Guide to Mutual Funds	Type	3 Yr. Performance Rank within Type/No. in Category					
		Volatility (within Type)					
				Percent Gain (or Loss) to April 1, 1987			
				One Year	Three Years	Ten Years	Percent Current Yield
Standard & Poor's 500-Stock Index				26.2	106.7	380.0	
Franklin Insured Tax Free Income	HGT	—	—	8.3	—	—	7.2
Franklin Option	OpInc	3/10	Average	10.2	58.9	304.8	1.9
Franklin U.S. Gov. Series	MBS	3/8	Average	9.5	53.9	115.4	10.7
Franklin Utilities Series	Sec	11/35	Low	11.6	94.5	314.9	6.8
Freedom Gold & Government	Gold	—	—	14.0	—	—	6.4
Freedom Regional Bank	Sec	—	—	17.4	—	—	2.0
Fundamental Investors	G&I	4/72	High	25.5	113.1	408.1	2.3
Fund for U.S. Gov. Sec.	MBS	8/8	High	7.2	44.1	129.4	9.4
Fund of America	G&I	65/72	Average	22.5	61.5	492.9	1.8
Fund of the Southwest	Max	63/66	Average	1.6	31.8	406.6	0.4
Gateway Option Income	OpInc	7/10	Low	12.7	44.6	—	2.6
General Securities	Max	49/66	Low	7.0	65.9	283.4	4.3
Gintel Capital Appreciation	Max	—	—	16.6	—	—	1.1
GIT Equity Trust—Sp. Growth	SCG	3/25	High	11.1	104.5	—	0.6
GIT Income Trust—Maximum Inc.	HYC	25/39	Average	8.0	53.9	—	11.0
GIT Tax-Free—High Yield	HYT	7/11	Average	10.4	52.4	—	7.0
Gradison Established Growth	Gro	26/118	Low	22.9	102.4	—	1.9
Gradison Opportunity Growth	SCG	7/25	Average	11.0	84.6	—	0.3
Growth Fund of America	Gro	70/118	Average	22.7	85.1	789.6	1.4
Growth Industry Shares	Gro	95/118	Average	15.7	67.7	450.3	1.5
G.T. Europe Growth	Intl	—	—	40.8	—	—	0.0
G.T. International Growth	Intl	—	—	44.2	—	—	0.0
G.T. Pacific Growth	Intl	12/13	Average	55.8	83.7	375.1	0.0
Guardian Park Avenue	Gro	4/118	High	22.4	128.9	632.3	1.3
Hamilton Fund	G&I	31/72	Average	20.3	94.2	241.2	4.5
Hancock (John) Bond	HGC	8/36	Average	9.5	65.4	144.3	9.3
Hancock (John) Global	Glo	—	—	32.2	—	—	0.0
Hancock (John) Growth	Gro	51/118	High	19.4	91.5	400.5	0.6
Hancock (John) Special Equities	SCG	—	—	7.1	—	—	0.0
Hancock (John) Tax-Ex. Inc. Trust	HGT	11/40	Average	11.8	61.0	67.4	6.5

Percent Maximum Initial Sales Charge	Percent Maximum Deferred Sales Charge	Expenses per $100	Minimum Initial Investment	IRA Minimum Initial Investment/Annual Fee	Assets as of Feb. 27, 1987 (in millions)	Phone Switch	Toll-free (800) + In State	Telephone
4	None	$ .63	$ 100	—/—	$ 183.4	Yes	632-2180	—
4	None	.95	100	2,000/10	40.9	Yes	632-2180	—
4	None	.54	100	2,000/10	15.2	Yes	632-2180	—
4	None	.74	100	2,000/10	596.7	Yes	632-2180	—
None	3	1.59	1,000	None/10	64.0	No	225-6258	800-523-3170 (Mass.)
None	3	1.52	1,000	None/10	52.6	No	225-6258	800-523-3170 (Mass.)
8½	None	.62	250	250/10	610.1	Yes	421-9900	213-486-9651 (Calif.)
4½	None	.91	500	50/None	1,160.3	Yes	245-4770	—
8½	None	.76	500	50/10	175.1	Yes	847-5636	—
7½	None	1.47	200	None/10	16.6	Yes	262-6686	—
None	None	1.49	500	500/10	43.9	Yes	354-6339	513-248-2700 (Ohio)
None†	None	1.00	100	100/10	17.3	No	—	612-332-1212
None	None	1.90	5,000	2,000/10	26.5	Yes	243-5808	203-622-6400 (Conn.)
None	None	1.35	1,000	500/12	20.3	Yes	336-3063	800-572-2050 (Va.)
None	None	1.10	1,000	500/12	16.7	Yes	336-3063	800-572-2050 (Va.)
None	None	1.16	1,000	—/—	55.6	Yes	336-3063	800-572-2050 (Va.)
None	None	1.79	1,000	1,000/5	48.2	Yes	543-1818	800-582-7062 (Ohio)
None	None	2.00	1,000	1,000/5	21.8	Yes	543-1818	800-582-7062 (Ohio)
8½	None	.66	1,000	250/10	1,052.5	Yes	421-9900	213-486-9651 (Calif.)
None	None	.90	200	200/10	79.3	No	—	312-346-4830
4¾	None	2.00	500	500/10	14.7	Yes	824-1580	—
4¾	None	1.90	500	500/10	15.7	Yes	824-1580	—
4¾	None	1.40	500	500/10	54.0	Yes	824-1580	—
8½	None	.71	300	300/10	166.8	No	221-3253	800-522-7800 (N.Y.)
8½	None	.89	1,000	250/7.50	267.0	Yes	525-7048	800-356-3556 (Colo.)
8½	None	.72	1,000	500/15	1,191.6	Yes	225-5291	617-572-4210 (Mass.)
8½	None	1.50	1,000	500/15	108.1	Yes	225-5291	617-572-4210 (Mass.)
8½	None	1.03	500	250/15	108.2	Yes	225-5291	617-572-4210 (Mass.)
8½	None	1.50	1,000	500/15	17.0	Yes	225-5291	617-572-4210 (Mass.)
4¾	None	.71	1,000	—/—	368.3	Yes	225-5291	617-572-4210 (Mass.)

†Fund may impose an exit fee.

Alphabetical Guide to Mutual Funds	Type	3 Yr. Performance Rank within Type/No. in Category					
		Volatility (within Type)					
			Percent Gain (or Loss) to April 1, 1987				
				One Year	Three Years	Ten Years	Percent Current Yield
Standard & Poor's 500-Stock Index				26.2	106.7	380.0	
Hancock (John)—U.S. Gov. Sec.	USG	2/13	Average	7.6	56.4	151.2	8.3
Hancock (John)—U.S. Guar. Mort.	MBS	—	—	9.3	—	—	9.4
Hartwell Growth	Max	33/66	High	41.6	82.9	689.1	0.0
Hartwell Leverage	Max	29/66	High	44.3	91.5	688.0	0.0
Heartland Value	Max	—	—	14.7	—	—	2.6
Heritage Capital Appreciation	Max	—	—	15.1	—	—	0.7
Hutton Bond & Income Series	HGC	2/36	High	7.1	76.6	—	8.7
Hutton Growth Series	Gro	86/118	Average	20.0	77.7	—	1.3
Hutton Inv. Series—Basic Value	Gro	—	—	16.5	—	—	2.3
Hutton Inv. Series—Gov. Sec.	USG	10/13	Average	7.3	45.0	—	10.4
Hutton Inv. Series—Option Inc.	OpInc	9/10	Average	11.8	42.1	—	2.4
Hutton Inv. Series—Precious Metals	Gold	—	—	90.1	—	—	0.9
Hutton National Muni Bond	HGT	5/40	Average	14.1	66.3	—	7.3
Hutton Special Equities	SCG	12/25	Average	13.2	74.2	—	0.0
IDS Bond	HYC	7/39	High	11.7	65.6	200.7	8.6
IDS Discovery	SCG	18/25	Average	20.4	60.9	—	0.9
IDS Equity Plus	G&I	21/72	High	25.6	98.7	371.4	1.9
IDS Extra Income	HYC	16/39	Average	13.4	59.3	—	10.0
IDS Federal Income	USG	—	—	9.1	—	—	7.8
IDS Growth	Gro	23/118	High	32.7	104.2	849.3	0.5
IDS High-Yield Tax-Exempt	HYT	2/11	High	11.8	60.1	—	7.4
IDS International	Intl	—	—	47.8	—	—	0.4
IDS Managed Retirement	G&I	—	—	28.3	—	—	1.8
IDS Mutual	Bal	9/17	Average	20.9	92.3	298.7	5.6
IDS New Dimensions	Gro	10/118	High	28.9	114.7	704.3	1.5
IDS Precious Metals	Gold	—	—	93.6	—	—	0.4
IDS Progressive	Max	50/66	Low	16.9	65.7	457.2	2.9
IDS Selective	HGC	10/36	Average	11.3	63.5	194.6	8.5
IDS Stock	G&I	45/72	High	24.4	85.9	292.4	2.4
IDS Strategy—Aggressive Equity	Max	—	—	35.2	—	—	0.0

Percent Maximum Initial Sales Charge	Percent Maximum Deferred Sales Charge	Expenses per $100	Minimum Initial Investment	IRA Minimum Initial Investment/Annual Fee	Assets as of Feb. 27, 1987 (in millions)	Phone Switch	Toll-free (800) + In State	Telephone
8½	None	$ .90	$ 500	$250/$15	$ 212.0	Yes	225-5291	617-572-4210 (Mass.)
8½	None	.91	1,000	500/15	431.7	Yes	225-5291	617-572-4210 (Mass.)
None	None	2.90	1,000	500/10	20.3	Yes	645-6445	212-308-3355 (N.Y.)
None	None	1.80	2,000	500/10	39.2	Yes	645-6445	212-308-3355 (N.Y.)
4½	None	1.70	1,000	500/10	35.6	Yes	558-1015	800-242-1001 (Wis.)
3	None	2.00	1,000	1,000/10	49.7	Yes	—	813-578-3800
None	5	1.79	500	500/25	497.0	No	334-2626	212-742-5000 (N.Y.)
None	5	1.77	500	500/25	1,505.0	No	334-2626	212-742-5000 (N.Y.)
None	5	1.59	500	500/25	460.0	No	334-2626	212-742-5000 (N.Y.)
None	5	1.67	500	500/25	6.6	No	334-2626	212-742-5000 (N.Y.)
None	5	1.96	500	500/25	68.0	No	334-2626	212-742-5000 (N.Y.)
None	5	2.37	500	500/25	55.0	No	334-2626	212-742-5000 (N.Y.)
4	None	.66	500	—/—	1,306.0	No	334-2626	212-742-5000 (N.Y.)
None	5	2.20	500	500/25	275.0	No	334-2626	212-742-5000 (N.Y.)
3½	None	.62	2,000	50/15	2,018.8	Yes	328-8300	612-372-3131 (Minn.)
5	None	.70	2,000	50/15	288.9	Yes	328-8300	612-372-3131 (Minn.)
5	None	.51	2,000	50/15	441.1	Yes	328-8300	612-372-3131 (Minn.)
5	None	.84	2,000	50/15	1,064.6	Yes	328-8300	612-372-3131 (Minn.)
5	None	.73	2,000	50/15	199.7	Yes	328-8300	612-372-3131 (Minn.)
5	None	.54	2,000	50/15	892.2	Yes	328-8300	612-372-3131 (Minn.)
5	None	.60	2,000	—/—	4,018.2	Yes	328-8300	612-372-3131 (Minn.)
5	None	1.13	2,000	50/15	301.0	Yes	328-8300	612-372-3131 (Minn.)
5	None	.99	2,000	50/15	470.0	Yes	328-8300	612-372-3131 (Minn.)
5	None	.59	2,000	50/15	1,465.8	Yes	328-8300	612-372-3131 (Minn.)
5	None	.63	2,000	50/15	671.6	Yes	328-8300	612-372-3131 (Minn.)
5	None	2.00	2,000	50/15	37.7	Yes	328-8300	612-372-3131 (Minn.)
5	None	.71	2,000	50/15	197.0	Yes	328-8300	612-372-3131 (Minn.)
5	None	.66	2,000	50/15	1,264.7	Yes	328-8300	612-372-3131 (Minn.)
5	None	.53	2,000	50/15	1,533.6	Yes	328-8300	612-372-3131 (Minn.)
None	5	1.76	2,000	50/15	256.4	Yes	328-8300	612-372-3131 (Minn.)

Alphabetical Guide to Mutual Funds	Type	3 Yr. Performance Rank within Type/No. in Category	Volatility (within Type)	Percent Gain (or Loss) to April 1, 1987			
				One Year	Three Years	Ten Years	Percent Current Yield
Standard & Poor's 500-Stock Index				26.2	106.7	380.0	
IDS Strategy—Equity	G&I	—	—	13.7	—	—	2.7
IDS Strategy—Income	HGC	—	—	9.0	—	—	7.3
IDS Tax-Exempt Bond	HGT	21/40	High	10.7	57.9	92.3	6.9
Income Fund of America	EqI	15/46	Average	12.6	83.2	316.6	6.8
Insured Quality Tax-Free Bond	HGT	32/40	Average	7.2	53.3	—	6.5
International Investors	Gold	3/11	Average	85.4	38.7	1,122.4	2.2
Investment Co. of America	G&I	7/72	Average	23.4	109.0	469.3	2.8
Investment Portfolio—Equity	Gro	106/118	Low	15.6	60.2	—	0.0
Investment Port.—Gov. Plus	USG	—	—	6.6	—	—	8.8
Investment Port.—High Yield	HYC	6/39	Average	19.6	66.9	—	8.3
Investment Port.—Option Inc.	OpInc	—	—	9.6	—	—	7.7
Investment Quality Interest	HGC	9/36	High	6.4	64.4	—	10.9
Investment Trust of Boston	G&I	48/72	Average	14.2	83.7	264.3	2.4
Inv. Tr. of Bost. High Inc. Plus	HYC	22/39	Average	10.5	55.5	—	10.5
Investors Income	EqI	35/46	Low	15.1	62.5	179.4	8.7
Investors Research	Max	12/66	High	28.5	106.0	649.6	0.4
IRI Stock	Gro	37/118	High	6.4	97.2	—	1.3
ISI Growth	Gro	110/118	Low	7.9	44.5	215.9	1.3
ISI Trust	G&I	71/72	Low	13.1	44.9	190.2	5.3
Ivy Growth	Gro	56/118	Low	21.7	90.2	552.3	3.7
Janus Fund	Max	48/66	Low	10.2	66.5	628.4	4.6
Janus Value	Max	—	—	6.5	—	—	5.6
Janus Venture	SCG	—	—	21.1	—	—	4.6
JP Growth	Gro	80/118	Low	15.4	81.4	335.3	2.6
JP Income	EqI	25/46	Average	8.4	74.3	—	8.7
Kemper Growth	Gro	89/118	Average	23.9	73.5	512.5	0.7
Kemper High Yield	HYC	4/39	Average	19.7	70.4	—	10.5
Kemper Income & Cap. Pres.	HGC	19/36	Low	10.0	59.4	165.4	10.1
Kemper International	Intl	9/13	Average	30.6	104.4	—	1.2
Kemper Municipal	HGT	18/40	Average	11.5	58.2	111.5	7.3

Percent Maximum Initial Sales Charge									
	Percent Maximum Deferred Sales Charge								
		Expenses per $100							
			Minimum Initial Investment						
				IRA Minimum Initial Investment/Annual Fee					
					Assets as of Feb. 27, 1987 (in millions)				
						Phone Switch			
							Toll-free (800) +		Telephone
								In State	
None	5	$1.86	$2,000	$50/$15	$ 117.6	Yes	328-8300	612-372-3131 (Minn.)	
None	5	1.75	2,000	50/15	144.6	Yes	328-8300	612-372-3131 (Minn.)	
5	None	.60	2,000	—/—	948.7	Yes	328-8300	612-372-3131 (Minn.)	
8½	None	.55	1,000	250/10	814.0	Yes	421-9900	213-486-9651 (Calif.)	
4¾	None	1.50	100	—/—	35.3	Yes	—	713-751-2400	
8½	None	.86	1,000	None/10	966.0	Yes	221-2220	212-687-5200 (N.Y.)	
8½	None	.41	250	250/10	4,348.2	Yes	421-9900	213-486-9651 (Calif.)	
None	5	2.14	250	250/10	262.9	Yes	621-1048	312-781-1121 (Ill.)	
None	5	1.99	250	250/10	5,856.4	Yes	621-1048	312-781-1121 (Ill.)	
None	5	2.09	250	250/10	283.5	Yes	621-1048	312-781-1121 (Ill.)	
None	5	2.11	250	250/10	421.3	Yes	621-1048	312-781-1121 (Ill.)	
4½	None	1.06	100	100/None	159.0	Yes	—	713-751-2400	
7	None	1.00	500	250/10	76.1	No	451-0502	617-542-0213 (Mass.)	
6¾	None	1.50	1,000	250/10	21.6	No	451-0502	617-542-0213 (Mass.)	
4½	None	1.52	200	200/10	24.3	Yes	262-6686	—	
8½	None	.80	None	None/10	103.0	No	—	213-595-7711	
4½	None	1.80	2,000	2,000/10	12.6	Yes	328-1010	612-853-9500 (Minn.)	
8½	None	1.50	None	None/10	13.2	Yes	441-9490	302-652-3091 (Del.)	
8½	None	1.21	None	None/10	107.2	Yes	441-9490	302-652-3091 (Del.)	
None	None	1.29	1,000	None/6.50	187.6	Yes	235-3322	617-749-1422 (Mass.)	
None	None	1.00	1,000	500/10	519.3	Yes	525-3713	303-333-3863 (Colo.)	
None	None	2.00	1,000	500/10	21.5	Yes	525-3713	303-333-3863 (Colo.)	
None	None	1.90	1,000	500/10	42.7	Yes	525-3713	303-333-3863 (Colo.)	
8	None	.89	300	25/10	26.8	Yes	—	919-378-2453	
8	None	.91	300	25/10	20.1	Yes	—	919-378-2453	
8½	None	.78	1,000	250/10	332.7	Yes	621-1048	—	
5½	None	.68	1,000	250/10	429.0	Yes	621-1048	—	
5½	None	.69	1,000	250/10	239.6	Yes	621-1048	—	
8½	None	1.23	1,000	250/10	213.7	Yes	621-1048	—	
4½	None	.52	1,000	250/10	1,172.6	Yes	621-1048	—	

Alphabetical Guide to Mutual Funds	Type	3 Yr. Performance Rank within Type/No. in Category						
		Volatility (within Type)						
			Percent Gain (or Loss) to April 1, 1987					
				One Year	Three Years	Ten Years	Percent Current Yield
Standard & Poor's 500-Stock Index				26.2	106.7	380.0	
Kemper Option Income	OpInc	8/10	Average	13.3	43.2	—	9.0
Kemper Summit	Gro	83/118	Average	21.1	78.8	641.4	0.0
Kemper Technology	Sec	13/35	Average	27.0	88.5	452.5	1.1
Kemper Total Return	Bal	10/17	Average	24.2	90.1	482.2	2.9
Kemper U.S. Gov. Sec.	MBS	1/8	High	8.6	60.3	—	10.5
Keystone B-1	HGC	20/36	High	7.0	58.7	173.3	9.0
Keystone B-2	HYC	18/39	Average	9.8	57.1	202.4	9.5
Keystone B-4**	HYC	33/39	Average	9.9	47.3	203.0	11.7
Keystone International	Intl	6/13	Average	54.1	123.7	370.4	0.7
Keystone K-1	EqI	20/46	Average	17.5	77.1	269.9	5.3
Keystone K-2	Gro	62/118	Average	24.4	86.8	327.8	1.3
Keystone Precious Metals	Gold	5/11	High	88.6	25.3	591.4	1.8
Keystone S-1	G&I	51/72	Average	22.6	83.4	248.8	1.6
Keystone S-3	Gro	93/118	Average	21.4	71.0	372.9	1.3
Keystone S-4	Gro	103/118	Average	19.3	63.9	418.9	0.1
Keystone Tax-Free Trust**	HGT	33/40	Average	9.5	53.2	—	7.6
Kidder Peabody Equity Income	EqI	—	—	13.2	—	—	2.3
Kidder Peabody Gov. Income	USG	—	—	6.1	—	—	7.5
Kidder Peabody Sp. Growth	Gro	—	—	11.7	—	—	0.2
Legg Mason Special Invest. Trust	SCG	—	—	12.4	—	—	0.2
Legg Mason Total Return Trust	Gro	—	—	9.5	—	—	1.6
Legg Mason Value Trust	Gro	44/118	Average	9.2	94.0	—	1.3
Lehman Capital	Max	44/66	Average	19.5	69.3	987.0	0.6
Lehman Investors	G&I	47/72	Average	22.6	84.8	451.8	2.3
Lehman Opportunity	Max	32/66	Average	9.6	83.2	—	2.1
Lepercq-Istel Trust	G&I	72/72	Low	13.8	42.6	252.0	3.2
Leverage Fund of Boston	Max	47/66	Average	20.6	67.8	300.9	0.0
Lexington GNMA Income	MBS	5/8	Low	10.7	50.2	114.1	8.7
Lexington Goldfund	Gold	1/11	Average	73.2	50.2	—	0.5
Lexington Growth	Gro	54/118	Average	25.2	90.6	355.4	1.4

** Fund closed to new investors.

Percent Maximum Initial Sales Charge	Percent Maximum Deferred Sales Charge	Expenses per $100	Minimum Initial Investment	IRA Minimum Initial Investment/Annual Fee	Assets as of Feb. 27, 1987 (in millions)	Phone Switch	Toll-free (800) +	In State	Telephone
8½	None	$ .85	$1,000	$250/$10	$ 613.6	Yes	621-1048		—
8½	None	.48	1,000	250/10	391.9	Yes	621-1048		—
8½	None	.60	1,000	250/10	683.4	Yes	621-1048		—
8½	None	.72	1,000	250/10	978.8	Yes	621-1048		—
4½	None	.48	1,000	250/10	3,723.2	Yes	621-1048		—
None	4	1.00	250	None/10	543.7	Yes	225-2618		617-338-3400 (Mass.)
None	4	1.00	250	None/10	950.6	Yes	225-2618		617-338-3400 (Mass.)
None	4	.86	250	None/10	1,635.4	Yes	225-2618		617-338-3400 (Mass.)
None	4	1.49	250	None/10	117.9	Yes	225-2618		617-338-3400 (Mass.)
None	4	.86	250	None/10	611.9	Yes	225-2618		617-338-3400 (Mass.)
None	4	.98	250	None/10	357.6	Yes	225-2618		617-338-3400 (Mass.)
None	4	1.44	250	None/10	98.5	Yes	225-2618		617-338-3400 (Mass.)
None	4	1.13	250	None/10	145.9	Yes	225-2618		617-338-3400 (Mass.)
None	4	1.05	250	None/10	297.0	Yes	225-2618		617-338-3400 (Mass.)
None	4	.83	250	None/10	725.4	Yes	225-2618		617-338-3400 (Mass.)
None	4	.83	10,000	—/—	1,058.4	Yes	225-2618		617-338-3400 (Mass.)
None	5	1.13	1,500	500/None	63.8	Yes††	—		212-510-5041
None	5	1.91	1,500	500/None	164.0	Yes	—		212-510-5041
None	5	1.45	1,500	500/None	33.4	Yes	—		212-510-5041
None	None	2.50	1,000	1,000/10	55.6	Yes	822-5544		800-638-1107 (Md.)
None	None	2.20	1,000	1,000/10	46.6	Yes	822-5544		800-638-1107 (Md.)
None	None	2.10	1,000	1,000/10	783.9	Yes	822-5544		800-638-1107 (Md.)
5	None	1.13	1,000	250/10	126.0	Yes	221-5350		212-668-8578 (N.Y.)
5	None	.57	500	250/10	465.7	Yes	221-5350		212-668-8578 (N.Y.)
None	None	1.16	1,000	250/10	108.7	Yes	221-5350		212-668-8578 (N.Y.)
None	None	1.67	500	500/10	27.6	Yes	—		212-702-0174
None	None	1.51	1,000	50/10	29.7	No	225-6265		617-482-8260 (Mass.)
None	None	.86	1,000	250/10	147.2	Yes	526-0056		—
None	None	1.50	1,000	250/10	37.6	Yes	526-0056		—
None	None	1.32	1,000	250/10	39.0	Yes	526-0056		—

††Family permits switching only through brokers.

Alphabetical Guide to Mutual Funds	Type	3 Yr. Performance Rank within Type/No. in Category					
		Volatility (within Type)					
		Percent Gain (or Loss) to April 1, 1987					
				One Year	Three Years	Ten Years	Percent Current Yield
Standard & Poor's 500-Stock Index				26.2	106.7	380.0	
Lexington Research	Gro	52/118	Average	19.6	91.2	341.8	3.7
L.G. Fund for Growth	Gro	22/118	High	24.3	104.3	—	1.7
L.G. U.S. Gov. Securities	USG	—	—	8.8	—	—	9.2
Liberty Federated High Income	HYC	19/39	Average	11.2	57.0	—	11.8
Liberty Tax-Free Income Fund	HGT	36/40	Average	10.3	51.8	79.6	6.9
Limited Term Muni	ITT	—	—	8.5	—	—	6.5
Lindner Dividend**	EqI	30/46	Average	18.5	68.9	648.6	5.1
Lindner Fund**	Gro	90/118	Low	22.5	73.0	874.9	7.2
LMH Fund	G&I	67/72	Low	10.5	59.8	—	4.0
Loomis-Sayles Cap. Development**	Gro	1/118	High	40.0	160.7	1,149.5	0.3
Loomis-Sayles Mutual	Bal	1/17	High	23.3	119.3	364.0	3.0
Lord Abbett Affiliated	G&I	16/72	Average	23.9	103.5	395.8	4.3
Lord Abbett Bond Debenture	HYC	31/39	Average	10.3	49.8	204.7	11.0
Lord Abbett Dev. Growth	SCG	23/25	Average	10.5	30.9	443.9	0.0
Lord Abbett Tax-Free Inc.—National	HGT	—	—	11.9	—	—	7.4
Lord Abbett U.S. Gov. Sec.	USG	1/13	Average	9.1	60.6	189.4	10.6
Lord Abbett Value Appreciation	Gro	38/118	Average	12.5	96.4	—	2.3
Lowry Market Timing	Max	65/66	Average	(4.8)	16.8	—	3.5
Mass. Capital Development	Gro	105/118	Average	11.6	61.2	772.4	1.2
Mass. Financial Bond	HGC	7/36	Average	10.9	66.2	178.8	8.8
Mass. Fin. Development	G&I	41/72	High	18.6	88.8	485.1	1.5
Mass. Fin. Emerging Growth	SCG	6/25	High	19.8	86.5	—	0.0
Mass. Fin. Gov. Guaranteed	USG	—	—	7.5	—	—	9.2
Mass. Fin. Gov. Sec. High Yield	USG	—	—	8.6	—	—	9.5
Mass. Fin. High Inc. Trust	HYC	26/39	Average	12.1	52.3	—	12.8
Mass. Fin. Intl. Trust-Bond	Glo	8/11	Average	27.6	85.0	—	6.2
Mass. Fin. Man. High Yd. Muni Bond**	HYT	10/11	Low	8.5	44.2	—	9.5
Mass. Fin. Managed Muni Bond	HGT	14/40	Low	11.6	60.1	167.3	6.8
Mass. Fin. Special	Max	36/66	Average	25.0	80.4	—	0.7
Mass. Fin. Total Return Trust	Bal	6/17	Average	19.6	97.7	320.7	4.8

** Fund closed to new investors.

Percent Maximum Initial Sales Charge	Percent Maximum Deferred Sales Charge	Expenses per $100	Minimum Initial Investment	IRA Minimum Initial Investment/Annual Fee	Assets as of Feb. 27, 1987 (in millions)	Phone Switch	Toll-free (800) +	In State / Telephone
None	None	$ .95	$1,000	$250/$10	$ 141.9	Yes	526-0056	—
4¾	None	2.12	1,000	250/10	24.8	Yes	543-8721	800-582-7396 (Ohio)
4	None	1.49	1,000	250/10	53.1	Yes	543-8721	800-582-7396 (Ohio)
4½	None	1.06	500	50/10	391.6	Yes	637-8511	412-288-1561 (Pa.)
4½	None	.93	500	—/—	409.8	Yes	245-4770	—
2¾	None	1.00	2,500	—/—	120.4	No	847-0200	505-984-0200 (N.M.)
None	2	.95	2,000	250/10	67.0	No	—	314-727-5305
None	2	.58	2,000	250/10	386.4	No	—	314-727-5305
None	None	1.25	2,500	500/10	82.7	No	422-2564	800-522-2564 (Conn.)
None	None	.74	250	25/10	301.6	Yes	345-4048	617-578-4200 (Mass.)
None	None	.84	250	25/10	250.0	Yes	345-4048	617-578-4200 (Mass.)
7¼	None	.32	250	250/9	3,657.0	Yes	223-4224	212-425-8720 (N.Y.)
7¼	None	.61	1,000	250/9	782.6	Yes	223-4224	212-425-8720 (N.Y.)
7¼	None	.87	1,000	250/9	289.1	Yes	223-4224	212-425-8720 (N.Y.)
4¾	None	.66	1,000	—/—	257.6	Yes	223-4224	212-425-8720 (N.Y.)
4¾	None	.82	500	250/9	514.1	Yes	223-4224	212-425-8720 (N.Y.)
7¼	None	.86	1,000	250/9	318.7	Yes	223-4224	212-425-8720 (N.Y.)
4¾	None	1.46	1,000	100/10	42.9	Yes	—	713-751-2400
7¼	None	.73	250	250/5	1,084.2	No	343-2829	617-423-3500 (Mass.)
7¼	None	.79	250	250/5	348.7	No	343-2829	617-423-3500 (Mass.)
7¼	None	.88	250	250/5	296.6	No	343-2829	617-423-3500 (Mass.)
7¼	None	1.11	250	250/5	313.9	No	343-2829	617-423-3500 (Mass.)
4¾	None	1.18	250	250/5	496.0	No	343-2829	617-423-3500 (Mass.)
4¾	None	1.35	250	250/5	984.0	No	343-2829	617-423-3500 (Mass.)
7¼	None	.80	250	250/5	1,263.4	No	343-2829	617-423-3500 (Mass.)
7¼	None	1.43	250	250/5	154.8	No	343-2829	617-423-3500 (Mass.)
4¾	None	1.04	250	250/5	440.5	No	343-2829	617-423-3500 (Mass.)
4¾	None	.69	250	250/5	989.7	No	343-2829	617-423-3500 (Mass.)
7¼	None	1.25	250	250/5	147.1	No	343-2829	617-423-3500 (Mass.)
7¼	None	.78	250	250/5	416.8	No	343-2829	617-423-3500 (Mass.)

Alphabetical Guide to Mutual Funds	Type	3 Yr. Performance Rank within Type/No. in Category					
		Volatility (within Type)					
			Percent Gain (or Loss) to April 1, 1987				
				One Year	Three Years	Ten Years	Percent Current Yield
Standard & Poor's 500-Stock Index				26.2	106.7	380.0	
Mass. Investors Growth Stock	Gro	73/118	Average	20.8	83.9	399.8	1.5
Mass. Investors Trust	G&I	40/72	High	23.8	89.4	314.7	2.5
Mathers Fund	Gro	65/118	Average	22.9	85.8	478.0	2.0
Medical Technology	Sec	10/35	High	23.0	94.8	—	1.1
Meridian Fund	Gro	—	—	9.2	—	—	0.4
Merrill Lynch Basic Value	G&I	32/72	Average	18.0	93.9	—	3.3
Merrill Lynch Capital	G&I	19/72	Average	18.5	99.6	476.4	1.6
Merrill Lynch Corp.—High Inc.	HYC	21/39	Average	12.5	56.1	—	11.2
Merrill Lynch Corp.—High Qual.	HGC	14/36	Average	9.3	62.7	—	8.6
Merrill Lynch Corp.—Intermed.	HGC	23/36	Average	9.1	58.0	—	8.3
Merrill Lynch Equi.-Bond I	G&I	63/72	Low	8.3	64.0	—	4.2
Merrill Lynch Fed. Sec.	MBS	—	—	8.7	—	—	8.3
Merrill Lynch Fund for Tomorrow	Gro	59/118	Average	16.6	88.2	—	0.4
Merrill Lynch International	Glo	—	—	26.9	—	—	1.8
Merrill Lynch Muni—High Yield	HYT	6/11	Average	11.9	58.5	—	7.4
Merrill Lynch Muni—Insured	HGT	34/40	Low	10.3	52.4	—	7.1
Merrill Lynch Muni—Ltd. Mat.	ITT	14/15	Low	5.7	22.2	—	5.5
Merrill Lynch Natural Resources	Sec	—	—	62.5	—	—	0.4
Merrill Lynch Pacific	Intl	1/13	High	74.5	195.9	867.7	0.4
Merrill Lynch Phoenix	G&I	42/72	Low	16.0	87.2	—	4.2
Merrill Lynch Sci.-Tech.	Sec	24/35	Average	20.7	50.5	—	0.7
Merrill Lynch Special Value	Gro	107/118	Average	2.0	57.4	—	0.3
MidAmerica High Growth	Max	56/66	Average	14.7	59.6	285.6	1.2
MidAmerica Mutual	Gro	85/118	Low	13.3	78.3	322.8	3.1
Midwest Inc.—Inter. Term Gov.	USG	11/13	Low	6.9	41.6	—	7.7
Midwest Tax-Free—Limited Term	ITT	12/15	Average	6.4	24.1	—	5.6
Monitrend Mutual	Max	—	—	6.8	—	—	1.3
Mutual of Omaha America	USG	9/13	Average	5.9	46.8	135.8	8.5
Mutual of Omaha Growth	Gro	42/118	Average	23.0	94.7	256.5	1.1
Mutual of Omaha Income	EqI	34/46	Average	9.1	62.9	178.0	8.3

Percent Maximum Initial Sales Charge	Percent Maximum Deferred Sales Charge	Expenses per $100	Minimum Initial Investment	IRA Minimum Initial Investment/Annual Fee	Assets as of Feb. 27, 1987 (in millions)	Phone Switch	Toll-free (800) +	Telephone
							In State	
7¼	None	$ .56	$ 250	$250/$5	$1,021.9	No	343-2829	617-423-3500 (Mass.)
7¼	None	.55	250	250/5	1,407.4	No	343-2829	617-423-3500 (Mass.)
None	None	.77	1,000	None/10	160.8	No	—	312-236-8215
None	None	1.40	1,000	500/None	62.5	Yes	262-3863	—
None	None	1.91	2,000	2,000/10	20.1	No	446-6662	800-445-5553 (Calif.)
6½	None	.61	250	250/20	1,021.4	No	—	609-282-2800
6½	None	.64	250	250/20	679.3	No	—	609-282-2800
4	None	.71	1,000	250/20	788.8	No	—	609-282-2800
4	None	.66	1,000	250/20	294.2	No	—	609-282-2800
2	None	.62	1,000	250/20	133.1	No	—	609-282-2800
4†	None	1.50	1,000	250/20	16.7	No	—	609-282-2800
6¼	None	.50	1,000	250/20	7,106.9	No	—	609-282-2800
None	4	.98	500	250/20	797.8	No	—	609-282-2800
6½	None	2.71	1,000	250/20	319.1	No	—	609-282-2800
4	None	.56	1,000	250/20	2,009.9	No	—	609-282-2800
4	None	.60	1,000	250/20	2,444.1	No	—	609-282-2800
1	None	.42	1,000	250/20	771.7	No	—	609-282-2800
None	4	.96	500	250/20	515.1	No	—	609-282-2800
6½	None	1.12	250	250/20	493.3	No	—	609-282-2800
6½	None	1.18	2,500	250/20	125.2	No	—	609-282-2800
6½	None	1.39	1,000	250/20	295.2	No	—	609-282-2800
6½	None	1.19	250	250/20	108.2	No	—	609-282-2800
8½	None	1.00	10	10/10	13.9	No	553-4936	800-342-4490 (Iowa)
8½	None	.93	10	10/10	36.1	No	553-4936	800-342-4490 (Iowa)
2	None	1.10	1,000	250/10	63.1	Yes	543-8721	800-582-7396 (Ohio)
2	None	1.16	2,500	—/—	32.3	Yes	543-8721	800-582-7396 (Ohio)
3½	None	2.50	2,500	250/10	31.6	No	251-1970	201-886-2300 (N.J.)
None	None	.98	250	None/10	54.5	Yes	228-9596	800-642-8112 (Neb.)
8	None	1.11	250	None/10	39.9	Yes	228-9596	800-642-8112 (Neb.)
8	None	.77	250	None/10	133.6	Yes	228-9596	800-642-8112 (Neb.)

†Fund may impose an exit fee.

Alphabetical Guide to Mutual Funds	Type			3 Yr. Performance Rank within Type/No. in Category			
				Volatility (within Type)			
				Percent Gain (or Loss) to April 1, 1987			
				One Year	Three Years	Ten Years	Percent Current Yield
Standard & Poor's 500-Stock Index				26.2	106.7	380.0	
Mutual of Omaha Tax-Free Inc.	HGT	4/40	High	15.8	66.8	86.1	6.9
Mutual Qualified Income	G&I	43/72	Low	23.6	86.1	—	3.6
Mutual Shares Corp.	G&I	50/72	Low	22.0	83.6	649.5	3.3
National Aviation & Tech.	Sec	21/35	Low	15.5	76.1	357.8	6.1
National Bond	HYC	30/39	High	5.4	49.9	143.5	14.4
National Federal Sec. Trust	USG	—	—	6.3	—	—	10.9
National Growth	Gro	101/118	Average	11.5	64.6	198.9	1.7
National Industries	G&I	68/72	Average	17.8	55.8	190.1	0.9
National Real Estate Stock	Sec	—	—	7.7	—	—	3.0
National Sec. Tax-Exempt	HGT	9/40	Average	12.2	61.8	87.3	7.2
National Stock	G&I	39/72	Average	13.5	90.1	308.3	4.0
National Telecomm. & Tech.	Sec	25/35	Average	17.1	48.5	—	0.8
National Total Income	EqI	8/46	High	16.6	94.2	366.9	5.3
National Total Return	EqI	13/46	Average	15.6	86.3	391.9	4.7
Nationwide Bond	HGC	27/36	Average	7.5	55.8	—	8.8
Nationwide Fund	G&I	11/72	Average	22.8	107.2	267.8	2.3
Nationwide Growth	Gro	11/118	Average	21.0	114.7	488.8	2.8
Neuberger & Berman Energy	Sec	23/35	Low	27.3	64.6	331.8	3.9
Neuberger & Berman Guardian	G&I	34/72	Average	21.4	91.2	462.7	3.1
Neuberger & Berman Liberty	HYC	17/39	High	14.5	59.2	157.6	7.8
Neuberger & Berman Manhattan	Max	8/66	Average	21.9	116.8	530.4	0.8
Neuberger & Berman Partners	Gro	40/118	Low	16.9	95.2	640.7	2.1
Neuwirth Fund	Gro	27/118	High	9.7	102.4	362.5	0.0
New Economy	Gro	18/118	Average	19.7	106.9	—	1.6
New England Bond Income	EqI	41/46	Low	10.1	55.6	132.2	7.9
New England Equity Income	G&I	37/72	Average	16.5	90.4	383.5	2.5
New England Growth	Gro	6/118	High	33.8	122.1	935.8	0.4
New England Retirement Equity*	G&I	2/72	High	27.5	117.4	525.5	0.9
New England Tax-Exempt Income	HGT	8/40	High	10.9	62.9	—	6.6
New Perspective	Glo	3/11	Average	34.3	99.2	549.0	1.8

*Open to IRA investors only.

Percent Maximum Initial Sales Charge	Percent Maximum Deferred Sales Charge	Expenses per $100	Minimum Initial Investment	IRA Minimum Initial Investment/Annual Fee	Assets as of Feb. 27, 1987 (in millions)	Phone Switch	Toll-free (800) +	In State / Telephone
8	None	$ .61	$1,000	—/—	$ 287.7	Yes	228-9596	800-642-8112 (Neb.)
None	None	.68	1,000	1,000/10	679.4	No	553-3014	212-908-4047 (N.Y.)
None	None	.70	1,000	1,000/10	1,708.2	No	553-3014	212-908-4047 (N.Y.)
4¾	None	1.23	1,000	1,000/10	92.9	Yes	654-0001	—
7¼	None	.94	250	100/5	713.1	Yes	223-7757	212-661-3000 (N.Y.)
6¾	None	.84	500	100/5	1,450.1	Yes	223-7757	212-661-3000 (N.Y.)
7¼	None	.91	250	100/5	74.6	Yes	223-7757	212-661-3000 (N.Y.)
None	None	1.68	250	—/—	32.6	No	367-7814	303-220-8500 (Colo.)
7¾	None	1.50	500	100/5	15.8	Yes	223-7757	212-661-3000 (N.Y.)
5¼	None	.79	1,000	—/—	90.8	Yes	223-7757	212-661-3000 (N.Y.)
7¼	None	.85	250	100/5	282.0	Yes	223-7757	212-661-3000 (N.Y.)
4¾	None	1.75	1,000	1,000/10	64.3	Yes	654-0001	—
7¼	None	.90	250	100/5	125.9	Yes	223-7757	212-661-3000 (N.Y.)
7¼	None	.88	250	100/5	313.5	Yes	223-7757	212-661-3000 (N.Y.)
7½	None	.68	250	250/10	30.1	No	848-0920	800-282-1440 (Ohio)
7½	None	.62	250	250/10	431.1	No	848-0920	800-282-1440 (Ohio)
7½	None	.65	250	250/10	212.2	No	848-0920	800-282-1440 (Ohio)
None	None	.88	500	250/9	436.8	Yes	367-0770	—
None	None	.73	500	250/9	597.6	Yes	367-0770	—
None	None	2.00	500	250/9	12.3	Yes	367-0770	—
None	None	1.10	500	250/9	422.9	Yes	367-0770	—
None	None	.89	500	250/9	681.5	Yes	367-0770	—
None	None	1.78	1,000	250/10	31.7	No	225-8011	—
8½	None	.66	1,000	250/10	909.4	Yes	421-9900	213-486-9651 (Calif.)
6½	None	1.02	250	25/25	57.2	Yes	343-7104	
6½	None	1.19	250	25/25	40.9	Yes	343-7104	—
6½	None	.84	250	25/25	422.5	Yes	343-7104	—
6½	None	.90	25	25/25	134.3	Yes	343-7104	—
4½	None	.85	250	—/—	129.8	Yes	343-7104	—
8½	None	.66	250	250/10	1,013.1	Yes	421-9900	213-486-9651 (Calif.)

Alphabetical Guide to Mutual Funds	Type	3 Yr. Performance Rank within Type/No. in Category		Percent Gain (or Loss) to April 1, 1987			Percent Current Yield
			Volatility (within Type)	One Year	Three Years	Ten Years	
Standard & Poor's 500-Stock Index				26.2	106.7	380.0	
Newton Growth	Gro	88/118	Average	21.6	76.0	473.7	1.3
Newton Income	HGC	35/36	Low	4.9	37.2	116.3	8.4
New York Venture	Gro	13/118	Average	19.7	113.9	733.7	0.9
Nicholas Fund	Gro	47/118	Low	16.8	92.7	851.2	2.2
Nicholas Income	EqI	39/46	Low	11.4	57.1	132.7	9.1
Nicholas II	SCG	2/25	Average	22.4	116.5	—	2.1
Noddings-Calamos Conv. Income	EqI	—	—	12.4	—	—	4.4
Nomura Pacific Basin	Intl	—	—	57.2	—	—	1.2
North Star Apollo	Max	61/66	Low	14.5	38.9	—	1.5
North Star Bond	HGC	22/36	Average	7.5	58.1	—	8.6
North Star Regional	Gro	21/118	Average	25.7	105.9	—	1.9
North Star Reserve	USG	—	—	5.7	—	—	4.6
North Star Stock	Max	34/66	Low	23.7	82.0	380.1	1.7
Northeast Investors Growth	Gro	5/118	High	26.6	125.2	—	0.4
Northeast Investors Trust	EqI	21/46	Low	16.4	76.7	199.8	10.4
Nova Fund	Sec	20/35	Average	35.9	79.5	—	0.0
Nuveen Municipal Bond	HGT	23/40	Average	10.7	57.2	102.0	6.7
Omega Fund	Max	14/66	Average	20.3	105.3	287.6	1.3
Oppenheimer Directors	Max	60/66	Low	12.3	45.9	—	2.1
Oppenheimer Equity Income	EqI	12/46	Average	19.3	87.3	434.2	4.8
Oppenheimer Fund	Gro	96/118	Average	9.1	67.2	245.7	0.4
Oppenheimer Global	Glo	4/11	High	35.9	99.1	646.6	0.3
Oppenheimer Gold & Special Min.	Gold	4/11	Low	76.5	28.5	—	1.1
Oppenheimer High Yield	HYC	35/39	Low	12.7	44.6	—	12.5
Oppenheimer Premium Income	OpInc	6/10	High	20.0	50.4	—	3.5
Oppenheimer Regency*	Max	55/66	Average	18.1	61.1	—	1.4
Oppenheimer Special	Gro	112/118	Low	9.7	36.1	497.6	3.5
Oppenheimer Target	Max	53/66	Average	5.5	63.0	—	0.5
Oppenheimer Tax-Free Bond	HGT	12/40	Average	10.8	60.8	107.7	6.6
Oppenheimer Time	Max	15/66	Average	26.3	105.0	727.3	1.1

*Open to IRA investors only.

Percent Maximum Initial Sales Charge									
Percent Maximum Deferred Sales Charge									
	Expenses per $100								
		Minimum Initial Investment							
			IRA Minimum Initial Investment/Annual Fee						
				Assets as of Feb. 27, 1987 (in millions)					
					Phone Switch				
						Toll-free (800) +		Telephone
							In State	
None	None	$1.23	$1,000	$500/$10	$ 42.5	Yes	247-7039	800-242-7229 (Wis.)
None	None	1.51	1,000	500/10	14.0	Yes	247-7039	800-242-7229 (Wis.)
8½	None	.99	1,000	250/10	253.8	Yes	545-2098	505-983-4335 (N.M.)
None†	None	.86	500	500/10	1,264.6	No	—	414-272-6133
None	None	.96	500	500/10	71.2	No	—	414-272-6133
None†	None	.79	1,000	1,000/10	349.4	No	—	414-272-6133
None	None	1.10	5,000	2,000/10	20.3	Yes	251-2411	800-821-6458 (Ill.)
None	None	1.40	10,000	***/None	72.9	No	833-0018	—
None	None	1.00	2,500	100/None	22.4	Yes	—	612-371-2884
None	None	.70	1,000	100/None	45.0	Yes	—	612-371-2884
None	None	.80	2,500	100/None	104.7	Yes	—	612-371-2884
None	None	.80	2,500	100/None	31.6	Yes	—	612-371-2884
None	None	.70	1,000	100/None	82.1	Yes	—	612-371-2884
None	None	1.87	1,000	100/5	27.8	Yes	225-6704	617-523-3588 (Mass.)
None	None	.72	1,000	100/5	365.5	Yes	225-6704	617-523-3588 (Mass.)
8	None	1.50	2,000	500/10	36.6	No	572-0006	617-439-9683 (Mass.)
4	None	.71	1,000	—/—	770.3	Yes	621-7210	312-917-7844 (Ill.)
5½	None	1.47	1,000	—/—	38.7	No	237-5047	617-357-8480
8½	None	1.05	1,000	250/7.50	266.9	Yes	525-7048	800-356-3556 (Colo.)
8½	None	1.03	1,000	250/7.50	595.3	Yes	525-7048	800-356-3556 (Colo.)
8½	None	1.01	1,000	250/7.50	287.0	Yes	525-7048	800-356-3556 (Colo.)
8½	None	1.60	1,000	250/7.50	456.9	Yes	525-7048	800-356-3556 (Colo.)
8½	None	1.61	1,000	250/7.50	47.3	Yes	525-7048	800-356-3556 (Colo.)
6¾	None	.89	1,000	250/7.50	729.7	Yes	525-7048	800-356-3556 (Colo.)
8½	None	.89	1,000	250/7.50	406.1	Yes	525-7048	800-356-3556 (Colo.)
8½†	None	1.11	1,000	250/7.50	177.6	Yes	525-7048	800-356-3556 (Colo.)
8½	None	.95	1,000	250/7.50	733.2	Yes	525-7048	800-356-3556 (Colo.)
8½	None	1.16	5,000	5,000/None	134.4	Yes	525-7048	800-356-3556 (Colo.)
4¾	None	.78	1,000	—/—	141.9	Yes	525-7048	800-356-3556 (Colo.)
8½	None	.96	1,000	250/7.50	339.2	Yes	525-7048	800-356-3556 (Colo.)

†Fund may impose an exit fee. ***Minimum investment $10,000; geared to IRA rollovers only.

Alphabetical Guide to Mutual Funds	Type	3 Yr. Performance Rank within Type/No. in Category		Percent Gain (or Loss) to April 1, 1987			Percent Current Yield
		Volatility (within Type)		One Year	Three Years	Ten Years	
Standard & Poor's 500-Stock Index				26.2	106.7	380.0	
Over-the-Counter Securities	SCG	11/25	Average	8.0	74.6	670.2	1.1
PBHG Growth	Max	—	—	46.6	—	—	0.4
Pacific Horizon Aggressive Growth	Max	1/66	High	38.0	208.5	—	0.1
Pacific Horizon High Yield	HYC	1/39	Average	12.8	82.2	—	10.7
Paine Webber America	G&I	54/72	Average	14.2	79.6	—	4.3
Paine Webber Atlas	Glo	2/11	High	35.8	151.4	—	5.0
Paine Webber Fixed Inc.—GNMA	MBS	—	—	9.2	—	—	11.2
Paine Webber High Yield	HYC	—	—	12.4	—	—	13.3
Paine Webber Inv. Grade Bond	HGC	—	—	8.6	—	—	11.1
Paine Webber Olympus	Gro	—	—	15.6	—	—	1.4
Paine Webber Tax-Ex. Inc.—Nat. Port.	HGT	—	—	10.9	—	—	6.9
Pax World	Bal	16/17	Average	12.1	67.1	258.0	3.1
Penn Square Mutual	G&I	57/72	Average	18.7	74.0	328.3	3.5
Pennsylvania Mutual**	SCG	13/25	Low	15.1	72.5	664.4	1.7
Permanent Portfolio	Sec	30/35	Low	14.6	23.8	—	0.0
Philadelphia Fund	G&I	64/72	Average	13.5	61.6	345.9	2.2
Phoenix Balanced Series	Bal	5/17	Average	19.3	102.6	406.3	4.1
Phoenix Convertible	EqI	26/46	Average	20.4	73.7	404.6	4.2
Phoenix Growth Series	Gro	15/118	Average	22.0	110.7	687.2	1.6
Phoenix High Quality Bond	HGC	28/36	Average	7.8	55.8	—	6.7
Phoenix High Yield Series	HYC	14/39	Average	14.6	60.0	—	12.0
Phoenix Stock Series	Max	17/66	Average	22.0	104.4	893.1	1.5
Pilgrim GNMA	MBS	—	—	7.1	—	—	9.8
Pilgrim High Yield	HYC	29/39	Average	11.4	50.5	177.9	11.8
Pilgrim MagnaCap	Gro	14/118	Average	17.0	113.0	432.5	2.3
Pilot Fund	Max	37/66	Average	26.4	79.0	367.3	0.8
Pine Street	G&I	22/72	Average	17.2	97.9	326.2	2.6
Pioneer Bond	HGC	31/36	Average	7.6	50.1	—	9.3
Pioneer Fund	G&I	60/72	Average	19.2	70.4	346.2	2.4
Pioneer Three	G&I	62/72	Average	14.6	68.3	—	1.9

** Fund closed to new investors.

Percent Maximum Initial Sales Charge	Percent Maximum Deferred Sales Charge	Expenses per $100	Minimum Initial Investment	IRA Minimum Initial Investment/Annual Fee	Assets as of Feb. 27, 1987 (in millions)	Phone Switch	Toll-free (800) +	In State / Telephone
8	None	$ .85	$ 500	$500/$5	$ 308.5	No	523-2578	215-643-2510 (Pa.)
7½	None	1.52	200	200/10	28.9	Yes	262-6686	—
4½	None	1.50	1,000	750/5	168.8	Yes	645-3515	—
4½	None	.29	1,000	750/5	32.9	Yes	645-3515	—
8½	None	1.15	1,000	1,000/10	106.8	No	544-9300	—
8½	None	1.52	1,000	1,000/10	249.9	No	544-9300	—
4¼	None	.66	1,000	1,000/10	3,264.8	No	544-9300	—
4¼	None	.69	1,000	1,000/10	847.7	No	544-9300	—
4¼	None	.68	1,000	1,000/10	672.3	No	544-9300	—
8½	None	1.23	1,000	1,000/10	130.8	No	544-9300	—
4¼	None	.72	1,000	1,000/10	396.8	No	544-9300	—
None	None	1.20	250	250/10	62.6	No	—	603-431-8022
None	None	.80	500	250/12	226.2	No	523-8440	800-222-7506 (Pa.)
None†	None	.98	2,000	250/10	369.7	No	221-4268	212-355-7311 (N.Y.)
None	None	1.17	1,000	1,000/8	75.3	No	531-5142	512-453-7558 (Texas)
8½	None	.83	None	None/5	115.6	Yes	221-5588	212-668-8111 (N.Y.)
8½	None	.75	1,000	100/10	243.9	Yes	243-1574	203-278-8050 (Conn.)
8½	None	.80	1,000	100/10	130.2	Yes	243-1574	203-278-8050 (Conn.)
8½	None	.78	1,000	100/10	388.3	Yes	243-1574	203-278-8050 (Conn.)
None	None	1.02	1,000	100/10	23.7	Yes	243-1574	203-278-8050 (Conn.)
7	None	.79	1,000	100/10	142.0	Yes	243-1574	203-278-8050 (Conn.)
8½	None	.85	1,000	100/10	109.4	Yes	243-1574	203-278-8050 (Conn.)
1½	None	1.00	1,000	500/10	346.6	Yes	334-3444	800-341-1080 (Calif.)
1½	None	1.50	1,000	500/10	36.2	Yes	334-3444	800-341-1080 (Calif.)
4¾	None	1.40	1,000	100/10	235.3	Yes	334-3444	800-341-1080 (Calif.)
4¾	None	1.22	100	100/10	80.1	Yes	—	713-751-2400
None	None	1.22	1,000	1,000/5	72.1	No	225-8011	—
4½	None	1.00	1,000	250/10	48.0	No	225-6292	617-742-7825 (Mass.)
8½	None	.68	50	250/10	1,494.0	No	225-6292	617-742-7825 (Mass.)
8½	None	.71	1,000	250/10	694.0	No	225-6292	617-742-7825 (Mass.)

†Fund may impose an exit fee.

Alphabetical Guide to Mutual Funds	Type	3 Yr. Performance Rank within Type/No. in Category		Percent Gain (or Loss) to April 1, 1987			Percent Current Yield
		Volatility (within Type)		One Year	Three Years	Ten Years	
Standard & Poor's 500-Stock Index				26.2	106.7	380.0	
Pioneer II	G&I	56/72	Average	17.9	75.3	566.8	2.4
Principal Pres. Gov. Plus	USG	—	—	6.2	—	—	7.6
Principal Pres. S&P 100	G&I	—	—	25.0	—	—	2.8
Principal Pres. Tax-Exempt	HYT	—	—	8.8	—	—	6.8
Princor Capital Accum.	Max	16/66	Average	23.2	104.7	412.4	1.8
Princor Gov. Sec.	USG	—	—	10.8	—	—	9.5
Princor Growth	Gro	49/118	High	25.1	91.6	396.8	1.1
Provident Fund for Income	EqI	33/46	Average	17.5	63.5	302.0	5.5
Pru-Bache Equity	Gro	25/118	Average	20.7	103.8	—	0.9
Pru-Bache Global	Glo	—	—	43.7	—	—	0.1
Pru-Bache GNMA	MBS	6/8	Low	8.9	48.9	—	7.5
Pru-Bache Gov.—Intermed. Term	USG	7/13	Low	8.2	51.8	—	8.6
Pru-Bache Gov. Plus	MBS	—	—	7.1	—	—	6.5
Pru-Bache Growth Opportunity	Gro	77/118	Average	17.4	82.4	—	0.0
Pru-Bache High Yield	HYC	12/39	Low	14.8	60.8	—	11.0
Pru-Bache High Yield Muni	HYT	3/11	Average	11.2	59.9	—	6.8
Pru-Bache IncomeVertible Plus	Sec	—	—	15.4	—	—	5.2
Pru-Bache Option Growth	OpInc	1/10	High	18.4	82.8	—	1.6
Pru-Bache Research	Gro	29/118	High	26.9	101.9	—	0.6
Pru-Bache Utility	Sec	2/35	Average	17.2	154.2	—	5.3
Putnam Convertible Inc. & Gro.	EqI	16/46	Average	16.3	82.5	416.4	5.4
Putnam Energy Resources	Sec	33/35	Low	27.7	20.0	—	2.8
Putnam Fund for Gro. & Inc.	G&I	26/72	Average	24.2	96.5	464.3	4.2
Putnam (George) Fund of Boston	Bal	12/17	Average	20.7	83.1	308.3	4.9
Putnam Health Sciences Trust	Sec	5/35	Average	26.6	118.3	—	0.9
Putnam High Inc. Gov.	USG	—	—	8.2	—	—	8.4
Putnam High Yield I**	HYC	20/39	Average	14.8	56.1	—	12.7
Putnam Income	HGC	18/36	Average	10.7	59.7	174.8	10.6
Putnam Information Sciences	Sec	22/35	Average	35.3	72.3	—	0.2
Putnam Intl. Equities	Glo	1/11	Average	29.3	153.6	646.7	0.5

** Fund closed to new investors.

Percent Maximum Initial Sales Charge	Percent Maximum Deferred Sales Charge	Expenses per $100	Minimum Initial Investment	IRA Minimum Initial Investment/Annual Fee	Assets as of Feb. 27, 1987 (in millions)	Phone Switch	Toll-free (800) + In State	Telephone
8½	None	$ .72	$ 50	$250/$10	$3,621.0	No	225-6292	617-742-7825 (Mass.)
4½	None	.70	1,000	1,000/10	34.2	Yes	826-4600	—
4½	None	.85	1,000	1,000/10	12.4	Yes	826-4600	—
4½	None	1.10	1,000	—/—	141.2	Yes	826-4600	—
8½	None	.93	300	250/15	80.7	No	—	515-247-5711
5	None	.60	1,000	250/15	64.8	No	—	515-247-5711
8½	None	.98	300	250/15	33.5	No	—	515-247-5711
7¼	None	.76	500	50/10	113.0	No	847-5636	—
None	5	1.52	1,000	None/10	414.8	Yes	872-7787	212-214-1234 (N.Y.)
None	5	2.01	1,000	None/10	567.2	Yes	872-7787	212-214-1234 (N.Y.)
None	5	1.39	1,000	None/10	290.7	Yes	872-7787	212-214-1234 (N.Y.)
None	None	.75	1,000	None/10	1,200.0	Yes	872-7787	212-214-1234 (N.Y.)
None	5	1.54	1,000	None/10	4,100.0	Yes	872-7787	212-214-1234 (N.Y.)
None	5	1.40	1,000	None/10	155.1	Yes	872-7787	212-214-1234 (N.Y.)
None	5	1.19	1,000	None/10	2,100.0	Yes	872-7787	212-214-1234 (N.Y.)
None	5	.90	1,000	None/10	1,200.0	Yes	872-7787	212-214-1234 (N.Y.)
None	5	1.99	1,000	None/10	392.2	Yes	872-7787	212-214-1234 (N.Y.)
None	5	1.53	1,000	None/10	79.2	Yes	872-7787	212-214-1234 (N.Y.)
None	5	1.73	1,000	None/10	271.1	Yes	872-7787	212-214-1234 (N.Y.)
None	5	1.42	1,000	None/10	1,800.0	Yes	872-7787	212-214-1234 (N.Y.)
8½	None	.83	500	250/5	1,106.0	Yes	225-1581	617-292-1000 (Mass.)
8½	None	1.77	500	250/5	54.6	Yes	225-1581	617-292-1000 (Mass.)
8½	None	.53	500	250/5	1,481.6	Yes	225-1581	617-292-1000 (Mass.)
8½	None	.58	500	250/5	373.4	Yes	225-1581	617-292-1000 (Mass.)
8½	None	1.00	500	250/5	300.2	Yes	225-1581	617-292-1000 (Mass.)
6¾	None	.82	500	250/5	9,839.5	Yes	225-1581	617-292-1000 (Mass.)
6¾	None	.57	500	250/5	2,493.9	Yes	225-1581	617-292-1000 (Mass.)
6¾	None	.73	500	250/5	271.9	Yes	225-1581	617-292-1000 (Mass.)
8½	None	1.14	500	250/5	147.1	Yes	225-1581	617-292-1000 (Mass.)
8½	None	.12	500	250/5	425.8	Yes	225-1581	617-292-1000 (Mass.)

Alphabetical Guide to Mutual Funds	Type	3 Yr. Performance Rank within Type/No. in Category					
		Volatility (within Type)					
		Percent Gain (or Loss) to April 1, 1987					
				One Year	Three Years	Ten Years	Percent Current Yield
Standard & Poor's 500-Stock Index				26.2	106.7	380.0	
Putnam Investors	Gro	33/118	Average	22.1	100.5	423.2	1.4
Putnam Option Income	OpInc	2/10	Average	18.4	63.4	—	1.1
Putnam Option Income II	OpInc	—	—	11.9	—	—	3.5
Putnam OTC Emerging Growth	SCG	1/25	High	27.5	129.7	—	0.0
Putnam Tax-Exempt Income	HGT	25/40	High	11.0	56.9	149.0	6.8
Putnam U.S. Gov. Guar. Sec.	MBS	7/8	Average	10.3	46.3	—	10.0
Putnam Vista Basic Value	Max	35/66	Average	25.4	81.7	597.8	3.1
Putnam Voyager	Max	5/66	Average	27.6	124.8	613.3	0.6
Quasar Associates**	Gro	7/118	High	19.0	119.3	1,161.1	0.0
Quest for Value	Max	38/66	Low	12.7	76.3	—	0.7
Reich & Tang Equity	Gro	—	—	15.7	—	—	2.0
Rochester Tax Managed	Gro	114/118	Low	3.2	25.8	228.6	0.0
Royce Value	SCG	16/25	Low	13.0	61.9	—	0.5
Safeco Equity	G&I	20/72	Average	21.6	99.5	372.7	2.1
Safeco Growth	Gro	108/118	Low	12.0	50.7	424.4	1.8
Safeco Income	EqI	4/46	Average	19.7	101.5	415.6	4.3
Safeco Municipal	HGT	15/40	Average	10.8	60.1	—	7.0
Scudder Capital Growth	Gro	35/118	Average	19.1	99.1	565.5	1.2
Scudder Development	SCG	20/25	Average	15.6	57.7	564.1	0.0
Scudder Gov. Mortgage Sec.	MBS	—	—	9.8	—	—	8.7
Scudder Growth & Income	G&I	36/72	Average	17.4	90.4	346.8	3.8
Scudder Income	EqI	36/46	Low	9.7	60.2	162.9	8.9
Scudder International	Intl	5/13	Average	40.5	125.1	501.3	1.1
Scudder Managed Muni Bond	HGT	31/40	Low	14.4	54.4	99.5	6.6
Scudder Tax-Free Target 1987**	ITT	7/15	Average	6.1	36.1	—	5.2
Scudder Tax-Free Target 1990	ITT	1/15	High	7.8	49.3	—	5.6
Scudder Tax-Free Target 1993	ITT	5/15	Average	9.8	41.8	—	5.9
Scudder Tax-Free Target 1996	ITT	—	—	9.5	—	—	5.8
Security Action	Max	39/66	Low	16.8	75.3	—	2.8
Security Equity	Gro	66/118	Low	18.0	85.5	415.3	2.8

** Fund closed to new investors.

Percent Maximum Initial Sales Charge	Percent Maximum Deferred Sales Charge	Expenses per $100	Minimum Initial Investment	IRA Minimum Initial Investment/Annual Fee	Assets as of Feb. 27, 1987 (in millions)	Phone Switch	Toll-free (800) + In State	Telephone
8½	None	$ .49	$ 500	$250/$5	$1,099.8	Yes	225-1581	617-292-1000 (Mass.)
8½	None	.73	500	250/5	1,210.7	Yes	225-1581	617-292-1000 (Mass.)
8½	None	.82	500	250/5	1,656.4	Yes	225-1581	617-292-1000 (Mass.)
6¾	None	1.46	500	250/5	106.3	Yes	225-1581	617-292-1000 (Mass.)
4¾	None	.53	500	—/—	965.3	Yes	225-1581	617-292-1000 (Mass.)
4¾	None	.56	500	250/5	1,176.6	Yes	225-1581	617-292-1000 (Mass.)
8½	None	1.02	500	250/5	253.8	Yes	225-1581	617-292-1000 (Mass.)
8½	None	.89	500	250/5	513.1	Yes	225-1581	617-292-1000 (Mass.)
None	None	1.18	1,000	1,000/10	162.0	No	221-5672	—
None	None	.18	2,000	250/7.50	106.4	No	862-7778	212-667-7587 (N.Y.)
None	None	1.22	5,000	250/7.50	132.8	Yes	221-3079	212-370-1248 (N.Y.)
8½	None	1.60	2,000	—/—	27.5	Yes	—	716-442-5500
None	1	1.98	2,000	250/10	165.6	No	221-4268	212-355-7311 (N.Y.)
None	None	.88	1,000	250/5	56.8	Yes	426-6730	800-562-6810 (Wash.)
None	None	.85	1,000	250/5	80.2	Yes	426-6730	800-562-6810 (Wash.)
None	None	.95	1,000	250/5	221.7	Yes	426-6730	800-562-6810 (Wash.)
None	None	.63	2,500	—/—	219.3	Yes	426-6730	800-562-6810 (Wash.)
None	None	.84	1,000	1,000/None	537.0	Yes	225-2470	—
None	None	1.25	1,000	1,000/None	396.8	Yes	225-2470	—
None	None	1.02	1,000	1,000/None	283.6	Yes	225-2470	—
None	None	.84	1,000	1,000/None	452.1	Yes	225-2470	—
None	None	.91	1,000	1,000/None	264.2	Yes	225-2470	—
None	None	.99	1,000	1,000/None	760.5	Yes	225-2470	—
None	None	.58	1,000	1,000/None	719.7	Yes	225-2470	—
None	None	.98	1,000	—/—	31.8	Yes	225-2470	—
None	None	.85	1,000	—/—	122.5	Yes	225-2470	—
None	None	.86	1,000	—/—	134.9	Yes	225-2470	—
None	None	1.00	1,000	—/—	24.3	Yes	225-2470	—
8½†	None	.90	50†††	50/10	103.5	No	255-2461	—
8½	None	.71	100	100/10	276.6	No	255-2461	—

†Fund may impose an exit fee. †††Available on contractual plan only.

Alphabetical Guide to Mutual Funds	Type	3 Yr. Performance Rank within Type/No. in Category					
		Volatility (within Type)					
			Percent Gain (or Loss) to April 1, 1987				
				One Year	Three Years	Ten Years	Percent Current Yield
Standard & Poor's 500-Stock Index				26.2	106.7	380.0	
Security Income	HGC	29/36	Average	7.1	54.6	152.7	11.4
Security Investment	G&I	69/72	Low	15.6	50.7	265.0	5.2
Security Tax-Exempt	HGT	39/40	Low	11.1	45.1	—	7.5
Security Ultra	Max	46/66	Low	10.3	68.9	586.3	3.9
Selected American Shares	G&I	6/72	Average	21.2	111.1	345.0	2.7
Selected Special Shares	Gro	99/118	Low	23.1	65.1	258.0	2.1
Seligman Capital	Max	28/66	Average	17.7	92.1	619.2	0.0
Seligman Common Stock	G&I	5/72	High	22.7	112.7	425.7	3.0
Seligman Commun. & Info.	Sec	6/35	Average	32.2	115.6	—	0.0
Seligman Growth	Gro	45/118	High	20.2	93.7	342.1	1.4
Seligman Hi. Inc.—Hi. Yield Bond	HYC	—	—	12.6	—	—	11.0
Seligman Hi. Inc.—Sec. Mort. Inc.	MBS	—	—	7.3	—	—	8.0
Seligman Hi. Inc.—U.S. Gov. Guar.	USG	—	—	2.1	—	—	7.3
Seligman Income	EqI	22/46	Average	9.9	76.3	260.2	7.8
Seligman Tax-Exempt—National	HGT	7/40	Average	13.4	64.8	—	7.1
Sentinel Balanced	Bal	7/17	Average	16.0	95.1	303.3	5.5
Sentinel Bond	HGC	21/36	Low	10.0	58.2	157.3	9.0
Sentinel Common Stock	G&I	3/72	High	24.7	114.8	442.4	3.3
Sentinel Growth	Gro	30/118	Average	23.7	101.4	507.3	1.5
Sentry Fund	Gro	28/118	Average	19.9	102.3	430.2	2.0
Sequoia Fund**	Gro	34/118	Low	18.7	99.2	651.1	3.4
Shearson Aggressive Growth	Max	6/66	High	40.9	118.0	—	0.0
Shearson Appreciation	Gro	17/118	Average	24.1	106.9	660.4	1.3
Shearson Fundamental Value	Gro	97/118	Low	20.2	66.4	—	4.0
Shearson Global Opp.	Glo	—	—	22.5	—	—	0.4
Shearson High Yield	HYC	27/39	Low	11.7	51.9	—	11.1
Shearson Managed Governments	MBS	—	—	8.8	—	—	8.5
Shearson Managed Muni	HGT	26/40	Average	11.2	56.5	—	7.3
Sigma Capital Shares	Max	13/66	Average	16.7	105.6	566.2	1.5
Sigma Income Shares	HGC	3/36	Average	11.2	72.0	164.5	8.1

** Fund closed to new investors.

Percent Maximum Initial Sales Charge	Percent Maximum Deferred Sales Charge	Expenses per $100	Minimum Initial Investment	IRA Minimum Initial Investment/Annual Fee	Assets as of Feb. 27, 1987 (in millions)	Phone Switch	Toll-free (800) + In State	Telephone
4¾	None	$1.01	$1,000	$100/$10	$ 49.3	No	255-2461	—
8½	None	.75	100	100/10	111.2	No	255-2461	—
4¾	None	1.00	1,000	—/—	17.2	No	255-2461	—
8½	None	.78	100	100/10	114.1	No	255-2461	—
None	None	.85	1,000	1,000/10	210.7	Yes	621-7321	800-572-4437 (Ill.)
None	None	1.08	1,000	1,000/10	39.7	Yes	621-7321	800-572-4437 (Ill.)
4¾	None	.78	None	None/10	248.0	No	221-7844	800-522-6869 (N.Y.)
4¾	None	.55	None	None/10	646.0	No	221-7844	800-522-6869 (N.Y.)
4¾	None	1.68	None	None/10	51.0	No	221-7844	800-522-6869 (N.Y.)
4¾	None	.57	None	None/10	711.0	No	221-7844	800-522-6869 (N.Y.)
4¾	None	1.08	None	None/10	82.0	No	221-7844	800-522-6869 (N.Y.)
4¾	None	1.06	None	None/10	56.0	No	221-7844	800-522-6869 (N.Y.)
4¾	None	1.10	None	None/10	180.0	No	221-7844	800-522-6869 (N.Y.)
4¾	None	.73	None	None/10	175.0	No	221-7844	800-522-6869 (N.Y.)
4¾	None	.76	None	—/—	149.0	No	221-7844	800-522-6869 (N.Y.)
8½	None	.68	250	250/10	55.6	Yes	233-4332	802-229-3900 (Vt.)
8½	None	.68	2,500	250/10	25.2	Yes	233-4332	802-229-3900 (Vt.)
8½	None	.64	250	250/10	571.8	Yes	233-4332	802-229-3900 (Vt.)
8½	None	.77	250	250/10	64.8	Yes	233-4332	802-229-3900 (Vt.)
8	None	.72	200	200/5	48.3	No	826-0266	800-472-0280 (Wis.)
None	None	1.00	—	—/—	783.0	No	—	212-245-4500
5	None	1.10	500	250/5	131.3	Yes	—	212-321-7155
5	None	.95	500	250/5	431.1	Yes	—	212-321-7155
5	None	1.00	500	250/5	108.4	Yes	—	212-321-7155
5	None	1.50	500	250/5	277.0	Yes	—	212-321-7155
5	None	.80	500	250/5	573.9	Yes	—	212-321-7155
5	None	.72	500	250/5	1,615.4	Yes	—	212-321-7155
5	None	.66	500	250/5	783.0	Yes	—	212-321-7155
8½	None	1.01	None	None/10	101.8	Yes	441-9490	302-652-3091 (Del.)
8½	None	.82	None	None/10	46.7	Yes	441-9490	302-652-3091 (Del.)

Alphabetical Guide to Mutual Funds	Type	3 Yr. Performance Rank within Type/No. in Category					
		Volatility (within Type)					
			Percent Gain (or Loss) to April 1, 1987				
				One Year	Three Years	Ten Years	Percent Current Yield
Standard & Poor's 500-Stock Index				26.2	106.7	380.0	
Sigma Investment Shares	G&I	12/72	Average	24.0	107.1	379.7	2.5
Sigma Special	Gro	36/118	Average	26.5	98.0	442.0	1.1
Sigma Tax-Free Bond	HGT	27/40	Average	8.8	55.7	—	6.5
Sigma Trust Shares	Bal	13/17	Low	16.3	83.0	270.4	5.0
Sigma Venture Shares	SCG	14/25	Average	8.2	70.0	655.5	0.4
Sigma World	Intl	—	—	39.3	—	—	0.0
Smith Barney Equity	Gro	60/118	Average	21.0	88.1	412.3	2.3
Smith Barney Inc. & Growth	G&I	27/72	Low	22.0	95.9	445.3	4.9
Smith Barney U.S. Gov. Sec.—Quar.	MBS	—	—	10.8	—	—	10.6
SoGen International	Gro	20/118	Average	31.3	106.1	601.5	2.8
Sovereign Investors	G&I	10/72	Average	17.3	108.1	365.5	3.9
Steadman Associated	EqI	46/46	High	0.6	26.7	96.9	1.0
Stein Roe & Farnham Cap. Opp.	Gro	58/118	High	37.6	88.8	564.5	0.1
Stein Roe & Farnham Stock	Gro	57/118	Average	27.6	89.3	359.4	1.3
Stein Roe Discovery	SCG	8/25	High	8.5	83.2	—	0.3
Stein Roe High-Yield Muni	HYT	4/11	Average	11.8	58.9	—	7.2
Stein Roe Managed Bond	HGC	12/36	Average	8.1	63.3	—	8.0
Stein Roe Managed Muni	HGT	1/40	High	11.6	69.2	125.5	6.7
Stein Roe Special	Max	22/66	Average	18.3	99.7	683.4	1.6
Stein Roe Total Return	Bal	14/17	Low	15.5	81.2	235.3	5.7
Stein Roe Universe	Max	40/66	Average	19.3	73.9	—	0.9
Strategic Investments	Gold	11/11	Average	79.5	(13.7)	757.7	4.7
Strategic Silver	Gold	—	—	42.3	—	—	0.0
Stratton Growth	G&I	55/72	High	11.7	76.1	332.3	1.2
Stratton Monthly Div. Shares	Sec	9/35	Average	8.7	105.5	242.5	7.4
Strong Income	EqI	—	—	21.0	—	—	9.6
Strong Investment	Bal	17/17	Average	8.8	64.5	—	3.8
Strong Opportunity	Max	—	—	46.2	—	—	0.2
Strong Total Return	Max	27/66	Average	18.2	93.4	—	2.5
Sunbelt Growth	Gro	94/118	Average	21.2	70.0	—	0.1

Percent Maximum Initial Sales Charge	Percent Maximum Deferred Sales Charge	Expenses per $100	Minimum Initial Investment	IRA Minimum Initial Investment/Annual Fee	Assets as of Feb. 27, 1987 (in millions)	Phone Switch	Toll-free (800) +	In State / Telephone
8½	None	$ .94	None	None/$10	$ 110.7	Yes	441-9490	302-652-3091 (Del.)
8½	None	1.26	None	None/10	18.6	Yes	441-9490	302-652-3091 (Del.)
4¾	None	1.03	None	—/—	15.3	Yes	441-9490	302-652-3091 (Del.)
8½	None	.99	None	None/10	47.2	Yes	441-9490	302-652-3091 (Del.)
8½	None	.95	None	None/10	83.2	Yes	441-9490	302-652-3091 (Del.)
8½	None	2.00	None	None/10	10.0	Yes	441-9490	302-652-3091 (Del.)
4	None	.85	2,000	1,000/2.50	82.9	No	221-8806	212-356-2631 (N.Y.)
5¾	None	.56	2,500	1,000/2.50	509.5	No	221-8806	212-356-2631 (N.Y.)
4	None	.35	2,500	1,000/2.50	524.5	No	221-8806	212-356-2631 (N.Y.)
4¼	None	1.39	1,000	1,000/10	89.1	No	334-2143	212-832-3073 (N.Y.)
5	None	.70	None	50/10	41.2	No	—	215-254-0703
None	None	2.88	500	500/10	24.8	No	424-8570	202-223-1000 (D.C.)
None	None	.95	2,500	500/10	276.6	Yes	621-0320	312-368-7826 (Ill.)
None	None	.67	2,500	500/10	285.1	Yes	621-0320	312-368-7826 (Ill.)
None	None	1.29	2,500	500/10	72.9	Yes	621-0320	312-368-7826 (Ill.)
None	None	.76	2,500	—/—	248.7	Yes	621-0320	312-368-7826 (Ill.)
None	None	.69	2,500	500/10	210.7	Yes	621-0320	312-368-7826 (Ill.)
None	None	.65	2,500	—/—	563.9	Yes	621-0320	312-368-7826 (Ill.)
None	None	.92	2,500	500/10	305.0	Yes	621-0320	312-368-7826 (Ill.)
None	None	.79	2,500	500/10	178.6	Yes	621-0320	312-368-7826 (Ill.)
None	None	1.22	2,500	500/10	104.7	Yes	621-0320	312-368-7826 (Ill.)
8½	None	1.46	500	500/10	90.2	Yes	527-5027	214-484-1326 (Texas)
8½	None	1.54	500	500/10	21.7	Yes	527-5027	214-484-1326 (Texas)
None	None	1.49	1,000	None/10	20.7	Yes	—	215-542-8025
None	None	1.24	1,000	None/10	54.1	Yes	—	215-542-8025
None	None	1.00	1,000	250/10	175.4	Yes	368-3863	—
1	None	1.10	250	250/10	377.8	Yes	368-3863	—
2	None	1.70	1,000	250/10	91.3	Yes	368-3863	—
1	None	1.10	250	250/10	652.3	Yes	368-3863	—
4¾	None	1.54	100	100/10	76.4	Yes	—	713-751-2400

Alphabetical Guide to Mutual Funds	Type	3 Yr. Performance Rank within Type/No. in Category					
		Volatility (within Type)					
			Percent Gain (or Loss) to April 1, 1987				
				One Year	Three Years	Ten Years	Percent Current Yield
Standard & Poor's 500-Stock Index				26.2	106.7	380.0	
Tax-Exempt Bond of America	HGT	30/40	Average	9.8	54.9	—	6.8
Templeton Foreign	Intl	11/13	Low	32.5	83.7	—	1.9
Templeton Global I**	Glo	7/11	Low	20.6	86.2	—	2.3
Templeton Global II	Glo	10/11	Average	9.6	67.6	—	2.2
Templeton Growth	Glo	9/11	Low	20.6	83.4	515.0	2.7
Templeton World	Glo	6/11	Average	19.6	90.4	—	2.5
Thomson McKinnon—Growth	Gro	8/118	Average	31.2	116.8	—	1.9
Thomson McKinnon—Inc.	EqI	43/46	Low	10.5	47.0	—	10.6
Thomson McKinnon—Opp.	Max	30/66	Average	18.3	90.6	—	0.0
Thomson McKinnon—Tax Exempt	HGT	—	—	10.5	—	—	5.8
Thomson McKinnon—U.S. Gov.	USG	—	—	9.1	—	—	9.8
Transatlantic Growth Fund	Intl	8/13	High	43.0	122.7	427.4	0.0
T. Rowe Price Equity Inc.	EqI	—	—	24.9	—	—	4.6
T. Rowe Price Growth & Inc.	G&I	70/72	Low	6.9	48.2	—	5.0
T. Rowe Price Growth Stock	Gro	12/118	Average	24.4	114.4	272.3	1.4
T. Rowe Price High Yield	HYC	—	—	15.2	—	—	11.3
T. Rowe Price International	Intl	4/13	Average	45.7	128.3	—	0.6
T. Rowe Price New Era	Sec	19/35	Average	31.0	82.1	466.7	1.6
T. Rowe Price New Horizons	SCG	19/25	Average	11.5	58.8	486.7	0.1
T. Rowe Price New Income	HGC	33/36	Average	7.4	48.4	169.3	8.2
T. Rowe Price Short Term Bond	HGC	36/36	Low	6.4	36.7	—	7.6
T. Rowe Price Tax-Free High Yield	HYT	—	—	13.1	—	—	7.2
T. Rowe Price Tax-Free Income	HGT	37/40	Average	11.0	50.5	112.0	6.6
T. Rowe Price Tax-Free Short-Intermed.	ITT	9/15	Average	7.5	27.9	—	5.5
Tudor Fund	Max	23/66	Average	25.6	99.2	792.4	0.0
Twentieth Century Growth	Max	10/66	High	33.4	111.3	1,232.2	0.4
Twentieth Century Select	Gro	16/118	High	23.7	108.4	1,198.2	0.9
Twentieth Century Ultra	Max	26/66	High	31.0	94.1	—	0.1
Twentieth Century U.S. Gov.	USG	12/13	Low	7.3	39.3	—	8.1
Twentieth Century Vista	Max	7/66	High	44.8	117.4	—	0.0

** Fund closed to new investors.

Percent Maximum Initial Sales Charge	Percent Maximum Deferred Sales Charge	Expenses per $100	Minimum Initial Investment	IRA Minimum Initial Investment/Annual Fee	Assets as of Feb. 27, 1987 (in millions)	Phone Switch	Toll-free (800) +	Telephone (In State)
4¾	None	$ .59	$1,000	$250/$10	$ 338.3	Yes	421-9900	213-486-9651 (Calif.)
8½	None	.90	500	500/10	222.9	No	237-0738	800-282-0106 (Fla.)
8½	None	.66	500	—/—	333.2	No	237-0738	800-282-0106 (Fla.)
8½	None	.76	500	500/10	577.4	No	237-0738	800-282-0106 (Fla.)
8½	None	.83	500	500/10	1,294.9	No	237-0738	800-282-0106 (Fla.)
8½	None	.71	500	500/10	3,905.2	No	237-0738	800-282-0106 (Fla.)
None	5	1.70	1,000	1,000/None	302.4	No	628-1237	212-482-5894 (N.Y.)
None	5	1.60	1,000	1,000/None	412.9	No	628-1237	212-482-5894 (N.Y.)
None	5	1.80	1,000	1,000/None	64.5	No	628-1237	212-482-5894 (N.Y.)
None	5	1.80	1,000	—/—	72.1	No	628-1237	212-482-5894 (N.Y.)
None	5	1.70	1,000	1,000/None	823.7	No	628-1237	212-482-5894 (N.Y.)
None	None	1.40	1,000	500/10	100.7	Yes	237-4218	212-687-2515 (N.Y.)
None	None	1.00	1,000	500/10	156.2	Yes	638-5660	301-547-2308 (Md.)
None	None	.96	1,000	500/10	438.8	Yes	638-5660	301-547-2308 (Md.)
None	None	.59	1,000	500/10	1,572.5	Yes	638-5660	301-547-2308 (Md.)
None	None	.99	1,000	500/10	939.6	Yes	638-5660	301-547-2308 (Md.)
None	None	1.00	1,000	500/10	871.5	Yes	638-5660	301-547-2308 (Md.)
None	None	.73	1,000	500/10	631.0	Yes	638-5660	301-547-2308 (Md.)
None	None	.73	1,000	500/10	1,311.8	Yes	638-5660	301-547-2308 (Md.)
None	None	.65	1,000	500/10	939.0	Yes	638-5660	301-547-2308 (Md.)
None	None	.94	1,000	500/10	218.0	Yes	638-5660	301-547-2308 (Md.)
None	None	.98	1,000	—/—	324.0	Yes	638-5660	301-547-2308 (Md.)
None	None	.61	1,000	—/—	1,558.8	Yes	638-5660	301-547-2308 (Md.)
None	None	.73	1,000	—/—	405.0	Yes	638-5660	301-547-2308 (Md.)
None†	None	1.01	1,000	250/10	211.2	Yes	223-3332	212-908-9582 (N.Y.)
None	None	1.01	None	None/10	1,260.4	Yes	345-2021	816-531-5575 (Mo.)
None	None	1.01	None	None/10	2,665.7	Yes	345-2021	816-531-5575 (Mo.)
None†	None	1.01	None	None/10	390.8	Yes	345-2021	816-531-5575 (Mo.)
None	None	1.01	None	None/10	334.7	Yes	345-2021	816-531-5575 (Mo.)
None†	None	1.01	None	None/10	241.1	Yes	345-2021	816-531-5575 (Mo.)

†Fund may impose an exit fee.

Alphabetical Guide to Mutual Funds	Type	3 Yr. Performance Rank within Type/No. in Category		Percent Gain (or Loss) to April 1, 1987			
			Volatility (within Type)	One Year	Three Years	Ten Years	Percent Current Yield
Standard & Poor's 500-Stock Index				26.2	106.7	380.0	
Unified Growth	Gro	55/118	Average	16.2	90.3	449.4	1.3
Unified Income	EqI	44/46	Average	8.2	41.3	—	6.6
Unified Mutual Shares	G&I	46/72	Average	13.7	85.6	288.8	3.1
United Accumulative	Gro	48/118	Low	19.7	92.3	437.8	2.1
United Bond	HGC	4/36	High	10.2	70.7	171.0	8.2
United Continental Income	Bal	3/17	High	14.6	107.5	369.3	3.6
United Gov. Securities	USG	—	—	9.3	—	—	8.1
United High Income**	HYC	8/39	Average	15.3	64.5	—	11.8
United Income	EqI	1/46	High	17.7	118.5	379.9	2.3
United International Growth	Intl	10/13	Low	28.7	96.8	521.5	0.9
United Municipal Bond	HGT	2/40	Average	12.7	68.0	82.1	6.9
United New Concepts	SCG	10/25	High	19.4	76.9	—	0.9
United Science & Energy	Sec	14/35	Average	27.1	86.7	401.2	1.2
United Vanguard	Gro	84/118	Average	19.2	78.7	764.9	2.1
United Services Gold Shares	Gold	10/11	Average	88.6	1.3	907.0	4.9
United Services Good & Bad Times	G&I	49/72	Average	16.4	83.6	—	1.9
United Services Growth	Max	62/66	Average	13.0	35.8	—	0.7
United Services New Prospector	Gold	—	—	106.0	—	—	0.0
United Services Prospector**	Gold	9/11	Average	96.5	19.1	—	0.0
USAA Cornerstone	Sec	—	—	46.5	—	—	1.6
USAA Gold	Gold	—	—	119.7	—	—	0.7
USAA Growth	Gro	91/118	Average	17.3	72.5	275.9	1.0
USAA Income	EqI	38/46	Average	10.2	57.4	176.3	10.4
USAA Sunbelt Era	SCG	15/25	Average	16.3	64.3	—	0.3
USAA Tax Exempt—High Yield	HGT	29/40	Low	12.1	55.0	—	7.5
USAA Tax Ex.—Intermed. Term	ITT	6/15	Average	8.3	41.6	—	7.1
USAA Tax Ex.—Short Term	ITT	10/15	Average	6.3	26.8	—	5.8
U.S. Gov. High Yield Trust	USG	—	—	5.8	—	—	8.1
U.S. Trend	Gro	92/118	Average	15.8	72.4	539.6	2.2
Value Line Fund	G&I	44/72	High	17.9	86.0	474.6	1.3

** Fund closed to new investors.

Percent Maximum Initial Sales Charge	Percent Maximum Deferred Sales Charge	Expenses per $100	Minimum Initial Investment	IRA Minimum Initial Investment/Annual Fee	Assets as of Feb. 27, 1987 (in millions)	Phone Switch	Toll-free (800) + In State	Telephone
None	None	$1.00	$ 200	$25/None	$ 28.9	Yes	862-7283	—
None	None	1.12	500	25/None	15.2	Yes	862-7283	—
None	None	1.02	200	25/None	22.4	Yes	862-7283	—
8½	None	.60	500	50/15	778.6	No	—	816-283-4000
8½	None	.64	500	50/15	347.2	No	—	816-283-4000
8½	None	.83	500	50/15	342.3	No	—	816-283-4000
4	None	.87	500	50/15	184.8	No	—	816-283-4000
8½	None	.81	500	50/15	1,347.7	No	—	816-283-4000
8½	None	.62	500	50/15	991.9	No	—	816-283-4000
8½	None	1.09	500	50/15	241.2	No	—	816-283-4000
4	None	.61	500	—/—	476.4	No	—	816-283-4000
8½	None	1.47	500	50/15	90.7	No	—	816-283-4000
8½	None	.83	500	50/15	217.0	No	—	816-283-4000
8½	None	.98	500	50/15	601.8	No	—	816-283-4000
None	None	1.27	100	None/10	321.6	Yes	824-4653	—
None	None	1.40	100	None/10	28.3	Yes	824-4653	—
None	None	1.52	100	None/10	10.1	Yes	824-4653	—
None†	None	1.51	100	None/10	73.1	Yes	824-4653	—
None†	None	1.89	—	—/—	74.9	Yes	824-4653	—
None	None	1.50	1,000	1,000/10	107.1	Yes	531-8000	—
None	None	1.50	1,000	1,000/10	59.9	Yes	531-8000	—
None	None	1.09	1,000	1,000/10	227.2	Yes	531-8000	—
None	None	.65	1,000	1,000/10	263.2	Yes	531-8000	—
None	None	1.05	1,000	1,000/10	148.2	Yes	531-8000	—
None	None	.50	3,000	—/—	1,028.8	Yes	531-8000	—
None	None	.57	3,000	—/—	401.7	Yes	531-8000	—
None	None	.65	3,000	—/—	269.9	Yes	531-8000	—
4¾	None	1.04	1,000	100/10	2,365.8	Yes	—	713-751-2400
7½	None	1.01	200	200/10	97.9	Yes	262-6686	—
None	None	.81	1,000	1,000/10	260.5	Yes	223-0818	—

†Fund may impose an exit fee.

Alphabetical Guide to Mutual Funds	Type	3 Yr. Performance Rank within Type/No. in Category					
		Volatility (within Type)					
				Percent Gain (or Loss) to April 1, 1987			
				One Year	Three Years	Ten Years	Percent Current Yield
Standard & Poor's 500-Stock Index				26.2	106.7	380.0	
Value Line Convertible	EqI	—	—	14.3	—	—	4.1
Value Line Income	EqI	23/46	Average	13.7	75.9	396.7	6.3
Value Line Leveraged Growth	Max	20/66	Average	25.1	102.3	745.8	0.5
Value Line Special Situations	Gro	113/118	Average	11.6	28.4	407.0	0.2
Value Line Tax Ex. High Yield	HYT	9/11	Low	10.9	48.8	—	8.1
Value Line U.S. Gov. Sec.	USG	3/13	High	8.7	56.1	—	10.1
Van Eck Gold Resources	Gold	—	—	113.5	—	—	0.0
Van Eck World Trends	Glo	—	—	38.3	—	—	1.5
Van Kampen Merr. Ins. Tax Fr. Inc.	HGT	—	—	10.0	—	—	6.7
Van Kampen Merr. Tax Fr. Hi. Inc.	HYT	—	—	14.0	—	—	7.8
Van Kampen Merritt U.S. Gov.	MBS	—	—	10.5	—	—	10.8
Vanguard Explorer*	Sec	32/35	Average	1.8	21.4	484.8	0.1
Vanguard Explorer II	SCG	—	—	10.5	—	—	0.2
Vanguard Fixed Inc.—GNMA	MBS	2/8	Average	10.2	55.5	—	9.4
Vanguard Fixed Inc.—High Yield	HYC	10/39	Low	16.2	63.0	—	11.1
Vanguard Fixed Inc.—Invest. Grade	HGC	15/36	Average	10.8	62.0	170.9	9.4
Vanguard Fixed Inc.—Short	HGC	34/36	Low	8.4	45.7	—	7.8
Vanguard Index Trust	G&I	14/72	Average	25.5	103.9	355.6	2.9
Vanguard Muni Bond—High Yield	HYT	1/11	Average	12.3	60.3	—	7.4
Vanguard Muni Bond—Ins. Long	HGT	—	—	10.6	—	—	7.2
Vanguard Muni Bond—Intermed.	ITT	2/15	High	11.1	49.2	—	6.9
Vanguard Muni Bond—Long Term	HGT	19/40	Average	12.0	58.1	—	7.3
Vanguard Muni Bond—Short Term	ITT	13/15	Low	6.2	22.5	—	5.3
Vanguard Naess & Thomas Spec.	SCG	24/25	Average	6.7	27.9	347.2	0.0
Vanguard Qual. Div. Port. I*	EqI	2/46	Average	20.9	117.7	616.0	6.7
Vanguard Qual. Div. Port. II	EqI	14/46	Average	14.6	83.9	189.4	8.5
Vanguard Sp. Port.—Gold & PM	Gold	—	—	90.2	—	—	1.4
Vanguard Sp. Port.—Health	Sec	—	—	27.6	—	—	1.1
Vanguard Sp. Port.—Serv. Econ.	Sec	—	—	13.2	—	—	1.8
Vanguard Sp. Port.—Technology	Sec	—	—	20.5	—	—	0.3

*Open to IRA investors only.

Percent Maximum Initial Sales Charge	Percent Maximum Deferred Sales Charge	Expenses per $100	Minimum Initial Investment	IRA Minimum Initial Investment/Annual Fee	Assets as of Feb. 27, 1987 (in millions)	Phone Switch	Toll-free (800) +	In State	Telephone
None	None	$1.31	$1,000	$1,000/$10	$ 95.0	Yes	223-0818	—	
None	None	.77	1,000	1,000/10	179.7	Yes	223-0818	—	
None	None	.96	1,000	1,000/10	426.6	Yes	223-0818	—	
None	None	1.01	1,000	1,000/10	241.6	Yes	223-0818	—	
None	None	.72	1,000	—/—	309.8	Yes	223-0818	—	
None	None	.76	1,000	1,000/10	210.5	Yes	223-0818	—	
7½	None	1.50	1,000	None/10	63.8	Yes	221-2220	212-687-5200 (N.Y.)	
7½	None	1.46	1,000	None/10	83.0	Yes	221-2220	212-687-5200 (N.Y.)	
4⁹/₁₀	None	.76	1,500	—/—	477.9	Yes	225-2222	—	
4⁹/₁₀	None	.67	1,500	—/—	279.5	Yes	225-2222	—	
4⁹/₁₀	None	.56	1,500	1,500/10	5,136.8	Yes	225-2222	—	
None	None	.76	—	500/10	302.9	No	662-7447	—	
None	None	1.17	3,000	500/10	69.0	No	662-7447	—	
None	None	.38	3,000	500/10	2,512.0	Yes	662-7447	—	
None	None	.45	3,000	500/10	1,457.9	Yes	662-7447	—	
None	None	.41	3,000	500/10	769.9	Yes	662-7447	—	
None	None	.38	3,000	500/10	413.5	Yes	662-7447	—	
None	None	.28	1,500	500/10	662.9	No	662-7447	—	
None	None	.33	3,000	—/—	1,016.4	Yes	662-7447	—	
None	None	.33	3,000	—/—	1,004.6	Yes	662-7447	—	
None	None	.33	3,000	—/—	1,190.0	Yes	662-7447	—	
None	None	.33	3,000	—/—	804.2	Yes	662-7447	—	
None	None	.33	3,000	—/—	1,159.2	Yes	662-7447	—	
None	None	.92	3,000	500/10	34.5	No	662-7447	—	
None	None	.52	—	500/10	193.1	Yes	662-7447	—	
None	None	.58	3,000	500/10	204.6	Yes	662-7447	—	
None†	None	.59	1,500	500/10	77.0	Yes	662-7447	—	
None†	None	.61	1,500	500/10	56.7	Yes	662-7447	—	
None†	None	.48	1,500	500/10	53.3	Yes	662-7447	—	
None†	None	.65	1,500	500/10	38.5	Yes	662-7447	—	

†Fund may impose an exit fee.

Alphabetical Guide to Mutual Funds	Type	3 Yr. Performance Rank within Type/No. in Category					
		Volatility (within Type)					
				Percent Gain (or Loss) to April 1, 1987			
				One Year	Three Years	Ten Years	Percent Current Yield
Standard & Poor's 500-Stock Index				26.2	106.7	380.0	
Vanguard Star	Bal	—	—	15.1	—	—	5.0
Vanguard Wellesley Income	EqI	18/46	Average	12.5	80.8	275.4	7.9
Vanguard Wellington	Bal	8/17	Average	21.0	92.4	345.5	5.2
Vanguard Windsor*	G&I	9/72	Average	22.1	108.6	593.5	4.9
Vanguard Windsor II	G&I	—	—	20.2	—	—	2.9
Vanguard W.L. Morgan Growth	Sec	17/35	Average	21.3	82.4	454.8	1.3
Vanguard World—Int. Growth	Intl	2/13	Average	37.3	139.3	—	0.6
Vanguard World—U.S. Growth	Gro	64/118	Average	12.8	86.2	421.2	2.1
Venture Income Plus	HYC	32/39	High	11.1	47.9	—	14.4
Venture Muni Plus	HGT	40/40	Average	6.0	30.3	—	8.9
Venture Ret. Plan of Am.—Bond	HYC	34/39	Average	7.8	44.9	—	8.8
Venture Ret. Plan of Am.—Equity	EqI	5/46	High	19.6	100.9	—	0.2
Washington Mutual Investors	G&I	8/72	Average	21.3	108.6	461.0	3.7
Weingarten Equity	Max	4/66	Average	28.6	128.2	1,025.8	0.7
Westergaard Fund	Max	64/66	Average	2.6	22.5	—	1.5
World of Technology	Sec	27/35	Average	23.7	46.3	—	0.0
WPG Fund	Max	25/66	Average	19.0	95.2	—	0.7
YES Fund	USG	13/13	High	7.6	31.4	—	10.1

*Open to IRA investors only.

Percent Maximum Initial Sales Charge	Percent Maximum Deferred Sales Charge	Expenses per $100	Minimum Initial Investment	IRA Minimum Initial Investment/Annual Fee	Assets as of Feb. 27, 1987 (in millions)	Phone Switch	Toll-free (800) + In State	Telephone
None	None	None	$ 500	$500/$10	$ 527.8	Yes	662-7447	—
None	None	.58	1,500	500/10	615.4	Yes	662-7447	—
None	None	.53	1,500	500/10	1,336.9	Yes	662-7447	—
None	None	.52	—	500/10	5,532.6	Yes	662-7447	—
None	None	.65	1,500	500/10	1,265.0	Yes	662-7447	—
None	None	.54	1,500	500/10	743.2	Yes	662-7447	—
None	None	.78	1,500	500/10	479.2	Yes	662-7447	—
None	None	.80	1,500	500/10	190.2	Yes	662-7447	—
8½	None	1.25	1,000	250/10	71.9	Yes	545-2098	505-983-4335 (N.M.)
None†	5	1.44	1,000	250/10	45.7	Yes	545-2098	505-983-4335 (N.M.)
None†	5	1.14	1,000	250/10	68.7	Yes	545-2098	505-983-4335 (N.M.)
None†	5	1.25	1,000	250/10	16.4	Yes	545-2098	505-983-4335 (N.M.)
8½	None	.52	250	250/10	2,367.1	Yes	421-9900	213-486-9651 (Calif.)
4¾	None	1.00	1,000	100/5	232.9	Yes	231-0803	800-392-9681 (Texas)
8½	None	2.25	1,250	1,250/None	16.2	No	—	212-940-0253
None	None	.78	250	250/None	10.0	Yes	525-8085	800-525-9769 (Colo.)
None	None	1.23	1,000	250/10	46.8	Yes	223-3332	212-908-9582 (N.Y.)
3¾	None	1.18	250	250/10	154.0	No	845-8406	800-521-5612 (Calif.)

†Fund may impose an exit fee.

Glossary

Asset allocation fund. A relatively new type of mutual fund that offers investors one-stop shopping for their portfolio requirements. These funds spread their assets among a variety of investments such as domestic stocks, foreign stocks, precious metals, and bonds, keeping the elements in a permanent fixed percentage or altering the mix in an effort to time the market and to enhance shareholders' returns.

Back-end load. See **Redemption fees.**

Bear market. One in which prices of stocks or bonds generally drop over a long enough period to indicate a downward trend in economic activity.

Bond. Interest-paying government or corporate security that obligates the issuer to pay the holder a specified sum, usually at specific intervals, and to repay the principal amount, or face value, of the bond at maturity.

Book value. The net asset value of each share in a company (assets at historical cost, minus liabilities, divided by the number of outstanding shares). It reflects the underlying value of the firm's property and financial assets.

Bull market. One in which overall prices of stock or bonds rise over a long enough period to indicate an upward trend.

Business cycle. A recurring pattern of economic contraction (recession) and expansion (recovery) with effects on inflation, growth, and employment.

Call option. See **Option.**

Capital gains distribution. The payout to a mutual fund's shareholders of the profits realized from the sale of stocks or bonds.

Certificate of deposit. Debt instrument, usually paying interest, issued by a bank.

Clone fund. A portfolio spun off by a popular fund when its manager decides the original has become too large to accept new investors. A clone follows its parent's investment philosophy and usually has a similar name and sometimes the same manager.

Closed-end fund. A mutual fund with a limited number of shares outstanding. Unlike conventional open-end funds, which continually sell and redeem their shares at net asset value, closed-end funds have a fixed number of shares that trade the way stocks do on exchanges or over the counter.

Commission. A broker's fee for buying or selling securities on a customer's behalf. With mutual funds, this fee is called a load and can be as much as 9% of the amount invested.

Common stock. Units of ownership of a public corporation. Owners typically are entitled to vote on the selection of directors and to receive any dividends on their holdings.

Consumer price index. Measure of change in consumer prices calculated monthly by the U.S. Bureau of Labor Statistics.

Convertible. Corporate bond or preferred stock that is exchangeable for a set number of common shares at a prestated price.

Credit rating. Evaluation of debt securities' credit risk, or likelihood of default, by rating services such as Moody's Investors Service and Standard & Poor's Corporation.

Default. Failure of a bond issuer to make timely payments of interest and principal as they come due.

Diversification. The spreading of one's investment risk by putting assets in a wide-ranging portfolio of securities.

Dividend. Distribution of earnings to shareholders. Mutual fund dividends are paid out of income generated by stocks and bonds in the portfolio. Distributions are usually made on a quarterly basis.

Dollar-cost averaging. An installment-purchase technique that involves investing a fixed amount of money in stocks or mutual fund shares at regular intervals, such as monthly or quarterly, rather than all at once. The objective is to buy fewer shares when prices are high and more shares when they are low.

Ex-dividend. Period between the announcement and the payment of a mutual fund's next dividend. An investor who buys shares during that interval is not entitled to the dividend. A fund that has gone ex-dividend is marked with an *x* in newspaper listings.

Exit fee. See **Redemption fees.**

Expense ratio. Amount, expressed as a percentage of total assets, that shareholders paid in the past year for mutual fund operating expenses and management fees. The expense ratio for stock funds averages 1.1% versus 0.9% for bond funds.

Face value. Also called par value, this is the amount the bondholder receives when the bonds are redeemed at maturity. Interest payments are based on the face value.

Family of funds. Group of mutual funds operated by a single investment management company or brokerage house. Shareholders in one of the funds can usually switch their money into any of the family's other funds, sometimes at no charge.

Front-end load. See **Load.**

Ginnie Mae. The nickname for the federally backed debt securities issued by the Government National Mortgage Association. A Ginnie Mae represents a pool of mortgages; investors receive the payments of interest and principal made by homeowners.

Gross national product (GNP). The total value of goods and services produced in the U.S. economy over a given period. The GNP growth rate is a key indicator of the status of the economy.

Growth fund. One whose main objective is capital appreciation rather than income. Growth funds buy mostly stocks that are expected to increase steadily in value over time.

Growth stock. Issue of an expanding company that has reported above-average growth of earnings over the last few years and is expected to maintain or increase its growth rate in the years ahead.

Hedge. A defensive investment strategy, often involving the buying or selling of options, to offset possible losses and thereby to reduce risk.

Income fund. A portfolio that is managed to generate steady income rather than capital gains. It invests in bonds, high-dividend stocks, and other income-producing securities.

Index. A statistical composite of selected stocks or bonds that is used to measure price fluctuations in the stock and bond markets. Stock market indexes such as those compiled by Standard & Poor's are also used for trading options based on the indexes.

Index fund. One whose portfolio attempts to duplicate that of an index such as the Standard & Poor's 500-stock index and whose performance therefore mirrors that of the market overall.

Individual Retirement Account (IRA). Personal retirement account that an employed person may be entitled to fund with tax-deductible contributions of up to $2,000 per year (or $2,250 a year for a couple with one working spouse). All earnings generated in the account accumulate tax-deferred until the funds are withdrawn. Early withdrawals—those made before age 59½—are subject to a 10% tax penalty as well as ordinary income taxes.

Institutional investors. Large holders—and typically active traders—of stocks and bonds, including such organizations as mutual funds, banks, insurance companies, pension funds, and college endowment funds. Most of the daily trading in the stock and bond markets is on behalf of these institutions.

Junk bond. A high-yielding bond with a speculative credit rating—for instance, BB or lower from Standard & Poor's—that reflects doubts about the issuing company's or government's credit strength.

Load. Commission or sales charge for buying fund shares through a broker, financial planner, or insurance agent. Some funds that sell directly to the public also charge loads. Funds that do not are called no-load funds.

Management fee. Charge against investor assets to cover the costs of managing the portfolio of a mutual fund. The fee is a fixed percentage of the fund's assets, typically 1% or less per year, and is disclosed in the fund's prospectus.

Margin. The amount of money a customer deposits with a broker when borrowing from the broker to buy securities.

Market timing. A strategy of buying or selling securities, including mutual fund shares, to take advantage of—or reduce one's exposure to—anticipated changes in market conditions. For example, fund shareholders might switch from a stock fund to a short-term bond fund or money-market fund when they think the stock market is about to fall.

Maturity. The date on which a bond's principal becomes due and payable.

Money-market fund. One that invests in short-term government securities, bank certificates of deposit, and other low-risk, low-return securities. These funds pay so-called money-market rates of interest, and withdrawals from them can be made anytime at a predictable per-share value.

Municipal bond. Bond issued by a state or local government. In most cases, the interest paid is exempt from federal taxes and, if the bondholder lives in the state where the bond was issued, from state and sometimes local taxes too.

Mutual fund. An investment company that raises money from shareholders and invests it in stocks, bonds, and other types of securities. Most mutual funds are open-ended—meaning that they continuously sell new shares to investors and stand ready to buy back shares at their net asset value. Funds offer investors the advantages of diversification, professional management, and low transaction costs, in exchange for which they charge a management fee.

Net asset value (NAV). The value of a share of a mutual fund. A fund computes its NAV daily by taking the closing prices of all securities in its portfolio, adding the value of all other assets such as cash, subtracting the fund's liabilities, and dividing the result by the number of fund shares outstanding.

Offer price. What investors would pay for a share of a mutual fund. If a fund has an initial sales charge, or load, the offer price equals the net asset value plus the load. A no-load fund's offer price and net asset value are the same.

Option. An agreement that gives the buyer the right to buy (call option) or sell (put option) 100 shares of a particular stock or stock index at a fixed price during a preset period. An option produces income, called a premium, for the seller, who gives up ownership of the securities if the option buyer exercises his right. For example, a call option buyer hopes the stock will rise in price by an amount that exceeds the premium paid for the option, while a put option seller hopes the stock will remain stable, rise, or drop by an amount less than his or her profit on the premium.

Over the counter. A transaction involving securities that are not listed and traded on a central exchange. Trading in these securities is conducted through the National Association of Securities

Dealers Automated Quotation system (NASDAQ), a computer-linked network of broker-dealers who stand ready to buy or sell certain stocks and bonds for their own accounts. Over-the-counter stocks are traditionally those of fairly small or closely held companies that do not meet the listing requirements of the New York Stock Exchange.

Preferred stock. A class of stock that pays a fixed dividend and has preference over common stock in the payment of dividends and the liquidation of the issuing company's assets. Preferred stockholders do not normally have voting rights.

Premium. The price an option buyer must pay to an option seller for the right to buy (call option) or sell (put option) a security at a fixed price during a preset period. The premium is determined by market supply and demand forces.

Prospectus. The official document that a mutual fund supplies to all prospective shareholders, identifying the fund's management company, outlining its investment objectives, and assessing the risks involved. A corollary document, called Part B or the statement of additional information, generally describes in detail the fees that are charged and often lists the fund's holdings as well.

Put option. See **Option.**

Real estate investment trust (REIT). An investment company, usually traded publicly, that manages a portfolio of real estate in order to earn profits for shareholders. Modeled after mutual funds, REITs invest in properties that range from shopping centers and office buildings to apartment complexes and hotels.

Redemption fees. Often called exit fees or back-end loads, they are deducted from money you take out of some funds when you redeem, or sell, shares. Some exit fees, which can be as high as 1% of the amount redeemed, decline to zero over a period of a few months or years; others remain constant. Back-end loads, also known as contingent deferred sales charges, typically are levied by load funds that do not have initial, or front-end, sales charges. The loads start at 4% to 6% on withdrawals during your first year in the fund and gradually decline to zero over four to six years.

Sector fund. One that restricts its holdings to the stocks of companies in a particular industry, service, or region. Sector funds are often grouped into families, and investors switch among funds as economic and market conditions warrant.

Securities and Exchange Commission (SEC). The federal agency responsible for registering and regulating interstate transactions of financial securities, including mutual funds.

Share. A unit of ownership in a corporation, such as a mutual fund, which has divided its ownership into equal parts represented by stock or share certificates.

Standard & Poor's 500-stock index. A popular measurement of the stock market's performance based on prices of 500 common

stocks listed on the New York and American stock exchanges or
traded over the counter.

Takeover. A change in the controlling interest of a corporation
through a friendly acquisition or merger or an unfriendly bid that
the management of the target company opposes.

Total return. The dividends, interest, and capital gains that a
mutual fund achieves in a given period. A total-return fund is one
that pursues both growth and income by investing in a mix of
growth stocks, high-dividend stocks, and bonds.

Treasuries. Debt obligations—bonds, bills, and certificates—that
are issued by the U.S. Treasury and secured by the federal government's full faith and credit. Income from Treasury securities is
exempt from state and local, but not federal, income taxes.

Turnover rate. Figure found in a mutual fund's prospectus that
indicates how actively the fund traded securities in the past
12-month period. The higher the turnover of a portfolio of securities, the greater the fund's brokerage costs. These costs, which are
not included in a fund's expense ratio, can cut your return
because they reduce the profits (or increase the losses) on securities trades. Most stock and bond funds have a turnover rate of
80% to 100% a year.

12b-1 fees. Named after a Securities and Exchange Commission
rule that permits them, these assessments against shareholders'
assets are levied by many mutual funds to help pay for promotion
expenses. Such 12b-1 fees are usually included in a fund's expense
ratio.

Volatility. The degree to which securities such as mutual fund
shares move up or down in price within a given period.

Yield. The dividend or interest income that a stock, bond, or
mutual fund share pays out in one year, expressed as a percentage
of the issue's price or the fund's net asset value.

Zero-coupon bond. A bond that makes no periodic interest payments but instead is sold at a discount from its face value. The
buyer of a zero receives the rate of return by the gradual appreciation of the bond, which is redeemable at face value on its
maturity date.

Appendices

APPENDIX **A. Comparing After-Tax Returns of Bonds**

There is no simple answer to the question of which type of bond fund will pay you the greatest after-tax return: a high-yielding but fully taxable corporate or a lower-yielding muni exempt from federal income taxes and perhaps state and local taxes. The correct choice ultimately depends on the funds' current yields, your federal tax bracket, and—if your state has an income tax—the state rate you pay. The formulas that follow, prepared with the help of analyst Nancy Utterback of Drexel Burnham Lambert, will help you figure what is best for you. The formulas are designed for comparisons of different categories of bonds but also are applicable to the funds that invest in them. Just substitute the funds' yields for those of the corresponding bonds cited below.

● If you do not have to take state taxes into account in comparing bond yields, use this formula:

Taxable-equivalent yield = the municipal's yield divided by (1–your marginal federal tax rate)

You may live in a state that does not levy an income tax. Or you may be trying to decide between a triple-tax-exempt muni and a bond that is exempt only from state and local taxes—say, a Treasury bond. Either way, the formula will let you calculate the taxable-equivalent yield of a tax-free bond—what a taxable bond would have to pay to give you the same return after taxes.

For example, take a retired couple in Florida in the 28% federal bracket. They are trying to decide whether to buy a Florida tax-exempt muni yielding 7% or a long-term Treasury issue yielding 7.5%. By dividing 7 (the muni yield) by .72, which is 1 minus .28, they learn that the muni yields the taxable equivalent of 9.7%. Since that is more than two percentage points above the Treasury's yield, the tax-free muni is the best choice for them.

● If you live in a state with an income tax, the following three-step calculation lets you figure what a fully taxable bond would have to pay to match the yield on a tax-free muni issued in your state. To arrive at that number, you need to determine your effective state rate—the percentage you pay in state taxes after deducting those taxes on your federal return—then your cumulative state and federal bracket.

STEP 1: *Your effective state tax rate = your nominal state tax rate* x *(1— your marginal federal tax)*

STEP 2: *Your total bracket = your effective state tax rate + your marginal federal tax rate*

STEP 3: *Taxable-equivalent yield = the in-state muni's yield ÷ (1— your total bracket)*

For example, a Los Angeles accountant who will be in the 33% federal bracket in 1988 and whose marginal state tax rate is 11% is debating whether to buy a California-issued tax-free muni yielding 6.5% or a corporate bond yielding 8.8%. She determines her effective state rate by multiplying .11 by .67, which equals .0737 or 7.37%. She then adds this effective state tax rate to her marginal federal tax rate (.0737 plus .33), to arrive at her tax bracket, which is 40.37%. Dividing 6.5 (the muni's yield) by .5963 (1 minus her total bracket of .4037) shows her that the muni yields the taxable equivalent of 10.9%, or more than two percentage points above the corporate bond. She picks the muni.

● Use this formula to calculate how high a yield you would have to get on an out-of-state muni, which is subject to your state's income tax, to match the yield on an in-state bond, which is free of state and local income taxes. Use Step 1 above to figure your effective state tax rate.

The out-of-state equivalent yield = the in-state muni yield ÷ (1— your effective state tax rate)

Now the Los Angeles accountant is trying to decide between the 6.5% California muni and a Utah tax-exempt yielding 6.8%. Dividing 6.5 (the California muni's yield) by .9263 (1 minus her effective state tax rate of .0737) shows that it would take an out-of-state bond yielding more than 7% to match the yield on the California bond. She buys the California issue.

Marginal Tax Rates, Federal Income Tax

Single Filers		Marginal Rate	Married Filing Jointly	
Taxable Income of at Least			Taxable Income of at Least	
$0		15%	$0	
$17,850		28%	$29,750	
$43,150		33%	$71,900	

APPENDIX B. Closed-End Funds: Total Return in NAV and Share Price

For the following list of widely held closed-end funds, the percent change in price over the periods shown indicates how the stock has appreciated, given supply and demand. The percent change in net asset value allows you to compare performance with that of open-end mutual funds. The percent discount (or premium) is the difference between a fund's stock price and its NAV as of December 31, 1986.

DIVERSIFIED STOCK FUNDS		% change to 12/31/86			Where Trades	Discount or Premium
		1 yr.	3 yrs.	10 yrs.		
Adams Express	Price	20.6	50.9	326.5	NYSE	-2.8%
	NAV	19.2	46.6	254.2		
General American	Price	11.3	13.9	343.4	NYSE	-7.9
	NAV	12.3	25.4	291.7		
Lehman	Price	19.5	19.2	334.7	NYSE	-1.6
	NAV	16.5	24.7	265.9		
Niagara Share	Price	12.9	3.5	250.1	NYSE	-7.8
	NAV	12.4	14.1	215.1		
Tri-Continental	Price	26.3	53.5	397.8	NYSE	+3.2
	NAV	23.9	50.2	278.9		
Central Securities	Price	15.2	37.0	580.0	ASE	-8.5
	NAV	13.9	38.4	380.3		
Claremont Capital	Price	17.4	104.1	1,121.8	ASE	+13.1
	NAV	13.9	54.5	601.1		
Engex	Price	27.1	480.2	NA	OTC	-11.4
	NAV	4.1	215.4	NA		
Source Capital	Price	11.0	85.3	928.0	NYSE	+7.8
	NAV	13.9	65.1	570.7		
SPECIALIZED FUNDS						
ASA Ltd.	Price	11.0	-22.5	530.6	NYSE	-50.3
	NAV	68.7	41.3	736.2		
Petroleum & Resources	Price	12.2	36.8	221.6	NYSE	+5.4
	NAV	2.9	20.4	202.6		
Emerging Medical Technology	Price	-3.7	NA	NA	ASE	-8.4
	NAV	-1.0	NA	NA		
Mexico Fund	Price	54.9	28.1	NA	NYSE	-34.0
	NAV	57.3	137.1	NA		
Z-Seven Fund	Price	89.3	NA	NA	PAC	+27.2
	NAV	31.4	NA	NA		
Japan Fund*	Price	18.9	77.2	348.8	NYSE	-26.0
	NAV	41.3	135.1	384.4		

APPENDIX B *(continued)*

BOND FUNDS		% change to 12/31/86			Where Trades	Discount or Premium
		1 yr.	3 yrs.	10 yrs.		
Bancroft Convertible	Price	16.6	70.7	431.4	ASE	+0.6
	NAV	15.2	56.8	292.1		
Castle Convertible	Price	8.2	20.0	507.4	ASE	-0.2
	NAV	8.3	24.6	345.0		
American Capital Convertible	Price	25.6	55.0	710.0	NYSE	+15.0
	NAV	16.5	46.3	482.0		
American Capital Bond	Price	20.0	72.0	192.2	NYSE	+9.8
	NAV	10.0	54.5	168.7		
AMEV Securities	Price	25.5	61.6	181.9	NYSE	+8.1
	NAV	12.3	48.6	150.3		
Fort Dearborn Income	Price	20.1	77.1	200.0	NYSE	-4.0
	NAV	17.3	72.6	176.6		
Intercapital Income	Price	—	76.2	218.7	NYSE	+14.9
	NAV	17.5	61.2	187.3		
John Hancock Income	Price	15.5	71.0	218.7	NYSE	+0.5
	NAV	13.5	56.9	172.6		
John Hancock Investors	Price	16.2	76.1	237.7	NYSE	+5.5
	NAV	13.1	59.1	200.2		
Mass Mutual	Price	37.9	109.5	545.5	NYSE	+8.6
	NAV	33.8	71.0	369.3		
Mass Mutual Income	Price	4.4	38.8	223.0	NYSE	+10.4
	NAV	10.5	40.3	153.1		
Montgomery St. Income	Price	12.0	71.3	189.6	NYSE	+10.6
	NAV	12.9	53.2	156.6		
Transamerica Income	Price	21.1	75.3	228.5	NYSE	+4.7
	NAV	16.0	62.9	194.9		

*Became open-end in 1987

Source: Thomas J. Herzfeld Advisors, Inc., Miami, Florida

APPENDIX C. The Standard & Poor's 500-Stock Index Total Returns (with Dividends Reinvested)

Percent gain or loss at year-end over previous 12 months

1967	+23.88	1974	-26.39	1981	-5.01
1968	+10.98	1975	+37.16	1982	+21.44
1969	-8.42	1976	+23.57	1983	+22.38
1970	+3.93	1977	-7.42	1984	+6.10
1971	+14.56	1978	+6.38	1985	+31.57
1972	+18.90	1979	+18.20	1986	+18.56
1973	-14.77	1980	+32.27		

Source: Standard & Poor's Corporation

APPENDIX D. How Annual Deposits of $1,000 Will Grow at Given Returns
Percent increase compounded annually

Year	5%	6%	7%	8%	9%	10%	11%	12%
1	$ 1,050	$ 1,060	$ 1,070	$ 1,080	$ 1,090	$ 1,100	$ 1,110	$ 1,120
2	2,153	2,183	2,215	2,246	2,278	2,310	2,342	2,374
3	3,310	3,374	3,440	3,506	3,573	3,641	3,710	3,779
4	4,526	4,637	4,751	4,867	4,985	5,105	5,228	5,353
5	5,802	5,975	6,153	6,336	6,523	6,716	6,913	7,115
6	7,142	7,394	7,654	7,923	8,200	8,487	8,783	9,089
7	8,549	8,897	9,260	9,637	10,028	10,436	10,859	11,300
8	10,027	10,491	10,978	11,488	12,021	12,579	13,164	13,776
9	11,578	12,181	12,816	13,487	14,193	14,937	15,722	16,549
10	13,207	13,972	14,784	15,645	16,560	17,531	18,561	19,655
11	14,917	15,870	16,888	17,977	19,141	20,384	21,713	23,133
12	16,713	17,882	19,141	20,495	21,953	23,523	25,212	27,029
13	18,599	20,015	21,550	23,215	25,019	26,975	29,095	31,393
14	20,579	22,276	24,129	26,152	28,361	30,772	33,405	36,280
15	22,657	24,673	26,888	29,324	32,003	34,950	38,190	41,753
16	24,840	27,213	29,840	32,750	35,974	39,545	43,501	47,884
17	27,132	29,906	32,999	36,450	40,301	44,599	49,396	54,750
18	29,539	32,760	36,379	40,446	45,018	50,159	55,939	62,440
19	32,066	35,786	39,995	44,762	50,160	56,275	63,203	71,052
20	34,719	38,993	43,865	49,423	55,765	63,002	71,265	80,699
21	37,505	42,392	48,006	54,457	61,873	70,403	80,214	91,503
22	40,430	45,996	52,436	59,893	68,532	78,543	90,148	103,603
23	43,502	49,816	57,177	65,765	75,790	87,497	101,174	117,155
24	46,727	53,865	62,149	72,106	83,701	97,347	113,413	132,334
25	50,113	58,156	67,676	78,954	92,324	108,182	126,999	149,334

Year	13%	14%	15%	16%	17%	18%	19%	20%
1	$ 1,130	$ 1,140	$ 1,150	$ 1,160	$ 1,170	$ 1,180	$ 1,190	$ 1,200
2	2,407	2,440	2,473	2,506	2,539	2,572	2,606	2,640
3	3,850	3,921	3,993	4,066	4,141	4,215	4,291	4,368
4	5,480	5,610	5,742	5,877	6,014	6,154	6,297	6,442
5	7,323	7,536	7,754	7,977	8,207	8,442	8,683	8,930
6	9,405	9,730	10,067	10,414	10,772	11,142	11,523	11,916
7	11,757	12,233	12,729	13,240	13,773	14,326	14,902	15,499
8	14,416	15,085	15,786	16,519	17,285	18,086	18,923	19,799
9	17,420	18,337	19,304	20,321	21,393	22,521	23,709	24,959
10	20,814	22,045	23,349	24,733	26,200	27,755	29,404	31,150
11	24,650	26,271	28,002	29,850	31,824	33,931	36,180	38,581
12	28,985	31,089	33,352	35,786	38,404	41,219	44,244	47,497
13	33,883	36,581	39,505	42,672	46,103	49,818	53,841	58,196
14	39,417	42,842	46,580	50,660	55,110	59,965	65,261	71,035
15	45,671	49,980	54,717	59,925	65,649	71,939	78,850	86,442
16	52,739	58,118	64,075	70,673	77,979	86,068	95,022	104,931
17	60,725	67,394	74,836	83,141	92,406	102,740	114,266	127,117
18	69,749	77,969	87,212	97,603	109,285	122,414	137,166	153,740
19	79,947	90,025	101,444	114,380	129,033	145,628	164,418	185,688
20	91,470	103,768	117,810	133,841	152,139	173,021	196,847	224,026
21	104,491	119,436	136,632	156,415	179,172	205,345	235,438	270,031
22	119,205	137,297	158,276	182,601	210,801	243,487	281,362	325,237
23	135,831	157,659	183,168	212,978	247,808	288,494	336,010	391,484
24	154,620	180,871	211,793	248,214	291,105	341,603	401,042	470,981
25	175,850	207,333	244,712	289,088	341,763	404,272	478,431	566,377

Index

References to figures and tables are in boldface type.